# *The Unmentionable Vice*

# The Unmentionable Vice

## Homosexuality in the Later Medieval Period

Michael Goodich

Dorset Press

This edition published by Dorset Press, a division of Marboro Books Corp., by arrangement with ABC-CLIO, Inc.

**Library of Congress Cataloging in Publication Data**
Goodisch, Michael, 1944-
The unmentionable vice.

Bibliography: pp. 143-155
Includes index.
1. Homosexuality, Male—Europe—History
2. Sodomy—Europe—History. 3. Homosexuality and Christianity—History. I. Title.
HQ76.2.E9G66 301.41'57'0902 78-13276

ISBN 0-88029-012-9
(Previously ISBN 0-87436-287-3)

# *Table of Contents*

# *Preface*

Paradoxically, the original idea for a study of homosexuality in the Middle Ages was a product of my study of Catholic saints whose lives, according to traditional theological canons, were not stained by those pangs of fleshly desire which ordinarily plague humanity. Unlike their Protestant successors, medieval hagiographers did not shrink from graphically portraying the lusts which tempted these pious men and women, all the better to illustrate the saints' skill in driving away the minions of Satan. The paradigm saint often succumbed to sexual temptation and through divine revelation turned his back on the world; in fact, this rejection of sexual urges was often the most important factor which contributed to his charismatic piety, expressed by abandonment of the world for a celibate monastery. In the sixteenth century, when the first Bollandists turned to Cardinal Bellarmine for support in publishing critical lives of the saints, this great tactician of the Counter-Reformation refused to help on the grounds that such tales would so scandalize the church that believers would be driven into the arms of the Protestants. In the Middle Ages, therefore, although sex was regarded as a necessary evil at best, its importance was at least recognized, and even emphasized, as an expression of human weakness.

More recently, church historians, mainly ecclesiastics, or believers, have preferred not to emphasize the church's repressive role in the history of sexuality in the light of more liberal attitudes prevalent today. Those few historians, like G. G. Coulton or Henry Charles Lea, who attempted to uncover the seamier side of medieval society intended to embarrass the church. Only recently, with the rise of the *Annales* school and of psychohistory, has sexuality been treated as a legitimate subject of historical study and have efforts been made to relate the vagaries of erotic life to psychogenetic or material transformations. In the past twenty years, as a result of the movement to abolish laws against victimless crimes, more dispassionate and scholarly works in the history of homosexuality have appeared by Bailey, Bullough, Karlen, and Rowse, among others; and even more general works such as those by V. H. Green and J. H. Mundy refer to sexual nonconformity as an integral part of any general view of the Middle Ages.

Research for this book was supported by a grant from the University of Haifa Research Fund. Furthermore, without the assistance of colleagues or friends who often directed me to relevant sources, or criticized selected portions of the manuscript, this work would never have been completed. Among those who shared their scholarly knowledge with me are William Bowsky, Vern Bullough, Louis Crompton, Henry Diament, Jay Gonen, Aryeh Grabois, Bert Hansen, John Mundy, and Douglas Roby. I would also like to thank those libraries in which I did my research, including the British Library (formerly the British Museum), Columbia University Library, New York Public Library, and the Jewish National and University Library (Hebrew University, Jerusalem). Special thanks is due to the staff of the University of Haifa Library; and to Barbara Singer and Faye Ginsberg for typing the manuscript. The greatest appreciation must go to my wife Marian, whose trained eye provided me with the most valuable editorial criticism and whose conversations helped clarify obscure passages in the text. I acknowledge with thanks the scholarly detail of Amanda Clark Frost, who edited the manuscript for Clio Books, and the painstaking care of Paulette Wamego, who proofread the galleys.

Parts of this study are based on previously published articles: "Sodomy in Ecclesiastical Law and Theory," *Journal of Homosexuality* 1 (Summer 1976): 427–34; and "Sodomy in Medieval Secular Law," *Journal of Homosexuality* 1 (Spring 1976): 295–302.

# *Introduction*

IN THIS VOLUME I attempt to present the evidence concerning the "unmentionable vice" (homosexuality) in European history from the eleventh to the early fourteenth century. Many patterns of behavior and thinking had precedents in Jewish and patristic literary sources, Roman law, and the Celtic or Germanic traditions, and changing material and social conditions influenced attitudes toward homoeroticism. These factors determined the vigor with which society dealt with sexual and moral outcasts. The precedents laid down by Augustine and the Church Fathers classified same-sex relations as an illicit form of lust (*luxuria*), contrary to nature, likely to consign its perpetrators to the fires of Hell. All forms of homoerotic relations were indiscriminately labeled as sodomy (*sodomia*) and were regarded in canon law and theology as the most heinous of sins, comparable to homicide. Throughout the following text all homosexual acts are referred to as sodomy, in keeping with medieval terminology. Many commentators confusingly use *sodomy* as a synonym for both bestiality and homosexuality. Many medieval discussions of the sins against nature attempted to categorize and determine which were the most serious and which the least. The other vices against nature included adultery, rape, illicit deflowering of a minor, masturbation, incest, and bestiality. Other transgressions were occasionally added: oral sex, sex with nuns, sex during menstruation, etc.[1]

Some theologians described sodomy as a form of sacrilege, or a sin against God, thereby heightening its seriousness. Indeed, the penalties exacted were often as great as those for homicide. By the thirteenth century, in keeping with the church's program of moral reform, Christian preachers were often supplied with alphabetical compendia of scriptural references. John Peckham's *Divinarum sententiarum,* for example, cites sixteen biblical passages dealing with sodomy, although some clearly refer to onanism and bestiality.[2]

Some historians interpret the rejection of homosexual behavior as a product of the perennial conflict between the values of the Judaeo-Christian tradition and the Graeco-Roman or pagan ethos. H. Montgomery Hyde and Arno Karlen hold that the Jewish prohibition against sodomy is rooted in God's injunction to Adam and Eve to increase and multiply and thereby disdain sexual behavior which frustrates that goal. The ancient Hebrews, concerned for their tribal and ritual purity, separated themselves from their neighbors and spurned [x] the human sacrifices, ritual castrations, temple prostitution, and sodomy practiced by the pagans although they adopted circumcision as a means of emphasizing their special calling. There is however evidence for a more naturalistic attitude toward sexuality during certain periods, but the Jews clearly condemned homosexuality and bestiality.[3]

Judaism condemns excesses of passion but voices none of the praise for virginity and celibacy characteristic of Christianity; rather, it condemns those who do not marry and populate the earth. The victory of Christian doctrine, representing the most moralistic and puritanical strain of Judaism, may have led, however, to the suppression of the freer sexual attitudes of the Greeks and Romans. The more liberal approach attributed to the pre-Christian tribes and ancient pagans nevertheless lay dormant and was reactivated by the revival of pagan, specifically Neoplatonic philosophy. Such renascences occurred during the twelfth and fifteenth centuries, when youth tried to ape the literary styles, philosophical poses, and moral codes of the ancients, including an indulgence in same-sex relations. It is sometimes forgotten that ancient sexuality was often the result of violence. Homosexuality, for example, more often involved the forced abuse of children or slaves than mutual esteem among free men and women. Temple prostitutes and catamites (boys kept for pederasty) were frequently sold and forced into service; they were not voluntary participants. The rape of minors was rarely punished.[4]

The greatest impetus to the study of homoeroticism has been the homosexual rights movement in Germany and the English-speaking world, under whose auspices an effort has been made to reform those antisodomy statutes that survived the French Revolution.[5] Several German states influenced by the Napoleonic Code decriminalized homosexual acts, but when the German Empire was created in 1871 it adopted the stricter Prussian criminal code, which again applied criminal penalties to homosexual offenses. The ensuing fight for repeal attracted the interest of such outstanding figures as August Bebel and Ferdinand Lassalle and led to the first genuine homosexual liberation movement. The result was the publication of a number of scholarly books and journals treating homosexuality, or "uranianism," as it was called, from a historical, medical, and ethnological perspective. Not surprisingly, the homosexual liberation movement arose simultaneously with a number of "life reform" movements favoring nudism, vegetarianism, the abolition of alcohol, and women's rights.

The lawyer Karl Heinrich Ulrichs (1825–1895) was among the first crusaders for homosexual rights. Ulrichs was an outstanding Latinist—he adopted the pseudonym Numa Praetorius—and in addition to his polemical tracts he contributed articles dealing with medieval law and uranianism in the fifteenth century.[6] Another such scholar-reformer was the pedophile and nudist Benedict Friedländer, founder of the Community of the Special. Following a long line of German classicists, Friedländer praised the great cultures of Greece and Renaissance Italy as products of sexual freedom, which Christian asceticism sought to repress. A third great sexologist, Magnus Hirschfeld (1868–1935), founded the Scientific-Humanitarian Committee and was the leading force for repeal of the repressive statutes on sex. Hirschfeld established the *Institut für Sexualwissenschaft,* site of the leading archive of sexology until its suppression by the Nazis, and edited two pioneering journals in the field of sexology, the *Jahrbuch für sexuelle Zwischenstufen* and the *Zeitschrift für Sexualwissenschaft.*[7] The majority of contributors to these journals, like Iwan Bloch and Richard Linsert,[8] and others associated with the sexual reform movement, were ardent socialists or anarchists. They went into exile or perished during the Nazi program of homosexual extermination. Their medical and psychological theories differed, but many of them viewed the sexual repression of the Middle Ages as a natural product of a reactionary religious ideology in the service of an exploitative feudal system. Most tended to idealize the social virtues of homosexuals.



The post–World War II period witnessed a revival of interest in the reform of laws against victimless crime. The Wolfenden Commission was created in Britain and it suggested changes in the laws relating to prostitution, homosexuality, and pornography. As a result, the works of Derrick Bailey, Gordon Westwood, James Cleugh, and others attempted to erase the stigma of disease from homosexuals by tracing the historical roots of prejudice and legislation against sodomy.[9] In America, the National Institute of Mental Health commissioned a task force to study homosexuality, and several papers were presented by physicians, psychologists, and other interested persons, including one historical paper based largely on D. S. Bailey that described religious attitudes toward the problem.[10]

Vern Bullough, in his comprehensive *Sexual Variance in Society and History,* notes that there was an interest during the early Middle Ages in modifying forms of sexual behavior in conformity with the Christian ideal of celibacy. At the same time, he notes that marriage and procreation were encouraged and nonprocreative sex (the various sins against nature) discouraged. These attitudes contrast markedly with the flexibility shown by eastern religions toward all forms of sexual expression. Celibacy became a clear prerequisite of clerical ordination in the West in the eleventh and twelfth centuries; Augustinian theology was reaffirmed and sins against nature were condemned and associated with leprosy and heresy. The rejection of sexuality was enshrined in the celibacy of the cloister. The repression of material pleasure, the constant emphasis on spiritual values as opposed to physical pleasure, led Christians to accuse heretics of enjoying the sensual pleasures the church denied to the orthodox.

Nevertheless, the repressive medieval attitude toward sexuality was plagued with contradictions, and the church sometimes encouraged deviations it allegedly condemned: transvestism and nudity, for example. The ambivalence of theory and practice is evident in both the cults of the Virgin and of courtly love. Bullough believes that heretics were probably no more deviant than the orthodox, but the Marxist historian Ernst Werner suggests that heresy may have attracted a greater proportion of persons inclined to indulge in deviant sexual acts.[11] James Cleugh's approach is similar to Bullough's. He notes that such sexual aberrations as flagellation, sodomy, and bestiality among the clergy were a natural reaction to the enforcement of clerical celibacy and the repressive morality of a fanatical religious code. Yet, according to Cleugh, the threat of Islam necessitated the creation of military orders, e.g., the Hospitalers, Templars, and Teutonic Knights, that exaggerated the cultivation of male comradeship and fostered contempt for women. This, he argues, inevitably led to same-sex relationships.[12]

The recent liberalization of public attitudes has encouraged scholarly studies of sexuality based on analyses of local archives. The most notable studies have been made by E. W. Monter, Guido Ruggiero, and J. L. Flandrin. Monter[13] notes that overt homosexuality was traditionally allowed among royalty and he cites the cases of Edward II of England, Frederick II of Prussia, and Henry III of France. Otherwise, severe repression was the rule, beginning with the association of homosexuality and heresy in the twelfth century. In the fifteenth century, the first cases were tried before secular tribunals, which regarded sodomy as a crime against God. Clerics and students were regarded as the most common offenders in southern Europe, whereas sailors were most frequently cited in England and the Low Countries, adding credibility to Richard Burg's contention that the swashbuckling pirates of the seventeenth and eighteenth centuries were often homosexual. Monter's study of several dozen trials for sodomy (involving both homosexuality and bestiality) held between the fifteenth and eighteenth centuries contrasts the urban Calvinist republic of Geneva with the rural Catholic canton of Fribourg, both noted for religious ferocity. In Geneva, such trials came in waves, peaking in 1560 and 1610. The victims of those proceedings were primarily foreigners, including Turkish prisoners taken during the war with Savoy and Italians who claimed to have acquired their habits in Italian universities. The largest group comprised young French artisans, refugees from the Wars of Religion. Their presence in Geneva resulted in young men outnumbering women, a factor which doubtless contributed to the increase of law cases. Beginning in the early seventeenth century, accusations of sodomy at Fribourg focused less on homosexuality than on bestiality, a result of the pastoral character of Fribourg. These accusations were usually linked with charges of sorcery, although those charges virtually disappeared by the late seventeenth century along with the easing of the war against witchcraft. Monter's study thus highlights the link between heresy and sodomy and the persistent parallel between religious zeal and the persecution of sexual deviants. 

Guido Ruggiero[14] examined the sex crimes recorded in Venice between 1338 and 1358, the period of the Black Death. He concluded that sex offenders (except for sodomites) were treated with relative leniency despite the apparent severity of the law because the judging bodies were given latitude in imposing penalties. Rape, the most frequently cited offense, was treated as a petty crime and usually punished with a fine. The most serious punishments were given to the rapists of *puellae* (young girls); lesser punishments were meted out to violators of married women and young single women. The criminals cited were mostly noblemen. The merchant elite of Venice tended to treat its own criminals leniently. Penalties were equally mild in cases of adultery and fornication, although slightly higher for adultery; women were rarely tried. Sodomy was treated as a major crime, on a par with poisoning and forgery. Nevertheless, it is mentioned infrequently in the records. A large group of noble and clerical sodomites was uncovered by the Signori di Notte in 1406–1407 and at least forty-one persons were involved; but the Council of Ten intervened, apparently to reduce the number of executions. The records also cite the case of a transvestite arrested on 12 March 1354 in which evidence was gathered, the accused forced to confess under torture, and then burned at the stake within one week. The mercy displayed against other sex offenders was not applied to convicted sodomites, who were burned, although the younger partners were often spared. The records indicate that most sex crimes were committed in boats or at the homes of victims and in areas of greatest population density. Despite the remarks of Boccaccio and other contemporary observers concerning the decline of morals after the plague, these records suggest there was no significant change in attitudes toward sexuality after 1348.

Flandrin's[15] discussion of late marriage, relying partly on the outstanding study of contraception by John Noonan, treats the problems caused by conflicts between theory and practice in the Middle Ages. Flandrin suggests that church doctrine on sexuality was never passively accepted, that each social milieu necessarily adapted Catholic theory to suit its special needs and traditions. There was, he suggests, a gap between the behavior of medieval Christians and their dogma. He maintains that the archetype of sex-only-within-marriage for purposes of procreation versus the amorous passion and pleasure-seeking of the court were polar opposites. Reality lay somewhere in the middle. Coitus interruptus and other forms of contraception were practiced despite the theoretical ban, and the broad definition of crimes against nature enunciated by the church apparently never gained popular acceptance. Flandrin argues that the church more strictly proscribed illicit sex acts that resulted in the conception of bastards than those that did not lead to conception. Contraceptive intercourse apparently was thought to mitigate the guilt of illicit fornication. In the seventeenth and eighteenth centuries, marriages were often not contracted until ten or fifteen years after puberty as a safeguard against overpopulation and to facilitate the accumulation of capital necessary to start a family. Flandrin argues further that it is difficult to imagine that youths could remain entirely celibate during such a long period. More likely, he suggests, masturbation or other nonprocreative sex acts, perhaps including homosexuality, replaced marital intercourse. It is unlikely, says Flandrin, that young people would have the sexual energy or appetite to marry and bear children after years of sublimation.

Despite the severity of the penitential code, all acts against nature, because of their infertility, were far more difficult to suppress than fornication. The fifteenth-century theologian John Gerson, for example, noted that unnatural sex occurred more often between unmarried people and that young people, especially between the ages of nine and twelve, often refrained from confessing sexual transgressions. Gerson and his contemporary Guy de Roye were aware of the difficulties involved in obtaining information in the confessional concerning such acts. Relying on the statutes of Cambrai (1300–1310), Flandrin notes that punishment of sodomitical acts between women and those committed by youths under twenty was not reserved to the bishop (as were cases involving men over twenty). Clearly, certain types of sodomy (according to age and sex) were considered less heinous. This distinction indicates that theory and practice often diverged despite clerical harangues. Thus the degree of guilt felt among the masses is difficult to determine and Flandrin consequently assumes that acts against nature were common in youth before marriage. The old forms of sexual segregation, the absence of a free choice in the selection of partners, and the predominance of economic criteria rather than romantic ones in marriage have survived until recently in rural areas like the Béarn. Flandrin thus argues that a "Cathar mentality" (a dualistic mentality) governed sexual life in the medieval period and that illicit and nonprocreative practices contrary to theological theory frequently occurred.

The evidence presented in this study supports the contentions of recent historians of sexuality. Until the eleventh century, occasional voices were heard condemning same-sex relations, but it was not until the Gregorian reform movement that a determined effort was made to impose the canons of Catholic sexual morality on an often indifferent public. The polemical lines were laid down in the eleventh and twelfth centuries in penitentials, biblical commentaries, and canon law that became the bases of a revitalized Christianity. Thereafter, discussions of the sin against nature were monotonously similar. A second, equally militant wave of moral "reform" was undertaken in the thirteenth century. The scholastics created a systematic philosophy that attempted to rationalize Catholic opposition to homosexuality. Simultaneously, secular law was mobilized in a war against heresy and sexual nonconformity; and the Inquisition became the militant, persecuting arm of the church. But persecution was still episodic and a willingness to prosecute homosexuals by burning as prescribed by law did not become evident until the fourteenth century.

## *Abbreviations*

| | |
|---|---|
| *AS* | Socii Bollandiani, *Acta Sanctorum quotquot tot orbe coluntur . . .* |
| *B.N.* | Bibliothèque nationale |
| *CSEL* | *Corpus scriptorum ecclesiasticorum latinorum* |
| *DDC* | R. Naz et al., *Dictionnaire de droit canonique* |
| *DHGE* | A. Baudrillart et al., *Dictionnaire d'histoire et de géographie écclériastique* |
| *DTC* | A. Vacant et al., *Dictionnaire de théologie catholique* |
| *LTK* | M. Buchberger et al., *Lexikon für Theologie und Kirche* |
| *Mansi* | *G. D. Mansi, ed., Sacrorum conciliorum et amplissima collectio* |
| *MGH. Leges* | *Monumenta germaniae historica. Leges* |
| *MGHS* | *Monumenta germainiae historica. Scriptores* |
| *PL* | *Patrologia latina* |
| *RIS* | L. Muratori, ed., *Rerum italicarum scriptores* |

# I

## *Homosexuality in the Middle Ages*

THE FIRST TESTIMONY to the existence of homosexuality in Europe in the Middle Ages appeared in the late tenth and early eleventh centuries. The reports are quite sparse and largely literary and they suggest that homosexuality was often regarded as a distinctly foreign import. In this period, deviant sex was not yet regarded as a serious threat to Christian morality. Catholic preachers were still occupied in trying to convert the semipagan population that occasionally threatened to return to its pre-Christian roots. The German poetess and playwright Roswitha of Gandersheim (935–975) described homosexuality as an Arab vice that true Christians would avoid. In the *Passio S. Pelagii,* she told the story of Pelagius, the young and handsome prince of Galicia who was taken as a hostage by the caliph of Cordoba, Abderrahman (ca. 921). The caliph heard of Pelagius's great beauty and when the youth was brought before him he attempted to embrace him. Steadfast in his faith, however, the young prince spurned the caliph, slapping his attacker in the face and drawing blood. For this he suffered martyrdom, defending his Christian morality against the sodomitical practices of the Arab conquerors. Another contemporary poem, *De Lantfrido et Cobbone,* composed in Latin by an unknown Anglo-Saxon and betraying a strong pagan influence, describes the love between the homosexual Cobbo and the bisexual Lantfrid, who during a voyage attempted to introduce Cobbo to the pleasures of heterosexual love with the assistance of his wife.[1] In both of these references, sodomy had already come to be associated with pre-Christian or non-Christian morality, just as the Jews identified it primarily as a Gentile vice.

By the mid-eleventh century, southern France had become the conduit through which many new fashions were to penetrate the north, and those in closest contact with Spanish Saracen culture may have aped the more liberal sexual tastes of the Moslems. Just as Romanesque architecture and courtly poetry have been traced to Spanish antecedents, so also other signs of freer self-expression may have non-Christian precedents. Around the turn of the millennium, the historian Ralph Glaber indicted the nobility of Aquitaine and the

Auvergne for its free morals and "effeminate" ways: "they shaved their faces and wore their hair parted [causing them] to look like mummers."

By the late eleventh century, the Provençal knights who took part in the Crusades in the East were described as milksops by their supposedly hardier Norman comrades-in-arms.[2]

## Anglo-French Deviation

By the mid-eleventh century, Anglo-French court circles had earned a reputation for sexual nonconformism and bawdiness. The mere quantity and variety of such accusations suggest some truth to what might otherwise be considered the ravings of fanatical clergymen bent on extending the restrictions of celibacy to the lay population, "turning the whole world into a monastery." Commenting on the degradation of the French clergy, which had become the object of a papal campaign to impose celibacy, Gregory VII wrote in 1074: "Among you all justice is treaded under foot. The most shameful, cruelest, foulest, and intolerable deeds are committed with impunity. As a result of such license, they become habits."[3] Such easy morals are found both among the upper clergy and the Anglo-French aristocracy. The unceremonious disposal by Philip I of France of his wife Bertha of Marbais, for example, and her replacement by the wife of one of his vassals created a minor scandal. Philip's cousin Henry IV of Germany was barely dissuaded by Peter Damian from divorcing his first wife, Adele of Turin; his second wife, Praxède, according to several chroniclers, was treated with the utmost cruelty. In 1119, Countess Hildegarde of Poitiers complained to the pope of the conduct of her husband, William IX, who had abandoned her and her children for the wife of the viscount of Chatellerault. This laxity produced another problem: a multiplicity of children born out of wedlock. Henry I of England, for example, fathered at least twenty-one known children, mostly illegitimate.[4]

While adultery, concubinage, consanguinity, rape, and clerical marriage are most frequently noted, homosexuality, the "crime against nature," also found a prominent place in the catalog of sexual misdemeanors attributed to the nobility. The descendants of William the Conqueror seem to have had an especially bawdy reputation, which brought them ill repute among the crusading churchmen of the age. William's son Robert Curthose, duke of Normandy, allegedly abandoned himself to "effeminacy" and set up a Venus of Sodom in his court; his regime was allegedly dominated by catamites and "effeminate men." In 1120, on a return trip to England from Normandy, Henry I's heir William and his natural son Richard, along with an entourage of servants, noblemen, and their wives, were all drowned in the famous "White Ship" off Barfleur. Such chroniclers as Henry of Huntingdon and Guillaume de Nangis claim that since almost all of the passengers were tainted with sodomy, their fate was the just reward for vice. Gervase of Canterbury likewise reports that the corpse of Henry I, before its transfer to the grave, gave off a disgusting stench, the natural product of his immoral behavior. During the reign of William Rufus, the second Norman ruler of England, the chronicler Orderic Vitalis (ca. 1090) bemoaned the long hair, feminine behavior, and sodomy that had become popular among Norman youth. And in rather graphic prose, John of Salisbury in his *Policraticus* (1159) described how noble parents pandered their sons and how feminine fashions were accepted by young Norman dandies.[5] Regarding allegations that Rufus was homosexual, such a sober historian as A. L. Poole says it is "tolerably certain that he indulged in unnatural vice." Noting the frequent allegations in contemporary chronicles that William's court encouraged "effeminacy," Jack Lindsay concludes, "Rufus seems certainly to have been homosexual, and in a semimilitary caste like that of the Norman nobles, sodomy was no doubt a common practice." This view, based on insufficient evidence, seems to have originated with the nineteenth-century historian E. A. Freeman.[6]

It is not surprising in this atmosphere of relaxed sexual restraints that pagan and indeed amoral literature should enjoy a certain vogue. The works of Ovid, in particular, exercised strong influence in noble circles and eventually became the objects of clerical censure during the controversies that flared up in the early thirteenth century over the antinomian doctrines of Amaury of Bène and David of Dinant and the introduction of Aristotle and Averroës to the arts curriculum at the University of Paris. One of the more widespread literary genres of the twelfth century, based upon reacquaintance with Cicero's *De Amicitia*, was the treatise on friendship, to which Peter of Blois and Hugh of St. Victor contributed notable examples.[7] But such works, adhering closely to their classical model, deal with spiritual friendship and rarely touch upon physical manifestations of love.

The Cistercian monk Aelred of Rievaulx (1110–1167), the son and grandson of a priest and himself a product of the libertine Anglo-French court circles, wrote two such treatises on friendship, *Speculum caritatis* (ca. 1142/43) and *De Spirituali amicitia* (ca. 1160), intended for the instruction of monks under his care. In his youth at the Scottish court, Aelred had been one of a group of young courtiers surrounding the sons of King David I; there he served as household steward and apparently conceived an infatuation for some unknown young companion. At twenty-four he entered the abbey of Rievaulx, where he eventually became abbot. His contemporary biographer, Walter Daniel, notes that unlike other abbots, who reacted with anger to physical contact between monks, Aelred allowed his monks to hold hands as a natural sign of affection. Like many a nascent saint, including Augustine and Francis, in young adulthood the abbot of Rievaulx was plagued by the alleged corruption of his soul, the "horrible stench" within him. In the lives of both Francis and Augustine, this self-hatred and discontent are specifically described as revulsion against lustful escapades. Given the life-style of the young courtiers of the twelfth century, this scrupulousness probably reflected Christian guilt over the pleasures of the flesh.[8]

Baudri de Bourgeuil, archbishop of Dol (1107–1130), is responsible for a considerable number of poems—addressed to students, ecclesiastics, and noblemen—that seem to have a strong homosexual slant. Baudri had close connections with the court of William the Conqueror, whose daughter, Adele, countess of Blois, along with the queen of France, supported Baudri's unsuccessful candidacy for the archibishopric of Orléans. In addition to active participation in church councils, Baudri wrote a number of works, including a chronicle of the First Crusade and lives of saints Samson of Dol, Robert of Arbrissel, and Hugh of Rouen. Among the recipients of his poems was the poet Marbod of Rennes (ca. 1035–1123). Marbod served as a teacher at the cathedral school of Angers and as bishop of Rennes; he later retired to the cloister of St. Aubin in Angers. He is survived by a number of prose biographies and accounts of visions as well as didactic and religious poems. In one poem he regrets having sinfully embraced young men in his youth. Another member of this Anglo-French circle, the wandering scholar Hilary, addressed a number of poetical epistles to beautiful young boys. An anonymous poem, perhaps of the same literary circle, the *Altercatio Ganymedis et Helenae,* discusses whether the love of young boys or girls is superior. The poet notes that pederasty, first invented by the ancient gods, continues to flourish in noble circles.[9]

The chronicler Guibert of Nogent (1064?–c.1125) in his *Autobiography* presents a detailed picture of the kind of environment in which such intellectuals were raised. In his youth Guibert displayed an interest in Ovid's work, copying the style of the Roman pastoral poets, writing "indecent and obscene poems," perhaps including verses in the genre that depicted the beauties of the various parts of the body, including the genitals. At the same time, he noted his agitation by certain unspecified lustful longings. Guibert described his father, on the other hand, as a man who did not respect the marriage vow and fathered several illegitimate children.[10]

In Dante's *Purgatory,* two troubadours, the Provençal Arnaut Daniel (fl. 1180–1200) and the Tuscan Guido Guinicelli (1240–1276?), are found in the sodomites' seventh circle. Certainly the courtly love ideal of unsatisfied love between the poet and his lady could conceivably lead to homosexuality as a means of satisfying the frustrated sexual impulses of the lover. One poem by the great courtly poet Guillaume IX of Aquitaine (1071–1127) speaks of his love for the girl Agnes and for a certain Arsene, perhaps a boy. The courtly knight, indeed, often addressed his damsel by such masculine titles as *mi dons, me dominus,* or *senhor.* Concerning the specific allegation of sodomy leveled by Dante, there is no clear evidence in either case. In one of his few surviving poems, Daniel does describe an oral-anal encounter between his two poetic rivals, Raimon de Derfort and Turc Malec. The poem, however, is a facetious polemic against the two poets, who were involved in a courtly quarrel with Arnaut, so its reliability is doubtful.[11]

## Heresy and Homosexuality

Despite such literary examples of variant sexual behavior, there is no evidence whatsoever of widespread persecution of sexual deviants until the thirteenth century. Before that time the church's attention was still largely devoted to the problems of adultery, consanguinity, and clerical marriage. And reform was often accomplished without any cooperation from the secular authorities. By the thirteenth century, however, the homosexual, whose sinfulness had allegedly been proven by the sulfurous destruction of Sodom and Gomorrah, had become the object of a program of extermination that paralleled the attack on apostates, judaizers, heretics, dabblers in the art of magic, and other politico-religious deviants.

As early as the late eleventh and early twelfth centuries, theologians had begun to associate heresy with sodomy and apply the same punishment to both. In 1049, at the same time that Peter Damian was launching an attack on clerical sodomy, a local synod excommunicated certain unnamed Gallican heretics along with "sodomites." In 1114, Abbot Guibert of Nogent, whom John Benton has recently labeled a "suppressed homosexual," noted that Henrician heretics at Bucy-le-Long near Soissons were accused of performing homosexual acts and engaging in sex with women *à tergo.*[12] Simultaneously, scriptural glossators grouped around Anselm of Laon linked heresy and sodomy as forms of sacrilege punishable by death. This identification of theological and sexual deviancy was soon given the force of law at the Council of Nablus in 1120 (see below, pp. 42–43).

The rejection of sexual intercourse in marriage by so many of the new heretical sects was often regarded by the church as sufficient proof of homosexuality. And, indeed, there are elements of heretical theology that could be interpreted as condoning freer sexual behavior. In an 1135 sermon against certain heretics who preached against marriage, Bernard of Clairvaux opposed the extremism of such sects, some of whom by rejecting marriage, according to Bernard, opened the door to excessive sexual freedom: "If you deprive the church of honorable marriage and an unstained bed, you will fill her with concubinage, incest, seminal emissions, masturbation, homosexuality, and every other kind of filthiness."[13]

The most widespread of these heretical sects, centered in southern France and northern Italy, were the Cathars, or Albigensians. Their attitude toward generative sexuality could be interpreted as tacit acceptance of all of the outrageous forms of sexual expression so thoroughly condemned by the church. In theory, Catharism, because of its hostility to the material world as a creation of the Devil, condemned marriage and indeed all sexuality whose ultimate result was generation of matter. In the *Summa quadripartita,* a polemical attack on the errors of the Waldensians and Albigensians, Alan of Lille notes that the Cathars even condemned marriage as a form of legalized adultery. They insisted that mankind should strive rather to free itself entirely from the works of Satan, that is, the material world; fornication merely satisfied the urge for generation and multiplication of the species and resulted in the perpetuation of Satan's minions. Because marriage could only be consummated through carnal relations, and thus through sin, it was to Cathars an execrable institution contrary to natural law.[14]

The Cathars, however, seem to have somewhat mitigated this extreme doctrine. The Cathar church was divided into two membership groups. The *perfecti* were expected to practice total abstention in order to purify themselves of earthly shackles. Christian polemicists claimed that the mere "believers," on the other hand, could (at least in theory) engage in the most extreme hedonism, even commit mortal sin, until the final rite of liberation, the *consolamentum,* had been administered. This sacrament might even be undergone at the point of death, after which time such unorthodox behavior was prohibited; but until that time, anything was allegedly permissible. Thus, while for the *perfecti* all sex acts were equally bad (and one could not draw up a list of relative evils as the Catholic theologians did), the believers were believed free to satisfy every lustful urge.

Like the early Christians themselves, the Cathars were soon divided up into a number of sects, largely along geographical lines. According to the Catholic polemicist Anselm of Alexandria, writing around 1266/7, one such sect was founded by the "bishop" Philip at Desenzano in the diocese of Brescia. This Cathar worthy, who had allegedly been apprehended with two Cathar women and forced to return to secular life, argued that "no man or woman can commit sin from the waist down," a view that supposedly attracted many followers. A similar opinion was attributed to the Albigensians of Languedoc in 1213 by the chronicler Peter of Vaux-de-Cernay. Writing in 1250/60, the author of the *Brevis summula contra errores notatos hereticorum* stated that some Italian Cathars denied that one could do penance after sinning and disputed the existence of purgatory. Both of these opinions effectively rejected the Catholic notions of sin and repentance.[15]

Nor was the church slow to accuse the heretics of every sexual misdemeanor from contraception to sodomy. By about 1170 A.D., the

Albigensian, because of his theology's presumed origins in Bulgaria, was occasionally called *bougre* or *bougeron,* which soon became a synonym for sodomite. The Old French *erite,* or heretic, was also used interchangeably for an Albigensian and a sodomite. This confusion has created problems in studying legislative references to sodomy, for it is sometimes uncertain whether the laws apply to homosexuality or to heresy, as in the *Coutumes de Touraine-Anjou.* Matthew Paris notes that in France usurers were also called *bugeros.* Several contemporary poets even describe the Lombards, Europe's chief bankers and usurers, as practiced pederasts in addition to their other vices.[16] Interestingly, the very same popular reform movements, like the Flagellants and Fraticelli, that attacked sodomy and heresy with such relish, also scorned the practice of usury and were often tainted with anti-Semitism; they frequently regarded philo-Semitism, Catharism, usury, and homosexuality as upper class, or noble, "vices."

The antinomianism of the most libertarian of medieval sects, the Brethren of the Free Spirit, could also be interpreted as permitting sexual deviation. But to what extent such rejection of the socially established morality was merely theoretical, and to what degree practiced, is difficult to estimate. The Dominican John of Schwenkfeld, for example, after examining some beguines of Silesia, claimed that they indulged in all forms of sexual license. A novice of the beguines allegedly heard that the sisters petted each other and placed their tongues in one another's mouths during sermons and masses. A member of the Italian sect of the Apostolic Brethren, whose theology was similar to that of the Brethren of the Free Spirit, confessed in 1299 at Bologna to believing that homosexual acts were licit if the participants were in a state of perfection. The chronicler Salimbene de Adam claimed that some members of the sect fornicated with both women and boys.[17]

In 1233, Gregory IX addressed the bull *Vox in Rama* to the archbishop of Mainz and the bishop of Hildesheim commending the activities of Conrad of Marburg against certain German heretics. In this letter, which has been regarded as early proof of the campaign against witchcraft, the pope noted that these heretics worshipped the devil by kissing the posterior of their leader and taking part in bisexual orgies. Similar rites were described in the 1336 trial of the Cologne Luciferian Lepzet, who confessed that the sectaries kissed the anus of their leader and then engaged in homosexual acts.[18] Such pseudosexual rites of initiation were also ascribed to the most well-known victims of sexual obscurantism, the order of Knights Templars. Because the use of torture always accompanied inquisitorial trials, however, it is difficult to judge whether the confessions of homosexual activity were true or the inventions of tortured witnesses.

In addition to the campaign against heretics, by the thirteenth century clerics and university students had begun to replace the nobility as the groups most frequently accused of sodomy. One of the few exceptions among critics was Philip of Novara, who described lust as a vice of old men who, because of fear of aging and death, became easily addicted to unnatural vices and perversion. Alexander of Roes, however, regarded lust as a clerical vice and sodomy as a specifically French sin. Because the clergy rules in France, he argued, the nobility and commonfolk have become infected. A French fabliau dealing with the amorous activities of a priest and a chevalier in pursuit of the same damsel quotes the fair lady as complaining of a pain in her posterior as a result of the priest's preference for sodomitical pleasures. On hearing this, the knight threatens to perform the same act several times upon the priest himself.[19] The satirical poet Walter Mapes attacks the Cistercian order, in his *De Nugis curialium* (ca. 1182/89) and singles out St. Bernard's nonhomosexuality as an exception among monks, a distinction which proved his sanctity. A certain marquis of Burgundy, Mapes reports, had asked the saint to cure his ailing son. Bernard ordered the body taken to a private room and, when everyone had left, he lay on the lad and prayed. As a result, the youth was revived. Mapes then added: "He was indeed the most unhappy of monks, for I have never heard of a monk who had lain on top of a boy and who did not immediately rise after him."[20] James of Vitry, writing about 1230, called the French a "proud, soft, feminine" people. He particularly condemned the students at the University of Paris for keeping prostitutes and practicing sodomy.[21] In 1270, the poet Guillot in his *Dit des rues de Paris* cited rue Beaubourg as a favorite homosexual trysting place in Paris; on the rue des Marmouzets the poet himself had been served by prostitutes. The fifteenth-century poet Antonio Beccadelli testified to the continued practice of sodomy in the learned and student circles found in Paris.[22]



## Political Charges of Deviation

The early fourteenth century, despite the virtual eradication of such widespread sects as Catharism and Waldensianism, witnessed the revival of charges of homosexuality against political foes, particularly in France. Among the accusations heaped upon the ill-fated Pope Boniface VIII in his struggle with Philip the Fair were heresy, usury, simony, and sodomy. The political nature of these charges is transparent. A hundred years later, during the conciliar period, in order to force the resignation of the reluctant Pope John XXIII, who had refused to appoint proctors for his abdication, the charges leveled against the pope at the Council of Constance included sodomy, incest with nuns, rape, and adultery. That only two days were required to file the charges and hear testimony indicates the degree of concern for truth.[23]

There is less doubt that the relationship between Edward II of England (1284–1327) and his favorites Hugh Despenser and Piers Gaveston had homoerotic elements. The *Vita Edwardi secundi,* by a monk of Malmesbury, notes that the king's connection with Gaveston predated the coronation. He is described as the king's bedmate and lover, for whom the king felt the greatest love and affection. As a result, despite his humble and foreign origin, he was granted many lands, married to Edward's niece, Margaret, daughter of Jeanne of Acre, and served as regent in the king's absence. Ultimately, baronial resentment resulted in Gaveston's assassination at the order of Earl Thomas of Lancaster. Writing fifty years later, a Cistercian chronicler flatly attributed the death to "too much sodomy"; Edward himself, it is reported, was killed in a similar manner by having a hot poker thrust up his "posterior."[24] While the case for Edward's sexual preferences seems well documented, several other monarchs, including Richard the Lion-Hearted, Frederick II of Germany, and Conradin of Sicily, have also been identified as sexual nonconformists. The Swedish St. Bridget in one of her visions was advised by the Virgin Mary to caution King Magnus Eriksson (1316–1374) against his sinful preference for sex with young men over sex with his own wife.[25]

The poet Dante, writing in the same period, describes in the seventh circle of the *Inferno*, the sufferings of a number of prominent political and artistic figures who had allegedly been damned for acts against nature. But none of these accusations can be proven; moreover, many of the denizens of Hell were in fact political opponents of the poet in his native Florence. Adimari Tegghiaio, for example, who had served as podestà of Arezzo in 1255, was a Guelph opponent of the Florentine commune during the famous battle of Monteperti (1266); he later joined the Florentine exiles at Lucca and acquired a reputation as an honest magistrate. The great Bolognese civil lawyer Accursius (d. ca. 1260) was also consigned to Dante's Hell. Yet he married twice and sired several children, displaying no recorded preference for sins against nature. Nor do his commentaries on the *Corpus iuris civilis* betray special liberalism in the treatment of sexual offenders. Another sufferer in the seventh circle was the former papal chaplain and bishop of Florence, Andrea dei Mozzi, who had been transferred from his Florentine see to the bishopric of Vicenza-on-the-Bacciglione, perhaps because of moral turpitude. Besides these political figures, Dante consigned to the sodomites' circle his teacher Brunetto Latini (1220–1294), a Guelph expelled from Florence in 1260, and the sixth-century poet Priscian. Once again, in neither of these cases is there clear evidence of the alleged sin against nature.[26]

The most notorious political accusation of sodomy was leveled against the entire order of Knights Templars, who were held responsible for the ignominious fall of Acre (1291) and the end of Crusader power in the East.[27] In the resulting persecution, several thousand Templars were executed or imprisoned and the venerable order was disbanded. Their considerable wealth in Europe itself became a welcome source of revenue for the hard-pressed crown of France, which in the early fourteenth century had been forced to undertake a series of desperate measures to relieve its financial crisis: devaluation of the currency, the expulsion of the Jews and the confiscation of their property, restrictions on the activity of the Lombard bankers within the kingdom, reduction of the outflow of gold from France to the papal treasury, and pillaging and destruction of leprosaria throughout France.

The first accusations of sexual unorthodoxy against the Templars apparently date from 1304 or 1305 in the Agen region of France, from whence the charges were relayed to King Jaime of Aragon and Lerida. Among other offenses, the Templars were accused of requiring new members to take part in a bizarre rite of admission that involved denying Christ, spitting on the Crucifix, and disrobing; various members of the order would then allegedly kiss the initiate on the mouth, lower waist, anus, or other area, sometimes including the penis. Many witnesses—some of whose testimony is suspect because they had been expelled from the order for various offenses or had undergone torture—claimed that the rule of the Templars permitted as sinless "acts against nature" between members.

While Pope Clement V apparently knew of these charges when he ascended the papal throne in 1305, he did not act until pressured to do so by Philip IV of France, who hurled charges of sexual misconduct against many of his political foes. On 24 August 1307, an official inquiry opened; despite some involvement of the Inquisition, the arrests, confiscations, torture, trial, and punishment were largely conducted by royal officials. By 13 October 1307, the arrest of all Templars throughout France was ordered; and by 22 November 1307, Clement V ordered all other princes to arrest the Templars and sequester their goods. For the next several years, despite some conflict between royal and ecclesiastical authorities, the task of cataloging the wealth of the order, gathering witnesses, hearing testimony, and passing judgment was carried out by hundreds of episcopal and royal tribunals. At the Council of Vienne (1311/12), the order was completely suppressed and its wealth was transferred to the Hospitalers; by 1314, the dignitaries of the order were placed in perpetual imprisonment by the church and executed by royal edict. While many of the Templars may indeed have been involved in same-sex relationships, the denunciations, torture, and political implications of the entire affair have made a dispassionate treatment of the case nearly impossible.

## Urban Vice

While charges of homosexuality in noble circles continued to be voiced in the later Middle Ages, by the fourteenth and fifteenth centuries the city emerged as the focus of such activity, with no social class being specified. Ports and trade centers, because of their large foreign and transient populations, were particular centers of sexual nonconformity. While in the earlier period sodomy had been regarded as a French vice, the Italians were now increasingly identified with the freer sexual mores that were to characterize the Renaissance. And in Italy, where political animosities often resulted in a strong anticlerical tradition, the state rather than the church began to take a more active role in the persecution of sexual deviants.

Italian communal records remain a storehouse of information regarding late medieval sexual mores. These documents, which include court proceedings, council minutes, arrest lists, and prison records, unfortunately have not yet been studied in depth. At Bologna, a noted university center, the four crimes punished by burning were rape, sodomy, heresy, and infanticide; all four of these crimes would have been treated with much less severity before the twelfth century. But by 1442 a sodomite priest had been condemned to death, and in 1412 one Nicola Campioli was condemned for performing sodomy in one of the chapels of the church of San Petronio.[28]

Venice was regarded as a flourishing center of pederasty, transvestism, lesbianism, and prostitution, no doubt because it was a bustling seaport with a large number of foreign, particularly Greek, unattached seamen in its midst. The city fathers made determined, if unsuccessful, attempts to halt the spread of such offenses. A superficial reading of Venetian court records reveals several examples of indictments for sodomy in the fourteenth century. In 1342, for example, one Giomello de Bonaldo was accused of stabbing the vagabond Marin Piero to death after forcibly raping him. In 1354, the transvestite Rolandinus Ronchaia was ordered burned for sodomitical acts. It is reported that Rolandinus, who had always looked and acted like a woman, had been married some years earlier at Padua but had been introduced to homosexuality after his wife's death. He then became a transvestite and was working as a female prostitute at the time of his arrest in Venice. In another case, in 1365, one Roberto de Marchesio was found guilty of forcing a twelve-year-old shipboy to commit sodomy with him during a voyage. In 1368, the town herald Benedetto was found guilty of first forcing, then cajoling (at two *denarii* a meeting) a certain thirteen-year-old boy named Antonio into an affair lasting three years. One meeting allegedly occurred on the steps leading to the meeting room of the Grand Council.[29]

The situation was apparently regarded as so grave by 1455 that two nobles were to be appointed for a year to find out where pederasts loitered and committed their illicit acts.[30] If those appointed should refuse to carry out their duties, they were to pay a fine of 100 lire. In 1460, the council described the existence of a sodomites union, a "collegium sodomitarum"; and in the following year, the physicians and barbers of Venice were ordered to report to the captains of the council within three days after treating any man or woman whose anus had been damaged by sodomy. In 1464, the capital punishment of burning was again enacted for all sodomites. In 1468, the widespread existence of women and boys who engaged in acts of sodomy for profit was noted; and in 1480, Venetian law even prohibited women from wearing men's hairstyles and clothes on the grounds that this was a kind of sodomy aimed at attracting other lesbian women. In 1500, the same capital punishment suffered by sodomites was extended to pimps who induced boys or women to commit sodomy.

The records likewise refer to specific spots in the city that were notorious as homosexual trysting places. In 1496, it was reported that the bordellos were a site of homosexual activity and that the red-light district of the Carampana quarter was a well-known gathering place for sodomites. Other reported meeting places included the field beside the Cruciferian monastery, the dark corners of the palaces of the dukes of Modena and Ferrara, and the city's gondolas and barbershops. The records also cite classes most prone to "unnatural vice": the clergy, foreigners, including a Turk cited three times in the late fifteenth century, and the nobility, who were wont (it is said) to engage in pederasty. Filippo Barro, for example, a member of the Grimani family, reportedly paid one hundred and thirty ducats for the services of one Pathicius Rabia. The homosexual prostitutes themselves often came from the large Greek contingent in the city; in 1469, the Greek Joannes Hierarchos was sentenced to death for sodomy. In 1462, several youths suffered castration, branding, and the removal of a nose for such offenses; and in 1443, a report even notes a transvestite homosexual.

The records of the city council of Cologne in 1484 afford a rare view of the alleged spread of homosexual activity north of the Alps.[31] During June and July of that year, as a result of repeated charges, the city council decided to hold an inquiry and hear testimony from local pastors concerning the frequency of sodomitical acts within their parishes. One priest estimated that there were two hundred active sodomites in the city, that is, 1–1.5 percent of the total population. The pastor of St. Cunibert noted that every year two or three persons confessed to him regarding that crime; the pastor of St. Apostolus told of a poor man who was forced through penury to serve the lustful needs of a wealthy married man. According to the pastor of St. Martin, the center of all this vice was the Haymarket area. On the other hand, several priests reported no contact whatsoever with sodomites. In Lucerne in 1414 and in Holland in 1446, complaints were also voiced about the widespread practice of sodomy. No doubt a more thorough study of municipal court and council records will reveal much more about sexual offenders in the free cities of the Empire, where such offenses were punished largely by communal rather than imperial officials because of the weakened central authority in Germany.

## Theory versus Practice

In sum, during the medieval centuries a number of groups at one time or another, including the clergy, nobility, university students, and heretics, were identified with sexual nonconformity. Geographically, France and Italy, the European heartland, were most frequently cited as hotbeds of disorder, although this may simply be the result of more adequate documentation; the mere struggle for survival on the periphery, in Germany, Spain, and Scandinavia, in the face of Mongol, Saracen, or pagan peril may have reduced sexual diversity to the level of a mere peccadillo. Urbanized Europe, however, seems to have been populated by a throng of religious puritans on the lookout for sexual deviance. The character of sexual life among the peasantry or rural folk is considerably more difficult to ascertain in the absence of literary or documentary evidence. Certainly, the close but severely supervised physical contact of a one-room shack is not likely to foster excessive sexual freedom.

The kind of mass judicial murder for homosexuality that was to occur in Holland in 1730/31 apparently never took place in the Middle Ages—or at least our records are silent.[32] For, as Flandrin argues, despite the antisexual rhetoric of the church, an awareness of the need to compromise in the face of social needs is evident. Prostitution was condemned, but overlooked; infanticide was equated with homicide, but often disregarded; and consangunity and concubinage sometimes appear to be more the rule than the exception. Acts of sodomy are considerably more difficult to uncover.[33] The sixteenth-century theologians, for example, often expressed the fear that the anti-ceremonialism of the Anabaptists would unleash a wave of sexual license—logic that seemed to imply that only the rituals of the faith served as defense against the release of repressed impulses. Many obviously feared that Christians might be transformed into uncontrollable beasts once the restraints of organized religion were removed. In fact, the metaphor of a dog wallowing in his own filth, lacking reason, is a frequent image for the sodomite or any other sexual deviant. Repeated ritual was the prescribed means of warding off unanticipated expressions of spontaneity.[34]

A more realistic view of medieval society makes room for the perennial conflict between Dionysian and Apollonian elements, license and repression, sexual experimentation and self-mortification. Concentration on the declarations of theologians fearful of free sexuality and the demons it might unleash creates a picture of a thoroughly monasticized world unable to overcome the stresses of urbanization and expansion that Europe experienced in the twelfth and thirteenth centuries. The sexual variety uncovered in 1323 in the small village of Montaillou by the inquisitor Jacques Fournier, which included promiscuity, homosexuality, bigamy, and illegitimacy on a wide scale, throws into considerable doubt the long-held notions of moral rigidity attributed to medieval society. Arnold ofVerniolle certainly had no difficulty finding young men to share the pleasures of his bed (see Appendix). The sexual relationships of the Clergue clan show an immoderate sexuality unexpected in a rural seigneury where all benevolently followed the lead of the local curate, Pierre Clergue. And Beatrice of Planisolles, although illiterate, was attracted to the intricacies of heresy and was not frustrated by the restrictions of the marriage couch from bestowing her sexual favors on a variety of partners.[35] Such a wide gap between official theology and local practice extended to so many areas of life that one is tempted to regard learned treatises, canon law, and the penitential code as the expressions of a high ideal rather than the reality of everyday life. For indeed when unusual conditions freed Europe briefly from the sexual tyranny of Augustinian Catholicism, as during the plague years of 1348/9 or the German peasant revolt of 1525, reports show that immoral behavior and antinomian prophecy threatened to overwhelm the rigidity of Catholic tradition.

In fact, those elemental drives that always threaten to destroy the order in which religion attempts to clothe the world were of continuing concern to the medieval consciousness; and much medieval culture, in keeping with Augustine's dualistic tendencies, attempted to come to grips with this conflict between the upper and lower selves, Satan and God, the animal demands of the flesh and the controlling force of reason. The church functioned in a world filled with temptations, many of them sexual, which were at all times to be avoided. A good example of the conflict is the autobiography of Otloh of St. Emmeram (d. ca. 1070), a remarkably frank record of dreams and illusions describing the sufferings of one Benedictine monk beset with a multiplicity of fears and temptations.[36] Otloh explains that the Devil constantly invents new arguments, often incredibly convincing ones; that "pious books tell one story and men's lives and habits another" suggested to Otloh that those supposedly God-inspired writers of Scripture, like men of our day, uttered pieties while practicing vice. Furthermore, the imperfections and disorder of the universe argue cogently for the nonexistence of the Deity, who, if he existed, would not allow such disorder to reign.

Suffering from insomnia after two severe illnesses, Otloh entered religion and in accordance with the new kind of religious ideal of his time wandered about from monastery to monastery. In his *Liber visionum,* Otloh repeats some of the most gruesome tales found in the *Vitae patrum* and Gregory the Great's *Dialogues* in order to frighten both himself and the reader away from sexual temptation. One example he uses is that of St. Equitius (A.D. sixth century) who was sorely troubled by carnal lust and turned to God for assistance. That night he saw himself castrated by an angel![37] John of Lodi's contemporary biography of that paragon of moral virtue, Peter Damian, likewise notes that after reaching puberty the saint was subjected to sharp carnal pains at night. He would then immediately rise from his bed, undress, and plunge naked into cold water until his limbs were thoroughly frozen. Then he would get out, say several psalms, by which time the "noxious heat" that had afflicted him would have receded.[38]

The persistent fear of sexuality characteristic of so much of medieval society and the paradoxical inability to stamp out its manifestations even in the confines of the cloister is evident in a story related by Abbot Peter the Venerable of Cluny (ca. 1122–1156).[39] Peter tells the tale of an unidentified lay brother, a carpenter of Cluny, during the abbacy of Hugh V (d. 1109). Lying in his dormitory bed just before the lights had been dimmed one night, a threatening apparition suddenly appeared above the carpenter: a great vulture flanked by two demon-like men involved in conversation. They had come to attack the monk sprawled on his bed but admitted that because he was protected by the cross, holy water, and his psalms, he was inaccessible. They spoke of having just come from Châlons, where they had tempted a certain knight belonging to Geoffrey of Donzy to commit adultery with his lord's wife, and from the monastery of Tournus (Saône-et-Loire), where they had made a master of the novices fornicate with one of his students. Baited by his fellow spirit, one of the demons picked up the monk's axe from under his bed and tried to chop off the carpenter's leg; but the monk withdrew in time, the blow fell on the bed, and the spirits disappeared. The monk later related this diabolical conversation to Abbot Hugh who, after making inquiries, found that the sinful deeds described had in fact been committed. The region of Châlons and Mâcon apparently long remained a center of sexual diversity, for in 1203 Innocent III initiated an investigation into the prevalence of clerical sodomy in Mâcon.[40]

The fear of homosexual race—which could be a source of continuing anxiety in a monastic, all-male environment in which beating was a regular feature of penitential discipline and education—is illustrated in a capital at Vezelay that depicts the abduction of Ganymede by Jupiter. As Ilene Forsyth notes, classical examples of this theme traditionally depict a handsome Jupiter playfully carrying off a pretty boy.[41] In this medieval example, however, Jupiter becomes a cruel bird who picks up a yelping dog along with the helpless child while the parent or guardian frantically attempts to fend off the satanic creature. The elaborate rules drawn up for the education and behavior of oblates, or children placed in monasteries at an early age by their parents, also indicate the fear of physical and/or homoerotic contact that the close, sexually segregated monastic environment could generate. The *Constitutions* of Hirschau (ca. 1000), for example, forbade any kind of familiarity between the boys, prohibiting the exchange of signs or smiles or even the sight of each others' faces. Clothes were not to be touched and an older monk was delegated to stand between the boys, supervising their every waking moment, including toilet activities. At St. Benigné, corporal punishment for the infraction of such rules was severe; moreover, the use of the rod was required lest the punishing master, through the use of his bare hands, himself break the rules against physical contact.[42]

These draconian regulations were somewhat mitigated in the twelfth century when new penitential systems reduced the need for physical brutality. In a conversation with a pious but stern abbot known for severe punishments, Anselm of Canterbury (1033–1109) notes that such merciless beating tends to breed criminous, sinful monks. He suggests rather the application of compassion, kindness, and fatherly love as the best means of rearing the future servants of God and bringing out their highest potential.[43] By the thirteenth century, the mendicant orders, aware of the burdens and dangers of child oblation, tried to eliminate this institution entirely. Still, there remained the temptations of adolescence. St. Bonaventure in his rules for novices, therefore, prohibited sleeping on one's back or in "any other lewd manner" (e.g., naked) with hands touching the body, buttocks protruding or insufficiently covered. In order to further drive away temptation, psalms were to be recited at night and an image of the crucified Christ borne in mind.[44]

Peter Damian, the most vocal spokesman for the antisexual campaign of the eleventh century and the author of the only extant tract against homosexuality, the *Liber Gomorrhianus,* is himself a classic case of the abandoned and brutalized child whose early privations drove him to puritanical extremes in later life. Born into a large, impoverished family, lacking a father, scorned by his brothers, Peter was rejected even by his mother, who was so depressed that she refused to nurse him. Near death—or was this infanticide?—he was saved by a priest's concubine, who severely berated the mother for such cruel neglect. Although Peter's mother then briefly fulfilled her maternal duties, the child was soon orphaned and was raised by an older brother and his cruel wife. This initiated the worst phase of his life, for he was here treated "as a slave," beaten constantly and mercilessly, fed on the meanest of foods. About age twelve, Peter was transferred to the care of another brother, whose kindness and concern apparently contrasted sharply with his other sibling's brutality. But the psychological damage already inflicted on the child was to have a lasting impact. Peter's whole career was devoted to self-degradation and denial—the life-style which was to become the religious ideal for the next two hundred years. His biographer takes careful note of the vile foods, fasts, bare feet, abstinence, and isolation, both spiritual and physical, that filled his life.[45]

Peter always describes sexuality in the most derogatory terms—as violation, sacrilege, profanation, contagion, or corruption. Sex is never the product of love, only of animal lust.[46] The pangs of birth are the just punishment for the pleasures of conception; the desire to bear children is a sign of the unwillingness to abandon, even after death, the sensual world. To Peter, we are all born in "hideous putrefaction and filth"; even bestiality is preferable to homosexuality on the grounds that only one, rather than two souls, is damned. As a shepherd, Peter had no doubt learned to appreciate animals over men, for in fact he speaks more favorably of the sex life of animals than of mankind: beasts, he says, are merely concerned with conception, not the satisfaction of lust. The human body is variously described as dirt, filth, or ordure, consumed by the fires of lust. Damian expresses pride that he has never allowed himself to derive pleasure from his body. In a cry of despair, he addresses the Virgin Mary: "Oh my glorious mother, mirror of virginal purity and standard of all virtue, how have I, a wretched and unhappy creature, offended you by the filthy putridness of my flesh, and have violated the chastity of my body, of which you are the mother and author!"

The particular venom with which Peter was to tackle the problem of clerical sodomy suggests a personal experience of traumatic impact.[47] Nevertheless, the reforms initiated by Peter Damian and others who took up his ideal of self-denial had at first only a limited effect. In its second stage, the program of sexual repression gained momentum with the rise of heresy, which seemed to confirm the worst fears of the reformers, who were quick to identify theological heterodoxy with sexual nonconformity.

λ

In the early eleventh century, homosexuality was identified primarily as a non-Christian vice, but by the end of the century a veritable wave of denunciations by the clergy against their noble cousins suggests a period of sexual experimentation, perhaps related to the transformation in family structure that characterized the eleventh century. Those same noble and royal Anglo-French circles whose behavior prompted accusations of sodomy were experiencing a crisis of overpopulation and a corresponding growth of material needs.[48] As a result of the rapid growth of the ruling class, a scramble for land occurred, leading to inter- and intra-familial warfare. Usurpations and lawsuits rose dramatically; lands were alienated and reacquired, sometimes by force. In order to guard against fragmentation of the inheritance, the system of primogeniture gradually developed, leading to the creation of a new class of disinherited younger sons. This excess population was partially absorbed by the church, the Crusades, the colonization movement, and the Norman conquests. This land greed often led to the loosening of the close family ties that had characterized the early Middle Ages.[49]

Narrative accounts from this period speak of a large number of aimless young knights who were neither married nor heads of families.[50] Their lives were characterized by impatience, turbulence, and instability; they wandered in constant search of glory, honor, rewards, and a patrimony that the new system of inheritance denied them. Such youths were usually accompanied by mentors selected by their parents, and these guides were themselves often unmarried "youth" of greater experience. More often these landless sons were incorporated into a group of friends, sons of their fathers' vassals. Until a suitable heiress was found, the tendency was to prolong the premarital stage. In the sixteenth and seventeenth centuries, Lawrence Stone has noted, this was to lead to a rise in illegitimacy, homosexuality, and other phenomena traditionally decried by the church.[51] Until the introduction of such knightly orders as the Templars, the pursuit of pleasure and adventure often found less than Christian channels. Such bands of impressionable, "immoral" youth were especially prevalent in Anglo-French circles. The *History* of William the Marshal, for example, describes a young knight surrounded by boon companions "whom he loves as his brother." The *familia* maintained by Hugh of Chester included young knights, clergymen, and courtesans who enjoyed sex, gambling, horsemanship, and other vices together. Orderic Vitalis describes how the preaching of Gerald of Avranches successfully convinced Roger de Warenne and four companions to abandon Hugh's entourage and enter the monastery of St. Evroult, "escaping as it were from the destruction of Sodom."[52]

By the twelfth century, although noble circles were still branded as sodomitical, the focus had shifted and it was the new heretical sects that were accused of sexual nonconformity. The war against religious dissent was fatefully joined with the battle against homosexuality, an association that lasted well into modern times. With the rise of universities peopled by young, single, male clerics, such intellectual centers as Paris and Bologna were noted as centers of uranianism (homosexuality), along with such commercial crossroads as Venice, which attracted foreigners and young men in search of employment. Nevertheless, instances of persecution only appear in the fourteenth century with the trials of the Templars, whose fate was as much the product of reasons of state as of moral turpitude.

# II

## *Gregorian Reform*

THE REINVIGORATION OF the papacy in the eleventh century and the recognition of the low moral tone of church and society called forth a program of moral and religious purification. The Gregorian reform movement has often been regarded as a turning point in European history during which Catholic Europe freed itself from its cultural subservience to the East and for the first time defined itself as a unique civilization.[1] In the political sphere, the church asserted its independence from secular authority, the pope established his preeminence in the ecclesiastical hierarchy, and the financial basis of the Church was assured through a more efficient marshaling of tithes, an end to the alienation of church property, and a strengthened bureaucracy. In the religious sphere, the most immediate and persistent aim of the reforming party was the transformation of clerical morals and the reduction of lay influence. Specifically, the sexual morality of the secular and monastic clergy came under severe attack. Although celibacy theoretically had been one of the requirements for the priesthood for some time, a considerable number of clerics lived openly with wives, concubines, sisters, mothers, and children and attempted to pass their livings on to their heirs, treating their positions and church properties as feudal benefices. The enforcement of clerical celibacy, according to the reformers, would serve a variety of purposes: 1) the alienation of ecclesiastical property would cease, 2) the clergy would be freed from the worldly need to support families, and could therefore devote itself to the needs of its flock, and 3) a celibate clergy would serve as a more plausible ideal to the semi-Christianized peoples of Europe. In addition, the enforcement of celibacy could potentially ease population pressure.

Beginning in the late tenth century, secular law, synodal and ecumenical legislation, and papal decrees attempted to obliterate concubinage and clerical marriage, or Nicolaitism, and to severely reduce cohabitation. Masses performed by married priests were declared illicit; the offspring of such clerics were branded bastards; offenders were excommunicated if they failed to give up their wives or paramours; their property was confiscated, and they were liable to more serious secular punishment. The repetition of these decrees over a several hundred year period, however, suggests that their impact remained limited and spotty. The repeated publication of a pamphlet by Ulrich of Imola (ca. 1060) supporting the marriage of the priesthood indicates that, at least at the outset, some opposition was voiced to this aspect of the reform program.[2] Ulrich argues cogently that clerical celibacy should be voluntary, lest sinful priests, deprived of an outlet, commit even graver offenses, like bestiality and sodomy, which have already infected much of the upper clergy. Furthermore, Ulrich contends, the hypocrisy that forced celibacy engenders might scandalize the laity and turn them away from the church. He notes that at the Council of Nicaea when the subject of celibacy was raised St. Paphnutius pointed out that such legislation would lead to clerical corruption and Donatism. Ulrich's letter, often attributed to St. Ulrich of Augsburg, was used time and again in the Gregorian period; and many judaizing or heretical sects, like the Waldensians, were even to assert the right of married laymen to perform priestly duties.

Aside from purely legislative acts, many of which were incorporated in the newly created canon law codes, new forms of monastic and common life were initiated that enforced stricter rules of conduct. In particular, the eleventh century witnessed the rise of the regular and secular canons, based upon a resurrected Augustinian rule. At such priories as St. Victor, Arrouaise, St. Ruf, and Prémontré and their daughter houses, clerics were brought together under one roof, sharing their property and supervising each other's morals. Similar groups of canons united around the great cathedrals, where they continued to minister to their flocks. Among the monastic clergy, a series of new orders arose under stronger central authority and exacting more severe penitential discipline. Among these were the Camaldulensians, Carthusians, Grandmontains, and Cistercians. This revitalization of the monastic life also provided a partial outlet for unemployed, undirected youth. At the same time, the papacy urged local bishops to make regular visits to supervise the morals of the clergy under their care.[3]

The anticlerical historian Henry C. Lea, author of works on the Inquisition and sacerdotal celibacy, insists that such rigid enforcement of clerical celibacy only aggravated a problem endemic to the church: "Deprived as was the priesthood of the gratification afforded by marriage to the natural instincts of man, the wife at best was succeeded by the concubine, at worst by a succession of paramours, for which the function of priest and confessor gave peculiar opportunity."[4] Lea claims that provided the priest didn't marry, all was forgiven. As a result of such "artificial asceticism," particularly in the monasteries, sexual immorality was rampant, for such a rigid sexual code was unenforceable. Alexander II, for example, in 1064, decided that a priest of Orange was not to be deprived of the communion for committing incest with his father's wife, lest he be driven to desperation; instead, he was allowed to remain in lower clerical orders. In 1066, Alexander likewise reduced the penance of a Paduan priest who had committed incest with his mother, and allowed the bishop to adjudicate further.

While the new disciplinary regulations and modes of living were at first exclusively concerned with the clerical and monastic population, the reformers soon turned their attention to the mores of the laity. And a population that until then had only been superficially Christianized began to experience the full brunt of Catholic morality. The first volley of this campaign among the laity was naturally directed against the widespread practices of adultery, concubinage, and clandestine marriage. Both Urban II and Paschal II, for example, pronounced anathema against the adulterous Philip I of France for his liaison with Bertrade of Montfort; more severe synodal legislation was enacted against rape and adultery, though the degree of temporal compliance is unclear. Marriage law was another area of persistent concern. An entire book in Anselm of Lucca's collection of canons is devoted to this subject, with the aim of establishing the indissolubility of the marriage vow.[5] But, like the other moral reforms, evidence of widespread compliance had to await the pontificate of Innocent III (d. 1216).

## The Codification of Canon Law

### *Regino of Prüm*

One of the most important early landmarks in morals legislation was Regino of Prüm's *Libri duo de synodalibus causis et disciplinis* (906),[6] which influenced the pattern of subsequent legislation and the development of canon law. This work was written at the request of Archbishop Ratbod of Trier and was dedicated to Hatto, archbishop of Mainz, with the aim of gathering together all Roman and Carolingian legislation to be used by local synods as a basis for their deliberations. The purpose was not to compose a thorough code of canon law but rather to provide the elders of the church with the tools to make their decisions. The first volume deals with ecclesiastical matters and persons, the second volume with the laity. The compilation focuses on the special concerns of the western church in the tenth century: drunkenness, the usurpation and laicization of local parish churches, the use of churches for nonreligious purposes, the occupation of clerics in nonreligious pursuits (tavern-keepers, hunters, etc.). But problems regarding sexual misdemeanors are covered extensively. In this respect, Regino's work reflects the tradition of penitential discipline based upon social status, age, clerical position, marital status, and sex of the sinner. Because of the unsystematic nature of the work, however, some of the prescriptions are contradictory.

Regino includes statements from a variety of sources, some unidentified, and many of which appear in later, more authoritative collections. His treatment of sodomy rests upon the classic canons of the Council of Ancyra (314), which provided the governing statutes concerning homosexuality in the early Middle Ages, quoted both in theological texts and Carolingian legislation.[7] These canons had passed through several versions since their appearance and are at times a bit obscure. In Regino's version, also found in Burchard of Worms, it is stated that those who fornicate "irrationally," if under twenty, must do fifteen years' penance; after five years, however, they may assist at the holy sacrifice, that is, communion. If they are over twenty and married, they must do twenty-five years' penance but may participate in the prayers after five years. If over fifty, they may only receive communion after thirty years. A second, somewhat ambiguous Ancyra canon quoted by Regino states that those who carry on "irrationally and pollute others with the leprosy of this branded crime [sodomy]" must be included among those penitents who are endangered by an unclean spirit. This suggests that they are either to be segregated with demoniacs or simply excluded from entering the church during services. The "leprous" character of sodomy, as first noted in the Ancyra code, was a phrase that was to creep repeatedly into discussions of this sin. The somewhat earlier canon of Elvira (305/306), which prohibited "corrupters of boys" from receiving communion, even at death, is not cited by Regino and rarely appears in medieval texts.[8] Regino also quoted the Theodosian statute (390) that provided death by burning for those men who "act the part of a woman",[9] unfortunately, it is not clear whether this refers to sodomy, transvestism, or homosexual marriage. Certainly, there is some conflict as to the appropriate penance: thirty years' penance or execution.

Regino also lists a number of more specific prescriptions, drawn from the Roman Penitential and the penitentials of Bede and Theodore of Canterbury.[10] In his treatment of sodomy, Regino notes that the penalties applied vary greatly, from ten years to a mere one hundred days, with clerics generally suffering the more severe penances of five to twelve years, depending on rank. The first category of penitent Regino considers among the laity includes boys and young men (variously styled *parvulus, puer,* or *juvenis*). The penances vary from a seven-day fast on bread and water for a boy "involuntarily oppressed" by an adult to one hundred days for boys having relations interfemorally. Concerning lesbian acts, the penalties ranged from three to seven years depending on whether the woman was a nun or if a dildo was used. The greatest range of penances refer to acts of anal intercourse between males, with penalties ranging from three to thirty years, depending on whether the offender was married, a cleric, or perpetually criminous. There seems to have been a wide choice of penances available to the confessor, for many of the penitential's suggestions are not attributed to specific authoritative sources. In the case of bestiality, however, a Carolingian capitulary was quoted requiring a harsh, though unspecified, penance. And the recommendation of St. Basil concerning the treatment of sodomite monks who dallied with youths is quoted in full.[11] Because children were often placed in monasteries for educational purposes, as candidates for full monastic membership, as orphans, or merely as insurance against the insecurities of the time, pederasty was presumably somewhat more widespread than other forms of homosexual liaison and consequently required more clearly defined restrictions. This Basilian rule provided that the monk found guilty of molesting a boy was to be publicly flogged, shaven, reduced in rank, spat upon, chained in prison for six months, and before vespers fed only a diet of bread and water three days of the week. For the next six months he was to be kept under the care of a spiritual guardian, segregated, and occupied with prayers, vigils, lamentations, and manual labor; he was to move about only under the supervision of two other brothers and he was kept from speaking with others, especially youths. This penance for wayward monks became a standard text in all later penitentials and was later inserted in Gratian's authoritative canon law collection of the twelfth century. In another passage drawn from Isidore of Seville, it is suggested simply that anyone found in suspicious circumstances with a youth should undergo a harsh penance.[12] Elsewhere, Regino notes that if a monk is found playing with boys and is known to have a weakness for them, he should be thrice admonished to fear God. If he persists, he should be severely reproached.

Regino's work was composed in the period preceding the revolutionary changes in family structure, agricultural productivity, and ideology that marked the eleventh century. The *Libriduo* collection mirrors contemporary secular law, which similarly exacted punishment on the basis of a criminal's social standing, demanding a higher monetary fine from a knight and physical punishment from a serf. The changing character of penitential literature should be understood in the context of a parallel transformation of secular law, leading to its passage from a disorganized, decentralized system of local tribal laws based on kinship ties to a sophisticated judicial system containing a combination of Roman, customary, and canon law and placing legal responsibility on the individual rather than the group. Like contemporary civil law, canon law and penitential codes prior to the tenth century had been localized and specific, each region and nation governed by a different tradition. Given the mobility and disorder that characterized the ninth and tenth centuries, such "laws," both civil and religious, may have been little honored.[13]

Beginning in the eleventh century, these traditions were supplemented by a body of reform legislation demanded by the newest social and economic advancements. In the field of morals legislation, the earlier penitentials, like Regino's and the still older *Roman Penitential,* had contained conflicting penalties, sometimes presented without citing source or provenance. These penitentials seem to have been intended as informal guides for the local clergy, to provide them with a number of possible penances that might be imposed on the erring congregant. As the eleventh-century reformers began to categorize and rationalize the law, such collections were arranged topically, and the sources of such legislation, whether synodal, patristic, scriptural, or papal, were noted. Canons of questionable or obscure origin were discarded. Before the eleventh century, practice might vary from community to community, bishopric to bishopric, and might even be improvised on the spot; an aggressive church now attempted to create a uniform code of canon law and thereby reduce the variations from region to region.

### *Burchard of Worms*

The eleventh century *Decretum* of Bishop Burchard of Worms (ca. 965–1025) may be regarded as the most influential medieval collection of canon law and penitential discipline.[14] Intended for the practical use of the local clergy, the *Decretum* was far more systematic than its predecessors. Book 19, which deals with penance, begins with instructions for confessors on how to conduct their inquiries and identify the penitent's sins. This is followed by an enumeration of various sins and their proper penances, with special attention to sins of the flesh. While Burchard's most immediate source was obviously Regino of Prüm, for his discussion of homosexuality he relied on the *Penitential* of Theodore of Canterbury, the *Roman Penitential,* the works of Isidore and Basil, and the by-now standard decisions of the Council of Ancyra. Lesbian activity, as in Regino's work, demands a penance ranging from three to seven years. Homosexual offenses are described in great detail, with penalties for all forms of sexual activity—intercrural, interfemoral, oral and anal intercourse, and mutual masturbation, among others. Again, the punishment is graded by age, rank, marital status, and frequency, running from ten days for masturbation by boys to life for a married man over fifty performing anal intercourse. Burchard even includes a passage concerning two brothers having sexual relations: they must abstain from meat for fifteen years.

### *Peter Damian*

The most persistent opponent of clerical vice during this period was Peter Damian (1007–1072), who wrote an enormous number of tracts, many devoted to the education of adolescents, in which he attempted to expunge every vestige of non-Christian behavior from the Catholic clergy.[15] Born in Ravenna in the late tenth or early eleventh century of a poor family, orphaned and then relegated to a cruel brother who employed him to tend pigs, Peter suffered many privations. Another brother, however, noting his potential, finally sent the youth to study at Faenza. By 1035 he had entered the Benedictine abbey of Fonte Avellana, near Gubbio, where he remained for the next twenty-eight years, serving as abbot after 1040. In addition to imposing rigorous austerities upon himself and his monastery, Peter devoted much of his career to the Gregorian reform movement, frequently taking the most restrictive puritanical position. His special wrath was directed against the sexual mores of the contemporary clergy and their manifold sins, from adultery to sodomy.

At the council of Reims (1048), Peter spoke out forcefully in favor of the strict enforcement of the traditional canons against sodomy.[16] He further noted that in the bishopric of Langres offices were acquired through simony, the marriage vow was violated, tyranny was exercised against the clergy, and sodomy was practiced. In his campaign to purify the church, Peter composed the only known tract specifically directed against homosexuality, the *Liber Gomorrhianus*.[17] It his apologia, Peter recalls that when necessary Jerome himself had spoken out against various heretical sects, Ambrose had declaimed against the Arians, and Augustine against the Donatists. Peter claims that the widespread and insidious vice of sodomy in holy orders demanded an equally forceful program of extermination. (He implies that the vice is somewhat less current among the monastic clergy than among the secular.) A subsidiary aim of the work was to prove the authenticity of certain canons against sodomy contained in Burchard of Worm's *Decretum* and to reject other, allegedly spurious, more liberal canons. By the twefth century, in fact, Peter's canons were accepted as the standard rules regarding sodomy.

According to Damian, the sodomitical vice is a cancer that stealthily infects even holy men. Consequently, much of Damian's polemic is directed against clerical and monastic sodomy. He begins by defining the four genres of *luxuria,* or lust against nature: autostimulation, mutual masturbation, interfemoral relations, and complete homosexual relations, each with its own appropriate penance. He notes that many churchmen shrink from demoting sodomites from their posts unless the accused have acted with eight or ten persons. Consequently, some sodomitical clerics not only retain their offices but have even been promoted. Damian, in contrast, emphasizes the enormity of this vice that provoked the sulphurous destruction of Sodom and Gomorrah (Gen. 19), the damnation of Onan (Gen. 38), and the death penalty prescribed for sodomites under Levitical law (Lev. 20). Gregory the

Great testified that such sinners were not to be promoted to clerical rank; this prohibition applied to all who committed capital crimes under the Mosaic law. Nor, says Damian, should this rule be relaxed under any circumstances, for an even higher standard of morality is demanded of the clergy than of laymen. Furthermore, Damian insists that not only are the sodomites themselves damned, but so also are those who give them license to pursue their evil ways.

Peter notes that certain "spiritual fathers" sodomize those placed in their care: either pastors with youthful members of their flock or abbots with their monks. This may be regarded as a form of unnatural spiritual incest, even worse than simple incest because crimes committed against the soul are more severe than crimes against the body. In order to hide their transgressions, claims Damian, clerical sodomites often confess to each other and, unembarrassed, receive a light penance—although certainly one criminal cannot absolve another. If those who violate virgins are demoted from the priesthood, he concludes, so should sodomites be cast out. According to custom, a sodomite must do ten years' penance; if in orders, he is to be demoted and must then do penance as a layman.

Peter then proceeds to recount the penitential canons then accepted for such vices, canons that to his mind were far too lenient. Under these regulations, a secular priest (*presbyter*) who has relations with a girl or prostitute incurs two years' penance of dry bread during three successive Lenten seasons, Tuesdays, Thursdays, Fridays, and the Sabbath; if with a nun or a male, the same penalty is exacted; a fast is added for five years if it is a repeated act. Similarly deacons, if they are not monks, do two years' penance, as do nonpriestly monks. A cleric (*clericus*) or a canon who has sexual relations with a girl, if he has not taken a monastic vow, does merely one-half year's penance; if he so acts frequently, two years' penance. Those who perform sodomy do ten years' penance; those who do it habitually, urges Damian, ought to be more severely punished. If the guilty are in orders, they are first degraded and then do penance as laymen. A man who engages in interfemoral sex does penance for one year; if he does so repeatedly, then two years; if *à tergo,* three years; if a boy, two years; if with an animal, ten years. A bishop who sodomizes an animal does ten years' penance after degradation; a *presbyter,* five; a deacon, three; and a *clericus,* two. Thus, if Peter is to be believed, until the eleventh century sodomy was not among the most severely punished vices and, as confirmed by Regino, the penalties varied greatly.

Peter describes the more severe penalties he would like to see accepted by the church. He does not believe that the same five-year penance should apply both to sex with other men and sex with nuns. The minimal punishment for sodomy should rather be ten years; for, he notes, despite widespread application, the aforementioned punishments are not to be found in any synodal or papal legislation, neither in the *Penitential* of Theodore of Canterbury nor the *Roman Penitential.* These punishments should therefore be eliminated and all further codes begin with the statutes of the Council of Ancyra. This recommendation suggests that, although the Ancyra precedent had appeared in earlier codes, its prescriptions were not necessarily used. Peter's higher penalties are as follows: for anal sex, those under twenty should do fifteen years' penance; those who are over twenty and married should do twenty years' penance; if married and over fifty, they should do penance until death. Such penalties would also apply to those who have sex with animals and men.

The *Liber Gomorrhianus* describes in the most detailed way the penalties to be imposed on clerical sodomites. A cleric or monk found kissing or otherwise sinning with adolescents or children was to be publicly beaten and degraded, shaven, spat upon, bound in chains, imprisoned for six months, and kept on a stringent diet of dry bread. For the next six months he was to be kept under the care of a spiritual guardian, segregated in a small cell, and occupied with manual labor and prayer, free to walk about only under the watchful eye of two spiritual brothers, prohibited from engaging in sinful conversation, or from consorting or talking with youths. Peter next describes, at his polemical best, the heinousness of the sodomitical vice, which he regards as a kind of spiritual leprosy that should exclude men from the enjoyment of clerical dignities. For a variety of reasons, in arguments that approach the heresy of the Donatists and Patarenes, who held that sinful priests could not perform the sacraments, Damian argues that God is loathe to receive the sacrament from the hands of the impure. Because sodomy is comparable to homicide, the bloodstained hands of a sodomite cannot licitly perform the sacrament.

Despite this plea in favor of a more restrictive treatment of clerical sodomites, Pope Leo IX commended Peter for his efforts but favored the reinstatement of penitent clergy and was only willing to punish those who engaged in such deeds for an extended period of time. Such at least was the situation in the mid-eleventh century before the offensive against immorality had gathered force.

### *Yves of Chartres*

References to homosexuality also occur several times in the works of the celebrated canonist-bishop Yves of Chartres (ca. 1040–1116).[18] In a letter of 1097/98 to Pope Urban II, Yves protests that a certain youth, nicknamed Flora, the scandal of France and the subject of numerous ribald street songs, was about to be made bishop of Orléans. Yves had tried to forestall this consecration by sending a sample lyric to the archbishop of Lyons and to Hugh of Die, noting that Philip I of France had even boasted that this Jean (alias Flora) had shared his bed. Nevertheless, complains Yves, despite a papal interdict invoked against Philip for his immoral conduct, the archbishop of Tours had crowned the king of France during Christmas and in return for this favor had simoniacally purchased a bishopric for his paramour Flora, who was both underage and guilty of "dishonest familiarity" with the archbishop and the archbishop's deceased brother.

Yves is also the author of an influential *Decretum*[19] that gives the authoritative conciliar, scriptural, patristic, and papal remarks on a variety of sins, including sodomy. Much of Yves's material is taken wholly from Burchard of Worms; sexual misdemeanors are treated in book 9, *De Incesta copulatione.* His condemnatory selections come from Augustine's *Confessions,* the *Contra Iulianum,* and *De Bono conjugali,* along with Ambrose's *De Abrahamo.* He also includes a brief selection from the Council of Elvira (canon 71) prohibiting communion, until death, to pederasts. The other more specific penances are drawn from Burchard.[20]

*Gratian*

Soon after Lateran Council II (1139) appeared Gratian's *Decretum* (or *The Concordance of Discordant Canons*) (ca. 1140), the work that was to supersede all previous collections and become the standard text of legal precedent in the church. This work contains five selections dealing with the sin against nature.[21] The first, also found in Yves of Chartres, comes from Augustine's *De Adulterinis conjugiis* and discusses the relative seriousness of the various kinds of illicit intercourse; the least serious is fornication, followed by adultery, incest, and various sins against nature; if unnatural sex is committed with one's wife, it is more reprehensible than if committed with a prostitute. In scholastic theology, this text became the basis for frequent discussions of the relative evil of the sins against nature.

The second Augustinian text is taken from the *Confessions* and deserves quotation:[23]

> Therefore the crimes which be against nature are to be everywhere and at all times both detested and punished; such as those of the men of Sodom were: which should all nations commit, they should stand all guilty of the same crime, by the law of God, which hath not so made men, that they should this way use one another. For even that society which should be betwixt God and us, is then violated, when the same nature of which He is author, is polluted by the preposterousness of lust.

This text emphasizes the "unnaturalness" of sodomy contrasted to the God-ordained natural order.

The third Augustinian selection is cited as taken from the pseudo-Augustinian *Contra Jovinianum,* although no such paragraph appears there.[24] Gratian testifies that "unnatural sex," as noted in Romans 1:26, is more shameful than both adultery and fornication. A selection from Ambrose confirms this view, noting that Lot's offer of his daughters to curious neighbors from Sodom is less sinful than the Sodomites' proposed unnatural sex with the angels or the violation of Lot's hospitality.[25]

The final text comes from the third-century jurist Paulus and is found in Justinian's *Codex.* This passage was repeatedly cited in both canon and secular law to justify the most extreme punishment of sodomites:[26]

> Anyone who persuades a boy who has been either abducted by him or by his corrupt accomplices to submit to lewdness or anyone who attempts to seduce a woman or a girl, or who does anything for the purpose of encouraging her in debauchery by paying her money or giving her gifts in order to persuade her, and any of these crimes is accomplished, shall be punished with death; and if it is not accomplished, he shall be deported to some island. Their corrupted accomplices shall suffer the extreme penalty.

### *Peter Lombard*

Peter Lombard's *Sententiarum libri quattuor* (ca. 1160), after the *Decretum* the second great theological text produced in the twelfth century, has remarkably little to say about sodomy, and the Lombard's glossators subsequently reflect this lack of concern.[27] In his discussion of the sacrament of marriage, he makes an oblique reference to the sin against nature as one of the impediments to a licit marriage. In another instance, he notes the gravity of adultery with citations from Pope Clement and Augustine, who regarded relations against nature as the most severe of sexual misdemeanors. Elsewhere, he defines the genres of unnatural sex; he includes fornication, *stuprum,* or the illicit seduction of a virgin, adultery, incest, and rape. Sodomy and bestiality are not mentioned.

Commentaries on the *Sentences* became one of the most widespread philosophical genres. Nearly all of the great medieval thinkers made some contribution to this form in which they expanded upon selected passages from the Lombard. But the master's sparse discussion of sodomy is reflected in many of the commentators. William of Auxerre, Peter of Palude, Peter John Olivi, and Francis of Meyronnes, for example, do not treat this theme. Alexander of Hales merely quotes two condemnatory passages from Augustine's *De Adulterinis conjugiis* and Jerome's epistle *Ad Amandum presbyterum.*[28]

### *Alan of Lille*

One of the most outstanding perpetuators of the reforming tradition in the late twelfth century was the humanist Alan of Lille (d. 1202). In his poem *Complaint of Nature* (1165/82),[29] Alan defines happiness as the fulfillment of one's natural purpose; in this sense, because sodomy frustrates the conception of children, it is unnatural, sinful, and conducive to unhappiness. As a result, sodomy becomes in this poem an extended metaphor for all forms of vice. An anonymous poem of the period similarly describes sodomy as perverse and fruitless, arguing that if such love had been practiced by our fathers, we ourselves would not exist. So contrary to nature is sodomy, the poet asserts, that even brute beasts do not disport themselves in such a way.[30]

In one of the most extensive homiletical treatments of various vices against nature, the *Sermones de peccatis capitalibus,* Alan introduces the view that the two most serious crimes are sodomy and homicide, both of which are described in Scripture as creating a loud disturbance that calls forth God's eternal wrath.[31] This view reflects the absorption by preachers of the standard gloss on Scripture, which had made a similar comparison. Alan's discussion is replete with scriptural quotations condemning the vice against nature, although he mixes the treatment of sodomy with onanism and bestiality. Alan also cites the passages found in Gratian.

The twelfth century also witnessed considerable refinement of the penitential manual over its disorganized, contradictory predecessors and an attempt to establish standard, nonlocalized procedures applicable throughout Christian Europe. The new penitential typically began with the brief, classic definition of the particular vice under discussion, followed by selections from authoritative sources to be considered by the confessor before imposing penance. Alan of Lille produced several such manuals containing the definitive documents subsequently inserted in all such penitentials. In a short version of his *Liber poenitentialis* (ca. 1199/1202),[32] he defines the vice against nature as the expending of one's seed outside its proper vessel; this may include a variety of vices, among them masturbation, anal and oral intercourse, sex with nuns, incest, bestiality, adultery, rape, and sodomy. A fast on bread and water for forty days during Lent for a period of seven years is prescribed for a man guilty of committing sodomy with his wife; for a habitual sodomite, the penance is to last fifteen years; for a minor, the fast lasts only one hundred days. In a longer version of the same penitential (ca. 1192), Alan suggests the same penalties and quotes the Ancyra statute that subsumes under the vice against nature relations with men or animals, "that is, a mare, cow, or donkey." Alan is relatively liberal, only providing a penalty if the act is committed twice: a forty-day fast for seven years if unmarried; if it is a habit, fifteen years; and if performed by a child, one hundred days on bread and water. Two further canons concern fornication with animals, one falsely attributed to the *Roman Penitential* and the other falsely ascribed to Pope Martin. The penalties run as high as thirty years, although communion is permitted at death. The nearly contemporary penitential of Bartholomew of Exeter (d. 1184) contains four selections dealing with the vice against nature: the Ancyra condemnation, paragraphs from St. Basil and the *Roman Penitential* and a canon falsely ascribed to Pope Martin against bestiality.[33]



## Scriptural Commentary

While the touchstone on which all discussions of sodomy rested was Scripture, this base was expanded in the twelfth century with references from the Church Fathers—Augustine, Jerome, Gregory, Isidore of Seville, and Basil, in particular—who were regarded as the standard authorities on religious questions. But because the great corpus of patristic literature had by the twelfth century become too great even for the educated cleric to absorb, a standard gloss on the Bible was needed for instructional purposes. While such glosses had been attempted in the early Middle Ages by such theologians as Isidore, Rabanus Maurus, and Walafrid Strabo, the eleventh-century biblical scholars, often working together in schools such as Laon, Bec, or Auxerre, made determined attempts to produce an acceptable concise biblical commentary that would contain citations from all the relevant authorities.[34] A parallel development occurred simultaneously in the Jewish community, where the commentary of Rashi was eventually accepted as the standard gloss. In Western Europe, the most successful such compilation, later called the *Glossa ordinaria,* was produced by Anselm of Laon (d. 1119) and his students at Laon and Auxerre. This commentary typically contained a small portion of text followed by considerable excerpts from the relevant authorities, with an occasional comment added by Anselm himself. Most of the subsequent commentaries departed little from this standard, and it may therefore be regarded as the necessary text on which all theological and homiletical discussions of sodomy rested for the next three hundred years. Naturally, the work of commentary continued in the schools, and a mass of such material remains still in manuscript form scattered throughout Europe.

It was not until the early fourteenth century that a second standard gloss, the *Postillae super totam Bibliam* by the Parisian theologian Nicholas of Lyre (ca. 1270–1349), was accepted alongside Anselm of Laon's work as the basis of all subsequent biblical study.[35] Nicholas's opus represented the most successful integration of scholastic theology and Scripture, betraying a special reliance on Thomas Aquinas and Rashi. The *Postillae* was commonly printed along with Anselm's *Glossa ordinaria.* The interlinear commentary attributed to Walafrid Strabo (d. 849) was printed between the scriptural lines; the commentary by Anselm appeared in the left and right margins, followed by Nicholas's text.

The first biblical text directly connected with the sin of sodomy concerns the conflagration at Sodom following the alleged advances made by the men of Sodom toward the heavenly messengers visiting Lot. While, as Derrick S. Bailey suggests, the sin of the Sodomites may not have been homosexuality, but rather inhospitality or a desire to mix "the heavenly and the earthly" via intercourse, there is no doubt that medieval thinkers regarded the sin of Sodom as homosexuality.[36] Anselm's commentary is replete with quotations from the Church Fathers comparing the lustful inhabitants of the five destroyed cities to those who abandon themselves to the five bodily senses and who will likewise burn in eternal fire (Gen. 18:28–33). Nicholas pays particular attention to the cries that burst from Sodom and reached up to heaven (Gen. 18:22:"The cry of Sodom is great"). He notes that this loud cry is characteristic of three grave sins: 1) the killing of innocents, for instance, Abel's murder by Cain (Gen. 4), 2) the sin against nature (Gen. 18:22), and 3) the defrauding of the laboring poor (James 5). The "clamor" described in these texts suggests the shameless failure of such sinners even to attempt concealment of their sins. He cites Ezekiel 16 and an unidentified Hebrew source to the effect that the Sodomites also suffered from an excess of food and leisure.

In Genesis 19:8–10 it is reported that Lot, rather than produce his guests for the curious Sodomites, offered his virgin daughters to them. Here Anselm quotes Augustine and Gregory.[37] Nicholas's commentary reflects the impact of scholastic theology. While he questions whether Lot sinned by offering his two daughters, he concludes that according to natural law the deflowering of a virgin is a lesser crime than sodomy; thus, in order to placate the Sodomites and avoid a graver offense and the attempted violence to his hospitality, Lot was correct to give his daughters.

The actual destruction of Sodom by fire and brimstone (Gen. 19:24) in Anselm is glossed with a citation from Gregory's *Liber regulae pastoralis,* which notes that sulphur represents the stink of the flesh and fire the ardor of earthly passion.[38] Walafrid Strabo argues that whereas the first sinners were exterminated in the waters of the Deluge, for they had offended the Lord through concupiscence, the Sodomites suffered a graver punishment—a deluge of sulphur and fire—because while the first race had sinned naturally, the people of Sodom had sinned unnaturally. Alcuin of York[39] is quoted to the effect that even infants were destroyed at Sodom along with their parents lest the slightest trace remain. Had they lived, they might have followed their parents' example and would consequently have been even more gravely punished; for the habits of the children are invariably traceable to the parents. Nicholas adds little to this.

In his gloss on Leviticus 20:13 and 18:22, which demanded stoning for acts of sodomy between men, Anselm of Laon maintained that mankind, as opposed to womankind, is distinguished by the strength of its soul and the perfection of its virtues. Men should therefore avoid becoming effeminate in word and action; the penalty for such a sin is death. Here, for the first time, Anselm associates the sins against nature with idolatry and interprets Leviticus 18:22 as a prohibition against idol-worship and the introduction of pagan philosophy into the church. This identification is extended in the gloss to Exodus 22:19, where sodomy is associated with the practice of the arts of magic, dabbling with the devil's work, and heresy, all of which lead to excommunication and death. Anselm further extends the prohibition against sodomy to include women, who represent dignity and are helpmates to men. Nicholas's contribution is slight, adding that bestiality is more unnatural than sodomy because it is committed with another species.

There is some controversy over whether Judges 19, "the outrage at Gibeah" committed by the Benjaminites, refers to sodomy.[40] Anselm, in fact, does not comment on this text but rather quotes Augustine.[41] Nicholas, however, states that it is commonly believed that the Benjaminites attempted to sodomize a visiting Levite. Josephus, he notes, on the other hand, interpreted their visit as a request that the man hand over his concubine, intending to kill him should he refuse.[42] Like Lot before him, the man presented his daughter rather than commit a greater evil, that is, a sin against nature and injury to hospitality.

In Jeremiah 23:14, the prophet directly compares the false prophets of Jerusalem to the idol-worshipping inhabitants of Sodom and Gomorrah. Anselm thereupon compares the prophets of Baal in Samaria to heretics in the church who turn the people away from God to the worship of demons. Nicholas specifically notes that the idolatry of these prophets included acts of both sodomy and adultery. The prophet Ezekiel (16:49–50) likewise indicted the people of Jerusalem for pride, overabundance of bread and idleness, disregard of the poor and needy, and acts of "abomination." Anselm's gloss relies on Jerome[43] in comparing the people of Samaria to heretics and the people of Sodom to the Gentiles who entered the church. The sins of Sodom are defined as pride, excess of bread, wealth, leisure and pleasure; they mistakenly thought their happiness permanent and turned away from God.

Scriptural commentators interpreted Lamentations 5:13, which describes the many sufferings of the Jews during the Babylonian Captivity, to mean the sodomization of youth by the oppressor. Anselm extends this to include the later Roman oppressors, who also were known for indulgence in sodomitical pleasures. Joel 3:8 extended the list of ancient pederasts to include the Chaldeans and Assyrians, who sold boys for abuse; the Jews allegedly acquired this habit through their association with these peoples.[44] In the first linkage of intellectuals with sexual nonconformity, Anselm adds that these immoral peoples could likewise represent the heretics and the "prideful doctors" (i.e., teachers and clerics) who are dissipated in word and example and give themselves over to the rites of the Gentiles. II Maccabees 4:12 likewise included the people of Ephesus among those who buggered young boys. The Book of Wisdom also speaks of the evils associated with idolatry, among them "confusion of sex" (14:26); both Anselm and Nicholas, however, interpret this as the use of anal intercourse to frustrate conception, rather than sodomy between men. Finally, the gloss on Ecclesiasticus 16:8 quotes Rabanus Maurus[45] to the effect that the ancient giants, steeped in earthly pleasures, were weighed down by the burden of sin, while heretics, confident of their own virtue, glory in their weighty wealth of dialectic and rhetoric.

Compared to this wealth of direct and or indirect references in the Old Testament, the New Testament contains few passages of relevance. The most extensive material comes from Paul's Epistle to the Romans (1:24–27) in which the apostle details the fleshly sins of the Gentiles. In his commentary, Anselm of Laon provides quotations from Augustine, Gregory the Great, and Ambrose that compare those who give themselves over to fleshly lust to the Gentiles who worship the creation rather than the creator.[46] Nicholas elaborates little except to repeat his view that bestiality is the most serious of the vices against nature. While I Corinthians 6:9 clearly states that "nor effeminate, nor abusers of themselves with mankind" shall inherit the kingdom of God, neither commentator finds it necessary to elaborate. The equation of sodomy and heresy as crimes that lead to eternal damnation and the Hell-fire ot Gehenna is again repeated in Jude 7:8. The much quoted verse in Ephesians 5:6—"for because of these things cometh the wrath of God upon the children of disobedience"—is identified by Nicholas of Lyre as a reference to the corrupt generation that perished during the Flood, although Anselm does not comment. Augustine seems to have become the source for the perennial identification of these lines with sodomy.

Thus, with Holy Scripture as a basic text, assisted by the standard commentaries of Anselm of Laon and later of Nicholas of Lyre, the medieval preacher or theologian was equipped with an arsenal of polemical tools and precedents in his fight against moral offenders. Homosexual acts were classed among the gravest of sins, responsible for the utter destruction of five cities; for the fire and brimstone of Sodom were the just reward for such sin and a similar fate awaited their imitators in the next world. Sodomy was also clearly linked with paganism and heresy, and such alien, idol-worshipping peoples as the Arameans, Romans, Chaldeans, and Egyptians were variously accused of pederasty and sodomy. A further refinement was added in the commentary of Nicholas of Lyre, who argues not only that the sin against nature is contrary to scriptural authority but that it also contravenes right reason, although it is less sinful than bestiality.

The eleventh century thus witnessed a transformation in the church's attitude toward private moral behavior and an attempt to realize the rigid sexual code implied, but not enforced, in pre-Gregorian Christian Europe. While the Carolingian penitentials, represented by Regino's disorganized and contradictory collection of canons, had given the local parish priest considerable latitude in his treatment of erring Christians, the Gregorian reformers attempted to establish a uniform penitential code based on acceptable precedents. The first goal was the degradation and expulsion of sinful, sodomous clergy; the second aim, the extension of such restrictions to the laity. As a result of the combined efforts of such reformers as Yves of Chartres and Peter Damian, certain canons selected from Scripture, Augustine, Ambrose, and the Council of Ancyra became the governing sources for all subsequent legislation and theological treatments of sodomy. Simultaneously, the cathedral schools undertook to thoroughly gloss Scripture, including those passages dealing with the crime against nature. The penitential came into its own by the end of the twelfth century, as the various vices were systematically organized and the suitable penance clarified in accordance with universally accepted canons. At all times, the new morality argued for severity and rigidity and against leniency and flexibility.

# III

## *Conciliar Legislation*

DESPITE THE REFORMERS' zeal, efforts at moral regeneration clearly encountered resistance, for it was not until the early twelfth century that the restrictive sexual ethic entered the realm of conciliar legislation. The diminution of lay influence in the church, which preceded the introduction of such legislation, afforded the moral crusaders the opportunity to implement their program. The twelfth century also witnessed a number of developments that favored more effective absorption of the increasing population and even demanded a higher birth rate to meet European expansion: the Crusader movement and the colonization of the East, the reconquest of Spain and displacement of the native population by Christian settlers, the establishment of new states and settlements in eastern Europe, the communal movement and the rise of commerce and industry, the drainage of swamps and land reclamation within Europe itself, the establishment of new religious orders with specialized tasks, and the foundation of new monasteries. All of these changes necessitated greater vigilance against the reduction of the birth rate among the laity through abortion, artificial contraception, or sodomy. Nonetheless, while the Gregorian legislation against moral laxity became church law by the early twelfth century, there is little evidence of any concerted attempt to enforce the statutes.

### Anglo-French Councils

The result of the reformers' activities following the scandalous reigns of William Rufus in England and Philip I in France was the enactment of the first conciliar legislation against clerical and eventually lay sodomy. The astonishing increase in the number of religious orders and the foundation of new monasteries, which presumably attracted a considerable number of unsuitable members, no doubt also aggravated the problem of sexual disorder in this period. The natural center of the reformers' drive was the Anglo-French church. In a letter of 1102/1103 addressed to William, archdeacon of Canterbury, Archbishop Anselm notes that the vice has become so widespread that few are embarrassed by it and many may be unaware of its gravity. He recommends that the age, marital status, and duration of time in which the sin had continued be considered by the confessor determining penance. This missive, written on the occasion of the Council of London (1102), warns against admitting sodomites to the priesthood; such persons who have become priests, says Anselm, should be instructed that they are sinning against God and will suffer damnation. In his report on the council, William of Malmesbury notes that it was decided that those who commit sodomy are behaving like animals and should be anathematized until they have undergone penance and have been absolved. The council further stipulated that monks or regular clergy guilty of such acts might not be raised to higher rank but should rather be demoted. If the culprit were a layman, he was to be deprived of his legal status, that is, reduced to serfdom or imprisonment; finally, only a bishop is permitted to absolve offenders.[1]

The most extensive synodal legislation dealing with sins against nature significantly comes from the Council of Nablus (Schechem),[2] held in 1120 in the Holy Land, the very same year that the sons of Henry I drowned in the White Ship, allegedly for homosexual offenses. This council, held in the presence of King Baldwin II of Jerusalem, Patriarch Gormund of Jerusalem, and various church and royal officials of the Crusader kingdom, was called with the general aim of correcting the morals of the Crusaders. The introduction to the canons alleges that the decline in Crusader morality was responsible for the recent defeat of the Christians under Roger of Antioch. In retrospect, we may attribute the prevalence of homosexuality to several causes: 1) a large proportion of the army was composed of Normans, who as we have seen had acquired a reputation for sexual unorthodoxy; 2) residence in the East inevitably resulted in the absorption of Muslim behavior patterns, which traditionally are more tolerant of homosexuality; and 3) the relative shortage of Christian women in the Crusader military camps no doubt increased instances of homosexual behavior. Because of the special semitheocratic character of the Crusader kingdom, this legislation represents the first clear-cut union of moral theology and secular law. For the first time, civil authority is made responsible for enforcing a Christian moral code. Burning was the penalty demanded for adult sodomites.

The Nablus statutes provide that if a child or anyone else is "defiled" by sodomy but cries out loudly in protest, only the sodomite himself will be burned; the involuntary sinner must do penance, but he is not to be punished by the law. Any individual who is forced to commit sodomy and conceals the fact, and then repeats the act, will be burned if the accusation is proved by positive investigative findings. But if a sodomite, before being accused, repents and, following penance, swears not to repeat his transgression, he may be readmitted to a church and judged according to religious canons. If, however, he again falls into sin and wants to repent, he is exiled from the Kingdom of Jerusalem. The persistence of this severe legislation in the Crusader states is indicated by its later inclusion in the thirteenth-century statutes of the bourgeoisie of Jerusalem, which are based upon the Nablus code.[3] Murderers, heretics, and traitors condemned as "enemies of God" were likewise to suffer capital punishment.

## Ecumenical Councils

Outside of Anglo-French circles sodomy was apparently still not yet regarded as the greatest menace to clerical morality. The ecumenical councils influenced by the Gregorian reform placed far greater emphasis on concubinage among the clergy and marriage within the prohibited degrees of consanguinity among the laity. At Lateran I (1123), the Nicene prohibition against these vices was repeated.[4] At Lateran II (1139), the decrees of popes Gregory VII, Urban II, and Paschal II against clerical cohabitation were noted and demotion and severe penance recommended. For the first time consanguinity and incest were equated, both of which were prohibited.[5]

The only ecumenical legislation clearly directed against the "sin against nature" is found in canon 11 of Lateran III (1179); this was also the first council to launch an attack against the spreading Cathar heresy. This canon, because of its somewhat vague terminology, deserves quotation in full:[6]

> 11. Clergy in holy orders, who maintain their wives incontinently in their homes, should either expel them, and live continently, or be deprived of ecclesiastical office and benefice. Whoever is caught involved in that incontinence which is against nature, and because of which "the wrath of God came upon the sons of disobedience" (Eph. 5:6), and five cities were consumed in fire (Gen. 14:24–25), if they are clerics, they should be deposed from clerical office and placed in a monastery to do penance; if they are laymen, they are to be excommunicated and completely isolated from contact with believers. If any cleric, without clear and necessary cause, should especially frequent nunneries, he should be restrained by the bishop, and if he does not cease, he should be deposed from his ecclesiastical benefice.

This canon was eventually inserted in the *Liber extra* promulgated by Gregory IX (1234) as a permanent part of canon law.[7] The statute includes prohibition of several forms of lust; clerical fornication and relations with nuns are clearly attacked. The unspecified "incontinence against nature" could conceivably be bestiality or sodomy, but the reference to the five cities destroyed by fire makes sodomy more probable. Interestingly, the prohibition is extended to laymen, following the precedent of the Council of Nablus.

The standard gloss on this text, by Bernard of Parma (ca. 1263), reflects the Bolognese education of its author and the growing impact of Roman law. Although this passage gets less attention than others dealing with concubinage, incest, and consanguinity, Bernard does take note of the Roman legal precedents in the *Codex* of Justinian, the gloss by Alanus (ca. 1210), and the *Novels,* all of which exacted capital punishment for sodomy.[8]

In sum, this Lateran decree, although especially directed against clerical vice, for the first time officially extended to the laity the prohibition of the sin against nature. The clerical sanctions suggest reference to the Basilian rule requiring demotion and claustration for erring clerks; laymen are subjected to excommunication and its attendant liabilities. Homosexuality is still not singled out for special treatment but is bracketed along with clerical concubinage and illicit relations with nuns as equal crimes. The bishop retains prime responsibility for the enforcement of this decree, just as he remained responsible for the pursuit and prosecution of heretics.

Like so many conciliar decrees concerning moral behavior, these prohibitions were presumably ineffective, for again in 1215 at the Fourth Lateran Council a similar decree was issued to strengthen the mechanism of punishment. This text, also included in Gregory IX's *Liber extra,* reads as follows:[9]

> 14. That the morals and conduct of clerks may be improved, let all strive to live continently and chastely, especially those established in holy orders; let them seek to avoid completely the sin of lust—particularly that on account of which the anger of God comes from heaven upon the sons of disobedience—in order that they may be able to minister in the sight of Almighty God with a pure heart and clean body. Lest too easy pardon afford an incentive to sin, we decree that they who are caught giving way to the sin of incontinence shall, in proportion to the degree of their sin, be punished according to the rules of canon law, which we wish to be most effectively and rigorously observed in order that those whom the fear of God does not hold back from evil, temporal punishment at least may restrain from sin. If anyone, therefore, suspended because of this, presumes to celebrate divine service, he shall not only be deprived of ecclesiastical benefices, but also for this twofold transgression be forever deposed from office. Prelates who venture to support such in their wickedness, especially for money or other temporal advantage, shall be subject to like punishment. Those who, in the manner of their country, have not renounced the marriage bond, shall if they fall into sin be punished more severely, since they can avail themselves of lawful matrimony. . . .

Here Bernard of Parma notes that the canon is divided into five parts: 1) a reference to clerical honesty and chastity, 2) the imposition of punishment, 3) the strengthening of this penalty, 4) the punishment of negligent and corrupt prelates, and 5) the particular incontinence of the Greek church [not quoted above]. The first part, he notes, orders the strictest chastity among clerics in holy orders and urges avoidance of the unutterable vice that prompted destruction of the five cities. The second clause requires that lest excessive complacency contribute to delinquency, those who are apprehended in the sodomitical vice should be punished in accordance with holy canons, which should be strengthened by the application of temporal punishment. Anyone suspended for this crime who presumes to celebrate the divine office shall lose all his ecclesiastical benefices in perpetuity. Prelates who allow such persons to continue in their deeds, and especially obtain money for it, shall equally suffer temporal penalties. The rest of this commentary deals with other forms of lust. In addition, Bernard refers the reader to four other sources: 1) the Third Lateran decree (1179), 2) Gratian's *Decretum,* 3) the *Codex,* and 4) the *Novels.*[10]

Thus, by 1215, the offensive against clerical vice had hardened considerably, paralleling the contemporary strengthening of sanctions against heresy. By the late twelfth century, sodomy had become a reserved sin for which only the local bishop or his representative could impose penance. Nevertheless, as several contemporary theologians were to point out, the episcopate had been somewhat lax in applying penalties against moral offenders within their dioceses.[11] The church therefore laid down specific penalties against bishops who failed to apply the full rigor of the law; and the papacy, through the ecumenical decree, now called on secular authority to assist in the enforcement of its edicts. A similar transformation occurred in the crusade against heresy, which now became the object of both religious and temporal legislation. Bernard of Parma's commentary, written about fifty years after the Fourth Lateran Council, reflects the increased impact of Roman upon canon law and the application of secular penalties against both lay and clerical moral offenders.

## Local Synods

Ecumenical legislation found local expression in the canons of synods and the instructions issued by bishops to the local clergy. Some statutes, like those of the Council of Paris (1212), even predate ecumenical legislation. Once again, these acts are restricted to the same Anglo-French circles that had expressed concern about sodomy a century earlier. The councils of Paris (1212), Rouen (1214), and Béziers (1246) are but three examples.[12]

In 1202, for example, Pope Innocent III asked the archbishop of Sens to undertake a general reform of the clergy in his diocese. Simultaneously, archbishops Hervé of Troyes and Eudes of Paris attempted to clarify the problems faced by clergy in their provinces, making use of the speculations of the Parisian schools as the basis for these labors. No doubt Eudes made ample use of the recently published *Penitential* of Alan of Lille (ca. 1192), dedicated to Henry of Sully. These synodal statutes specifically reserve such sexual transgressions as rape of virgins, incest, and the sin against nature for the consideration of the bishop or grand-penitentiary. The version of the text at the Abbey of St. Victor in Paris goes so far as to require papal adjudication in such cases.[13]

The constitutions of bishops Fulk Basset for London (1245/59), Alexander Stavensby for Coventry and Lichfield (1224/37), and Peter Quinel for Exeter (ca. 1287) all deal specifically with the need for priests to seek out and punish sodomites.[14] One of the fullest surviving episcopal registers, belonging to Archbishop Eudes of Rouen, notes that two Benedictines of Jumièges were apprehended in 1248 for acts of infamy (i.e., sodomy) and, pending an investigation, were sequestered in other monasteries.[15] The archbishop's visitation indicates that sodomy was regarded as a form of judicial infamy, whereby the individual loses the good esteem of upright and honorable men.

Other conciliar statutes likewise have a bearing on the mounting war against clerical immorality. The Parisian synod of 1212 prohibited nuns from sleeping together and required a lamp to burn all night in dormitories; at Rouen in 1214, a similar statute focused on clerics.[16] Among the Cistercians, the 1221 chapter-general specifically expelled convicted sodomites from the order permanently. The synod of Angers (1216/19) declared pederasty to be worse than adultery, for it turned men into monsters; the synod recommended a penance of seven years and discipline each day of the week.[17] Finally, the statutes of Paris (ca. 1196), Fritzlar (1246), Liège (1287), Cambrai (1300/10), and Angers (1216/19) all recognized sodomy as a "reserved crime," which meant referral to high ecclesiastical authority. Among other sins so designated were homicide, sacrilege, incest, deflowering of a virgin, the breaking of vows, and doing injury to one's parents.[18] In order to enforce these strict regulations, the Cistercian statutes of 1279 required all abbeys to build prisons in which sodomites, thieves, incendiaries, forgers, and murderers could be incarcerated at the abbots' discretion. Similar statutes were passed by the Dominicans in 1238 and the Carthusians in 1261.[19]

## Contemporary Jewish Law

Non-Catholic churches were also forced to deal with the problem of homosexuality. The Jewish faith, like Catholicism, was simultaneously undergoing a period of theological clarification and legal codification. The twelfth-century texts of such thinkers as Moses Maïmonides and Rashi, like the works of Peter Lombard and Gratian, were destined to become the standard textbooks of law and Scripture. Regarding homosexuality, however, the scriptural remarks that Christianity regarded as direct condemnations of the crime against nature were treated rather more equivocally by Jewish scholars. Such a respected biblical commentator as Rashi (1040–1105), for example, in his commentary on Genesis 18:20–33 is largely concerned with linguistic problems.[20] He does, however, note that the passages in Genesis prove that a case of capital punishment should only be decided after careful investigation. God warned that he would kill the transgressing sodomites only if they *persisted* in their ways; if they ceased, they would merely suffer severe punishment. Earthly judges are likewise urged to follow God's example. Thus, Rashi's interpretation contains a plea for mercy rarely found in Christian interpreters.

The Talmud, dating from the second and third centuries A. D., rather than the Old Testament, was to become the basis for most Jewish legislation and theological speculation regarding the sin against nature. Most of the relevant material was taken from the Talmud *Sanhedrin,* where a specific link is drawn between idolatry and sexual misconduct.[21] Homosexuality is invariably regarded as one of the grounds on which a whole people may be destroyed by God's wrath; the generations before the Flood, the people of Sodom, the Benjaminites, the Jews in exile, and the Aramaeans were all stigmatized with the practice of homosexual vice. The generation of the Flood allegedly wrote songs in praise of sodomy and the descendants of Ham continued this tradition. The divine presence of the Lord, the so-called Shekinah, was driven by the sins of Sodom into the seventh heaven, at the greatest distance from mankind; only the righteous generations from Abraham to Moses succeeded in returning it to the world. The idolatrous acts of the destroyed tribe of the Benjaminites allegedly included sodomy; and Joseph was supposedly the object of such desire by the Egyptian Potiphar.

The use of sodomy as a means of denigrating defeated foes is reported on several occasions. For example, when King Joash of Judah, who had set up idols, was defeated by the Syrians (Aramaeans), he was immorally abused and then killed. The four kings who claimed to be gods—Hiram, Nebuchadnezzar, Pharaoh, and Joash—all ended by "being treated as women." The legend of Ben Sira reports that Jeremiah once came on the wicked men of Ephraim in a public bath committing group onanism. Instead of repenting when he urged them to cease, they forced the prophet to follow their example, threatening to sodomize him should he refuse. Shortly thereafter, his virgin daughter came to the same public bath to bathe and conceived by absorbing the sperm released by her father. The son born was Ben Sira. Another notation in the Talmud concerns one of David's cases of judicial murder; a pious man was allegedly executed on the false testimony of two witnesses, who accused him of buggery.

One of the most thorough treatments of sexual behavior is found in the work of Moses Maimonides (1135–1204). References to sexual conduct are found in his great *Mishneh Torah* (or *Code*), a codification of Jewish law, and the *Guide to the Perplexed,* in addition to his medical writings, the *Medical Aphorisms,* and a short letter on sexual conduct addressed to Saladin's nephew. In the *Book of Holiness* (volume 5 of his *Mishneh Torah*), Maimonides lists the thirty-seven kinds of forbidden intercourse.[22] This tractate, while clarifying all of the forbidden positions in accordance with scriptural, Mishnaic, and Talmudic precedent, is more concerned with the prohibited degrees of marriage than with the sex act itself. While the penalties for illicit sex may seem draconian, Maimonides also praises the therapeutic value of sexual intercourse. The Jewish tradition, while condemning homosexuality, bestiality, adultery, and other "sins against nature," is at the same time permissive concerning relations within marriage. The Jews regarded sex as a positive fulfillment of human needs and allowed free sexual contact between married persons. This is in sharp contrast to Christian law, which provides virtually no place for sexual activity as a natural, healthy, and beneficial activity. Nor is there any truly orthodox Jewish tradition of monastic or eremitical life. Maimonides quotes the sages to the effect that all men lust after forbidden unions and a minority are in fact actually guilty of such acts. Consequently, a man should be married, since the married state is most conducive to piety. Although he recommends that semen not be expended to no purpose, every type of sexual activity is allowed within marriage.

Although the punishment for sodomy is stoning (Lev. 18:22), Maimonides limits its application. If the culprit is a scholar, for example, neither death nor stoning is to be inflicted without a first warning, since the intention is to distinguish between purely wanton acts and acts committed in error. If one of the participants is a minor aged at least nine years and one day, the youth is not punished, only the adult. If the child is even younger than nine and a day, then both the child and the adult are entirely exempt from punishment, although flogging for disobedience is recommended. Relations with a hermaphrodite by way of the latter's male organ is liable to punishment. In the case of intercourse with a "tumtum" (a person of doubtful gender) or with a hermaphrodite through the female organ, no crime is committed; nevertheless, flogging is recommended for disobedience. The hermaphrodite, however, is permitted to marry.

In all of the preceding cases, witnesses to the act itself are not necessary; it is sufficient to see the accused in close embrace, which constitutes presumptive evidence. On the other hand, there can be no conviction without at least two eye witnesses. Although lesbianism is prohibited as one of the sinful "doings in the Land of Egypt" (Lev. 18:3), there is no clear *legal* prohibition against female homosexuality and it is not subject to flogging. Such women are even permitted to marry members of the priesthood. As a preventive, however, flogging for disobedience is recommended and husbands are advised to keep their wives from associating with women known to engage in such practices.

Like Christian theologians, Maimonides regarded "heathens" (in this case, presumably including Moslems and Christians) as more prone than Jews to sodomitical acts with men and animals. The Jews are therefore not prohibited from seclusion with animals and other men, although it is not recommended. On the other hand, a Jew should not entrust his child to a nonbeliever for education, since non-Jews are more likely to be pederasts. In his *Guide to the Perplexed,* Maimonides also notes that heathen males customarily wear colorful women's garments before images of Venus and women don buckles and other armor before Mars. Consequently, Jews are forbidden to wear the garments of the opposite sex because lust and immorality are the probable result.[23]

In his commentary on the *Mishnah* (ca. 1168), Maimonides makes some additions to the preceding discussion. An initiator of a sex act is defined as one who inserts the entire glans penis; a consummator is one who inserts the entire penis.[24] Punishment for illicit sexual relations is incurred simply for insertion, regardless of whether emission occurs; there is some controversy as to whether punishment is exacted in the case of a nonerect penis. Furthermore, Maimonides defines an adult (who is subject to stoning for sodomy) as a male over thirteen years and one day old who has at least two pubic hairs, the sign of puberty. Anyone younger is a minor, as is one without the requisite hairs. The ethical treatise *Orchoth-Chayim* by Rabbi Abraham Hacohen of Lunel is far more terse than the works of Maimonides.[25] Hacohen merely states that adults are punished by stoning; acts with children under nine years and a day old are exempt from punishment.

The early fourteenth century *Sefer-Hahinukh* contains a convenient summary of the relevant sources intended for the instruction of children.[26] The discussion of *miscav zakhar* (sodomy) relies largely on selections from the Talmud and from Maimonides. Much attention is devoted to the prohibition aganist ritual male prostitution, allegedly widespread among the pagans. Citing Maimonides and the biblical commentator Nahmanides, this source claims that male prostitution remains prevalent among the Ismaelite peoples, that is, the Arabs.

# IV

## *The Fourth Lateran Council and Scholasticism*

THE ENACTMENTS OF the Fourth Lateran Council (1215) held during the pontificate of Innocent III brought to fruition many of the intellectual currents that had animated the church in the twelfth century.[1] The relative liberalism of the pre-Gregorian period came to a close and a more militant, aggressive phase opened in the history of the Catholic church. A number of resolutions bear directly on the reform of morals, with the special aim of enlisting the cooperation of the secular authorities in the pursuit of religious and moral nonconformists. The first few canons contain a reaffirmation of Catholic dogma on the Trinity and the sacraments, along with the condemnation of several heretical and schismatical movements. Some of these groups, like the Cathars and the followers of Joachim of Flora, had espoused ideas that could conceivably justify homosexual activity on theological grounds. Canon 3 established the mechanism—soon formalized as the papal Inquisition—whereby heretics were to be investigated, tried, and punished. In fact, this canon actually summarizes many of the precedents established during Innocent's pontificate. The very same procedures outlined therein were also used to prosecute sexual offenders, including adulterers, bigamists, and sodomites.

Condemned laymen and clerics were to be handed over to secular authorities for punishment, while clerics were to be expelled from their orders prior to such transfer. The property of the condemned was to be confiscated, and if he were a cleric, it was to be given to the church from which he had received his living. Those suspected of heresy were anathematized for a year; if by that time they had not proven their innocence, they were condemned as heretics. It was expected that the secular authorities, under clerical pressure, would swear to expel heretics from their lands; if a lay ruler failed to do so, the pope could dissolve the oath of fealty that bound his vassals to him. By the end of the thirteenth century, under the influence of the mendicant orders and the Guelph pro-papal party, these oaths to prosecute heresy had become part of the swearing-in ceremony of the podestà or captain of the people in many Italian cities; and sodomy was included among those crimes, along with heresy, which such officials swore especially to eradicate. Furthermore, the same indulgence granted to Crusaders in the Holy Land was to be granted to all Catholics taking up the cross to expel heretics; those who aided or abetted the heretic were to be declared infamous, or *intestabilis* (technically, incapable of serving as a witness or making a will), after one year, subject to all the legal liabilities this status conferred.[2]

The archbishops and the bishops or their archdeacons were further required to visit the parishes of the heretics at least once or twice a year and to appoint three men of good reputation responsible for the identification of heretics and all others whose "life and habits differ from the normal way of living of Christians." If the accused could not clear themselves by compurgation or ordeal, they were to be punished by canon law. Bishops unwilling to fulfill these obligations were to be deposed. This net of prohibitions and investigative procedure eventually spread wide, taking in not only heretics but also sexual nonconformists. An efficient mechanism for the persecution of religious, sexual, and sometimes even political opposition to Rome was thus created; and the state was called upon to fulfill its obligations to guarantee Catholic doctrine.

In order to further strengthen the Catholic faith in the face of this heretical threat and to bolster Christian values among the population, the bishops were ordered to appoint preachers and priests in sufficient numbers to hear confession and impose penance.[3] A master was to be appointed in each diocese for the education of local clergy and poor scholars; in each archdiocese, a qualified theologian was to be chosen and both were to be provided with sufficient revenues for their support. Another canon required all believers to confess, undergo penance, and receive the sacrament of the Eucharist at least once a year. If one wished to confess to another priest, the permission of one's own was required. Careful procedures were likewise laid down for hearing confession, requiring the confessor to determine the circumstances of the sinner and the sin in order to give proper advice. Doctors were exhorted to avoid remedies that might endanger the souls of their patients and to urge the sick to seek the aid and counsel of priests, since "illness is sometimes the result of sin." On the other hand, priests were warned not to betray the penitent; priests who revealed the sins disclosed during confession were to be deposed from their clerical office and shut up in a strict monastery to do penance for life.

All of the preceding provisions considerably strengthened penitential discipline and minimized the likelihood that a Catholic could escape the supervision of the local priesthood. These enactments, aside from providing employment for students of theology, also led to the appearace of a considerable number of penitential manuals for the assistance of the clergy. Thus, a second means of pursuing sexual dissidents—the confessional—was strengthened. Because the far-reaching changes of the twelfth century—urbanization, colonization, the rapid emancipation of the serf—had weakened the bond of the individual to his clan, these new supervisory techniques also provided a means whereby church and society could control its dissidents in the absence of familial pressures.

After addressing the problem of orthodoxy and its maintenance, the council turned to the reform of clerical morals. Provincial councils were instructed to investigate breaches of clerical behavior, and a special official in each diocese was to investigate abuses and recommend correctives. One canon specifically attacked the sin of lust and required the demotion of erring clerics in accordance with canon law. This canon quotes the same passage (Eph. 5:6) found in the Lateran III condemnation of sodomy—" . . . for because of these things cometh the wrath of God on the sons of disobedience"—that had long been interpreted as a reference to homosexuality. Like its predecessor, the Lateran IV canon was inserted in Gregory IX's collection.[4]

A similar canon recommended the reform of the morals of prelates.[5] Although concubinage and incest presumably remained more widespread among the clergy, on at least one occasion Innocent III had been required to deal with an alleged outbreak of sodomy. In a letter of 22 November 1203, Innocent acted on reports relayed to him by the bishop of Mâcon and ordered Bishop Robert I of Châlons, Abbot Hugh V of Cluny, and the Carthusian prior of Squillace to investigate alleged incidences of clerical sodomy in that diocese.[6] In this letter he repeats some of the standard polemics, comparing sodomites to brute beasts who wallow in their own filth or to the inhabitants of Babylon who were steeped in licentiousness and gluttony and turned away from God. The results of this inquiry are not known. Interestingly, the instance of monastic sodomy at Tournus reported earlier by Peter the Venerable occurred in the very same region. The involvement of the prior of the Italian Carthusian house at Squillace suggests perhaps that the disorders may have taken place in a local Carthusian priory.

In order to fulfill the twenty-first canon of the council, which required the episcopate to provide the tools necessary for successful preaching against heresy and hearing of confessions, a new innovation appeared in the penitential literature, the *summa.*[7] Such works were of two kinds: the general and the more specific. Peter Cantor's work, for example, the *Liber de sacramentis,* treats a considerable number of sacramental and social questions on a purely theoretical plane, clarifying the character and function of such priestly tools as excommunication and penance and detailing the forbidden degrees of marriage. The more specific *summae* on penance represent an improvement over the twelfth-century penitential manuals in that they present a systematic treatment of confession and penance rather than a mere verbatim transcription of the relevant canons with a minimal gloss. While some were more legalistic than others and some contained extensive quotations from Scripture, canonical sources, and other theologians, such works were popular rather than academic in tone. They gave to confessor and congregation a clear, concise, and easily consulted handbook. All of the transgressions a priest might encounter in his flock were classified and briefly described, along with the punishment to be imposed upon the penitent. Moreover, these *summae* attempted to justify in a rational way the Christian doctrines of penance and sin to a more sophisticated audience, one presumably prey to the snares of heresy.

Not surprisingly, most of these new-style penitentials were composed by members of the Dominican order, the recently founded order of mendicant preachers entrusted with active combat against the heretics. As the thirteenth century wore on, the crusade against religious heterodoxy was increasingly linked to the persecution of moral nonconformism, to the extent that legislation condemning the Cathars, Patarenes, practitioners of the magical arts, Ghibellines, and other theological heretics was joined to laws punishing sodomites, gamblers, prostitutes, pimps, incendiaries, drunkards, adulterers, and a host of other offenders against Catholic morality. And the order specifically entrusted with providing examples of piety to forestall such vices was the Order of Friars Preachers (Dominicans).[8]

The first such penitential manuals were produced in Paris at the nascent University of Paris and the other Parisian schools. This same period witnessed the rise of the more militant mendicant orders, especially the Dominicans, who were also soon invested with the administration of the Inquisition, the persecuting and investigating arm of the church. In fact, many of the Lateran decrees had already appeared in the decrees of the Council of Paris (1212), whose intellectual ground had been laid by discussions held in the schools of Paris and Chartres where such issues as usury, marriage, excommunication, and sexual morality had been discussed at great length in the *quaestio* literature. Simultaneously, learned circles in Paris were rocked by the introduction of the Aristotelian corpus with its accompanying commentary by Averroës and the appearance of a small circle of antinomian, allegedly free-loving heretics under the leadership of Amaury of Bène. This small sect has been regarded as the source of the Brethren of the Free Spirit, the most libertarian movement of the Middle Ages.[9] Caesarius of Heisterbach, in his admittedly prejudiced account of the Amaurians who flourished in Paris at the university and in court circles during the early thirteenth century, claimed that they interpreted I Corinthians 12:6 in the following way: "If anyone was 'in the Spirit,' they said, even if he were to commit fornication or to be fouled by any other filthiness, there would be no sin in him, because that Spirit, who is God, being entirely distinct from the body, cannot sin. Man, who is nothing, cannot sin so long as that Spirit, who is God, is within him, for He 'worketh in all.'" If indeed such was the doctrine held by this pantheistic sect, then all manner of sexual behavior would be allowed and the rigid code of Catholic restrictions would be irrelevant. Such a view had been held by the fifth-century Spanish Priscillianists, who were also accused of orgiastic rites. During their trial at Paris in 1210, the Amaurians were condemned for accepting the Joachitic notion that a third "Age of the Holy Spirit" was about to commence, during which time the sacraments established in the New Testament would be superseded by the Holy Spirit. Just as the Father had been incarnate in Abraham and the Son in Mary, so the Holy Spirit would be incarnate in each true believer until Judgment Day. Like the Carolingian philosopher John Scotus Eriugena, the Amaurian sect adhered to the essential immortality of all things and the presence of divinity in all Creation, a view supported by citations from the Pauline epistles (I Cor. 4:28 and Col. 1:16). Such views could, in one blow, do away with the mediating role of the clergy, the sacraments, and the Catholic doctrines of sin and penance and open the way to sexual libertinism.[10] In response to such threats to the church, a host of Parisian luminaries, such as Cardinal Robert of Courson (d. 1219) and Peter Cantor (d. 1197), had already undertaken to refine the more sketchy *Liber poenitentialis* that typified the twelfth-century moral program. The new manuals represented an ideal combination of theology and law and were far more practical in application than the speculative treatises on the vices and virtues. And while such an offense as homosexuality might merit a brief reference, subsumed under *luxuria* in the older works, the new *summae* provide greater details in response to the everyday needs of the preacher and confessor. These *summae* are perhaps our most valuable guide to the practice of religion at the parish level. They stand in marked contrast to the nonsystematic, pre-Gregorian penitentials with their conflicting and more liberal treatment of sin, a reflection of the freer attitude toward sexual offenses that probably characterized the pre-Christian epoch.

## Parisian Schools

The work of Peter Cantor (d. 1197) is especially important in providing the link between the speculation of the twelfth century and the systematic theology of the schools. Peter's *Summa de sacramentis,* however, deals more with theoretical problems, for example, the manner of administering penance, the limits of excommunication, and the distinction between mortal and venial sin, rather than the prescriptions for specific vices. In his *Verbum abbreviatum,* Peter equated sodomy with homicide in its seriousness as a sin against God's law and a contradiction of the divine injunction to increase and multiply. He argues that God's order specifically implied the nonandrogynous nature of humanity and prohibited sexual relations between members of the same sex because they inhibit conception. The very enormity of this crime is confirmed by the results of the sins of Sodom: no living creature can survive in the Dead Sea (see Gen. 19, Wisdom 1:10). A member of Peter's circle in Paris, Raoul Ardent, echoing Ulrich of Imola, went so far as to claim that the church would even prefer married clergy to those tempted by fornication, adultery, or sodomy.[11]

One of Peter's more active disciples was the chancellor of Chartres, Peter of Roissy (d. 1213?), a close associate of the popular preacher Fulk of Neuilly.[12] In the early thirteenth century, Peter of Roissy had a short but brilliant career converting usurers and prostitutes in Paris, before serving as chancellor and head of the cathedral school at Chartres (ca. 1204–1211). His major work, the *Manuale de mysteriis ecclesiae* (ca. 1208/1211), deals with a variety of problems in the liturgy and administration of the sacraments and follows the order of Peter Lombard's *Sentences.* In a number of chapters he touches upon sodomy.[13] In the discussion of the various impediments to admission to the priesthood, Peter notes that all those guilty of mortal sins that required episcopal adjudication and dispensation are barred from the priesthood. He notes, however, that "nowadays" sodomites and individuals guilty of incest easily receive episcopal dispensations. The observation that the sanctions against homosexuality, however severe, are not observed is found again and again in the contemporary theologians and suggests that a clear distinction must be made between theoretical formulations and practical application of such dogma. It was this gap between theory and practice that led to the severe penalties imposed on bishops who failed to carry out the law. In his treatment of the licit grounds for the dissolution of a marriage, Peter also noted that the sin of pederasty was sufficient basis for divorce.

One of the more influential manuals of penance emanating from Paris was the *Liber poenitentialis* by Robert of Flamborough (d. 1224), compiled between 1208 and 1215 and based on twelfth-century precedents, particularly Alan of Lille.[14] As penitentiary of the abbey of St. Victor in Paris, Robert served as confessor to many of the students at Paris. The penalties included in his work might therefore logically become the models for those imposed by his students on their own congregations. The specific texts he employs are also found in Yves of Chartres, Bartholomew of Exeter, Burchard of Worms, and Alan of Lille, though he does make some original remarks. Despite his audience, Robert continues the distinction found in Yves of Chartres between the punishment meted out to a *servus* and that to a freeman. He further notes that although many persons persist in regarding sodomy and bestiality as modest crimes, or even no crime at all, the severity of the penalties proves their seriousness.

Unlike the more theoretical practitioners of the penitential genre, Robert's manual was intended for use by future confessors who themselves had not yet had sufficient experience. It therefore contained several scenarios for a possible confrontation between a penitent who is himself a priest and his confessor. Noting that sexual relations must be investigated in the most precise fashion, Robert presents a possible interview:[15]

> Priest: Have you ever been corrupted by lust?
> Penitent: A good deal.
> Priest: Have you ever committed lust against nature?
> Penitent: A good deal.
> Priest: Even with a man?
> Penitent: A good deal.
> Priest: With a cleric or a layman?
> Penitent: With both.
> Priest: With married or unmarried laymen?
> Penitent: Both.
> Priest: How many of them were married?
> Penitent: I don't know.
> Priest: You therefore don't know their status?
> Penitent: Correct.
> Priest: Let us therefore get all the information we can. How long did you sin with them?
> Penitent: Seven years.
> Priest: What was your status at that time?
> Penitent: For two years I was a priest, for two years a deacon, for two years a subdeacon, and for a year an acolyte. I also sinned with other single persons, but I don't know how many or what their status was.
> Priest: Have you sinned with clerics?
> Penitent: Yes, with both secular and religious clergy.
> Priest: Tell me how many were secular and religious, what your status was at the time and what their status was, that is, whether they held any ecclesiastical offices, as archdeacons, deans, abbots, or bishops.
> Penitent: . . .
> Priest: Have you ever initiated any innocent person into that sin? Tell me how many, and what your status was at the time.
>
> Afterward the penitent may be asked if he had sinned against nature at any other time and if he had sex with anyone in any particular way. If he should ask what is meant by a "particular way," I would not answer him, for he would know. I never make mention of anything that might become an occasion for sinning, but rather speak of generalities that everyone knows are sins. I craftily draw the penitent out about masturbation and relations with women, although the manner of inquiry is not here described.
>
> Just as I ask men whether they committed acts against nature, I likewise ask women about every type of fornication. I ask about adultery, about every type of fornication, and finally about incest.

In another more abbreviated version of the same scene, the penitent might provide more complete information about his bed partners:[16]

Priest: Have you sinned with a man?

Penitent: With many.

Priest: Have you initiated any innocent persons into this sin?

Penitent: Yes, three students and a subdeacon.

Priest: Tell me about every person you abused, how long you did so, what your status and theirs was, whether clerics, and if laymen, whether they were married.

Penitent: I had sex while I was a subdeacon for half a year with three subdeacons, one of whom was married. At the time he and I polluted each other in turns, as occurred with the others.

Priest: Have you experienced a nocturnal emission?

Penitent: Frequently.

Priest: If it was caused by habitual intoxication or concupiscence, then it is a mortal sin; if not, then it is a venial sin.

Considering the atmosphere that pervaded Paris when Robert composed his penitential, these mock confessions may not be entirely fictional. It was in 1201 that the great evangelist Fulk of Neuilly led the campaign to purge the city of its prostitutes and pimps, and it was in 1210 that the Amaurian circle at the university was brought to trial. The thousands of young men who flocked to Paris as a result of the official founding of the university may well have satisfied their lustful drives in less than traditional ways, despite their status as minor clerks; as Jacques de Vitry pointed out, many classes were conducted a short distance from the brothels, so that the hagglings of pimps, prostitutes, and their customers was often mingled with the sounds of a learned lecture.

The *Summa confessorum* or Thomas of Chobham (ca. 1160–ca. 1240) comes from the same circle that produced Robert of Flamborough.[17] Thomas, a master of arts and theology, probably studied at Paris under Peter Cantor. He held a variety of clerical positions, primarily in Salisbury and London, and at least once served as an emissary of King John of England. His *Summa,* probably composed around 1216, follows the already standard precedent of subsuming the sins against nature under the types of lust. Unlike many other summists, however, Thomas devotes most of his discussion to bestiality rather than sodomy. Perhaps the work was intended for the use of rural, rather than urban, preachers who would necessarily handle such cases more frequently; it may therefore have attempted to clarify and answer some theoretical questions posed by penance rather than to provide a mere list of authorities.

Thomas's account begins with the traditional definition of the sin against nature taken from Peter Lombard: the use of an unnatural vessel during sexual relations. Thomas pairs this sin, one of the two most damnable crimes, with the sin of Abiron and Dathan, who forcibly attempted to usurp the priesthood from Aaron and Moses (Num.

16:1–33). The people of Sodom, like these two offenders, were consumed by the Inferno and every vestige of their deed was destroyed. Quoting Augustine's *Confessions,* Thomas notes that the Sodomites blasphemously perverted their intended, natural, God-given purpose. That Lot offered his virgin daughters to the two guests from Sodom rather than permit himself to be abused indicates that any natural fornication with women, even the seduction of unwed virgins, is preferable to the sin against nature. He adds, however, that unnatural sex with a woman is so odious that none of the offending man's consanguineous relatives may subsequently wed her. In the order of evils, Thomas rates unnatural sex between men and women as least sinful, auto-sex as more sinful, sex between members of the same sex even more so, and sex with animals as the most sinful of all. Regarding punishments for such vices, Thomas repeats the canons found in Yves of Chartres, Bartholomew of Exeter, and Robert of Flamborough. Elsewhere, Thomas recognizes the special temptations and dangers to which teachers of the young are subjected. Just as a confessor may be held responsible for his failure to impose a fitting penance, so a tutor may be responsible for the faulty morals of his charges. If boys are deficient in either learning or morals, Thomas points out, their teachers are worse than thieves–who merely steal money—for they rob the youth of both the good morals and the learning they have been paid to impart. Moreover, the defects of the teacher can be transmitted to the child, who himself might become a brigand or sinner because of the evil example of his teacher. Confessors are therefore required to impress on teachers their high duty and office.[18]

## Scholastic Philosophy

The penitentials composed by members of the Dominican order reflect the sophisticated legal training of their authors, who successfully integrated the latest conciliar decrees, precedents in Roman law, and literary citations with the earlier tried and true penitential formulas. The effort to base Christian polemic on rational grounds is evident in the greater resort to reasoned argument, which displaces the mere citation of authority characteristic of earlier examples of the genre. The *Liber de poenitentia* (1220) by the Dominican professor Paul of Hungary (d. 1242), one of the first converts to the Order of Preachers among the faculty of law at Bologna, is noteworthy on several counts.[19] First, the sin against nature is given a disproportionately greater place in the discussion of the vices of lust. Furthermore, this *Summa* presents a unique amalgamation of both canon and Roman law, along with considerable citations from the Fathers and Scripture and an extended quotation from Alan of Lille's *Anticlaudianus.* The emphasis on the crime against nature and the successful integration of Roman with canon law indicate a more scholarly, even university, audience made up of clerics, noblemen, and scholars; it was probably written for the



Dominican brethren of St. Nicholas at Bologna.

Paul's treatment is systematically organized in four parts: a definition of the crime against nature (sodomy in particular), a description of its causes, the reasons for its heinousness, and its proper punishment. Following a lengthy quotation from Alan of Lille's *Anticlaudianus*[20] describing the manifold characteristics of lust, Paul defines the sin against nature as the wasting of one's seed outside its normal vessel. In certain unnamed regions, Paul claims, men publicly pollute themselves in this way out of "courtliness" (*curialitater*), heedless of the evil involved. The reasons for the vicious character of the sin against nature are taken from the Augustinian passages in canon law: it is worse than incest, it violates the relationship with God, it is so evil as to be unmentionable. Paul further relies on the standard glosses to Jude 7 and Romans 1:24–26, which note that the terrible conflagration at Sodom and Gomorrah was meant as an example for later generations. Following Methodius, Paul also regards the sin against nature as a cause of the Deluge, for such sinners are destroyers of men and the worst emulators of Onan, who destroyed his own seed, depositing his sperm on the earth like a brute beast.[21]

Punishment is unequivocal. The sodomite is consequently consigned unredeemably to Hell. God was so angered at the Sodomites that he turned their city into the Dead Sea, where neither fish can live nor boats sail. Paul presents a lurid description of the Dead Sea as a metaphor for *luxuria* itself: its waters are unnavigable, undrinkable, filled with iron and feathers. On its shores are attractive fruits, but they contain embers and ashes in their cores. Its trees bear fruit that disintegrates at the touch. Lot's wife was transformed into a statue because the Deity did not want even the slightest vestige of this sin to remain lest Sodom be renewed. As noted in canon law,[22] sodomy is the most severely punished sin in both the Old and New Testaments. The sodomites are fittingly consigned to the flames of Hell for their searing passions. As a result of this crime, states Paul, starvation, pestilence, and earthquakes arise, for the sodomites are adversaries of God, murderers and destroyers of the human race, contradicting the godly injunction to increase and multiply. Paul notes that the Mosaic death penalty for homosexuality was confirmed in the civil law of Constantine; and the exile of the pederast in Roman law to an island is confirmed in canon law by the claustration of erring clerics in a monastery.[23] The punishment of the homosexual thus begun on earth is continued eternally in Hell.

Drawing from Ezekiel, Paul cites the basic cause of the sin against nature as an overabundance of bread, wine, oil, leisure, foreign food, and pride. He notes that there are four sins described in Scripture as so serious that they cry out (*clamant*) to God for retribution: sodomy, homicide, the oppression of widows, and withholding wages from laborers. These are all classed as crimes against nature: the sodomite acts directly against nature; the murderer extinguishes life; the oppressor injures natural piety; the withholder of a worker's wages contravenes natural equity.[24]

Paul argues that those most readily corrupted by sodomy are those with a good deal of free time, especially old men who waste their time eating, telling tales and gossiping instead of pursuing productive activities. Certain courtiers learned in drugs are likewise corrupted. Even clerics and monks not sufficiently devout in their prayers and afraid of the sufferings of the flesh do not heed the words of the Fathers of the church, like Jerome. And those who are steeped in wine more readily burst with the passions of lust. The surest way of purging this demon of licentiousness is through fasting and prayer, the one for purgation of the body, the other for purgation of the mind. Abstention, concludes Paul, extends not only to food but to all carnal attractions. Such exercise of the will must be continuous, without interruption, for this sin is a grave vice that pollutes both mind and body, day and night.

The work of William of Auvergne (ca. 1180–1249) deserves special attention because of the author's prominent position as bishop of Paris and confessor to Blanche of Castile, mother of St. Louis.[25] After serving as professor of philosophy at the University of Paris, when most of his more than thirty-seven works were written, William was appointed bishop of Paris in 1228. He subsequently weathered many conflicts with Rome and the student body at the university. Although his own writings indicate a wide range of sources, including both Jewish and Moslem authorities, he nevertheless took part in the infamous 1240 condemnation and burning of the Talmud. At the same time, he was one of the first to attempt an amalgamation of Christian theology and Aristotelianism and his work is regarded as a one of the foundation stones of scholastic philosophy.

William treats the types of licentiousness in his *Summa de poenitentia* in a dialogue between the confessor and penitent. Unlike most other theologians, William cites conscious masturbation as an even greater transgression than incest, on the scholastic grounds that the crime becomes more severe the closer one is to the person with whom it is committed—and one is closer to oneself than to one's mother. If the penitent argues that he did not know how serious his act was, claims William, he should be cautioned that ignorance is not an extenuating circumstance. William regarded all forms of unnatural lust as sacrilege, wherein lack of respect for the sacred is shown. The sinner is thus similar to a pig who wallows in, and even eats, his own filth. With passages drawn from Scripture (I Thess. 5:2, Prov. 6:12–15, Acts 5:3–5), William likens the sinner against nature to those who have secretly carried on their evil behavior and, before they can repent, are forced to face the consequences of their deeds, namely, death and damnation. For the day of the Lord, he notes, comes stealthily, and peace and security may be suddenly and unexpectedly shattered. The man who wastes his seed outside its proper vessel is doubly guilty, for rather than serving God he is offending nature through sodomy and homicide. This sin is so heinous, William adds, that preachers dare not name it, referring instead to the "unmentionable vice"; for, as Gregory the Great notes,[26] the air itself is corrupted by its mention, and the Devil himself is embarrassed. In Ezekiel 16:27, it is noted that even the shameless Philistines were shamed by such "whoredoms." God himself was so outraged that he refused to recognize the Sodomites as men, raining fire and brimstone on them; and the men of Sodom became mute in their confessions before God. Thus, William concludes, the confessor should admonish the sodomite in particular to repent, for he has only barely escaped eternal punishment.

Later in the *Summa,* William describes the various diseases caused by *luxuria,* such as insanity, headaches, and leprosy. As in the standard gloss on Scripture, he links androgyny and, by implication, homosexuality with the errors of the pagans and idolators. It is noted that in certain unnamed regions, the vice is openly practiced. In his summary, in accord with Methodius he regards sodomy as one of the causes of the Deluge; sodomites are marked as destroyers of humanity and imitators and worshippers of nature.

Perhaps the most systematic treatment of vice is found in the *Summa theologiae* of Thomas Aquinas (d. 1274).[27] In his treatment of the types of lust, Thomas first questions whether the crime against nature may be considered a form of *luxuria.* As proof of its noninclusion, he notes that Gratian does not number it among the forms of lechery. Further, as Aristotle notes, while lust is a form of human evil, unnatural sex is savage and nonhuman, and therefore not subsumed under the human sins. Furthermore, since lechery is an activity that serves generation, and unnatural lust does not lead to generation, it may not be included among the lecherous sins. On the other hand, St. Paul (II Cor. 12:31) condemned the "unclean," and Peter Lombard identified sinners against nature as practitioners of unnatural lust. Aquinas finally admits his agreement with Paul, on the grounds that unnatural sex is both contrary to right reason and conflicts with the natural pattern of sexuality as a fulfillment of procreative needs.

Thomas next considers whether unnatural sex is the worst form of lust. Against this proposition, there are four arguments: 1) it is not a sin against charity, for no one is injured; 2) it is not as much a sin against God as sacrilege is; 3) it is not necessarily committed against a person to whom one owes the greatest love, as incest is; and 4) *mollities,* or solitary self-abuse, would appear more severe because it is even further removed from the generative purpose of sexuality. But in the end Aquinas agrees with Augustine that the crime against nature is indeed the worst sin. It violates the natural goal of sexuality. It is contrary to reason because it harms a living person. In addition, since the plan of nature is God-ordered, unnatural sex, as a violation of the natural order, is a sin against God, like sacrilege. Among the serious vices against nature, the lowest in rank is self-abuse, while the worst is bestiality. In between, in order of severity, are sodomy with a member of the same sex and use of an improper vessel with a member of the opposite sex. Duns Scotus, like Aquinas, argued that the sin against nature violates both reason and perfection. And since nature inclines toward the absolute good, this sin detracts from such inclination. A parallel view was held by Raymund of Penyaforte and Alexander of Hales. These views were most widely disseminated in the encyclopedic *Speculum maius* (ca. 1250) of Vincent of Beauvais. With an arsenal of citations from Augustine, Gratian, Ambrose, and Jerome, Vincent demonstrates that sodomy is contrary to right reason.[28]

The Dominican preacher William Peraldus in his *Summa de virtutibus et vitis* (ca. 1274) deals at some length with the manifold proof of the evil of sodomy, which he, unlike Aquinas, regards as the worst form of *luxuria.*[29] Drawing most of his evidence from Scripture, he likens sodomy to homicide as a violation of the heavenly injunction to increase and multiply. The vice of the people of Sodom and the four other cities destroyed because of this enormity was so great that even innocents suffered in the conflagration, and in aping them we pervert our natures, becoming as brute beasts and separating ourselves from God.

Perhaps the most widely used *Summa confessorum* (ca. 1280/98), surviving in eleven incunabulum editions alone, was written by the Dominican lector John of Freiburg-im-Breisgau (d. 1314).[30] But despite its breadth, John treats sodomy only briefly and adds little to the earlier treatments. John relies on the standard Augustinian selections found in canon law and the condemnation found in Romans that demands degradation and claustration for clerics and excommunication and condign satisfaction for laymen. He also adds some comments from Raymund of Penyaforte to the effect that the punishment of Sodom proves the heinousness of the crime the mere mention of which pollutes the lips and ears.

## Related Vices

Despite the refinements introduced by the scholastics in defining the crime against nature, the Augustinian definition of use of an improper vessel for the disposal of semen remained in force. Included in the definition might be any number of sex acts, among them sodomy. The term *sodomia* itself also included bestiality, or sexual relations with animals, which was governed by the Ancyra statutes and a canon attributed to Martin of Braga requiring penances ranging from ten days to fifteen years, depending on the status of the penitent. In accordance with the tradition of Leviticus 20:16, the offending beast was to be killed, burned, and buried, lest its existence rekindle memories of the crime; the Jewish penalty of stoning for the sinner was moderated by Christian penance.[31] Thomas of Chobham notes that he himself has seen people undergoing penance for this crime; they are permanently barred from wearing shoes, instead wearing sandals without soles; they may never wear linen, enter a church, eat meat or fish, drink intoxicants, or wear the garments of a knight (*miles*). The severity of this rule, he notes, may only be diminished because of illness or after many years of penance.[32]

The widest definition of the term sodomy remained that found in Burchard of Worms's *Decretum,* which had unsystematically and uncritically noted every possible act, suggesting that the confessor had the widest latitude in imposing penance. Many of the deeds mentioned, like the use of a dildo, mutual masturbation, anal entry, sex between brothers, and oral sex, which may be regarded as acts against nature because they frustrate conception, are rarely mentioned in the other penitentials. Furthermore, since Burchard quotes many conflicting sources and the possible penalties are so varied, the confessor is given virtual free rein to use his discretion. The penalties range from ten days for masturbation to fifteen years for sexual relations between brothers; the penalty for lesbian acts is typically lower than for homosexual acts between men.[33]

Nocturnal emission presented the theologian with peculiar problems, for it is frequently involuntary and yet at the same time it fulfills the classical definition of a sin against nature (emission of semen into an improper vessel). As early as the fifth century, John Cassian (d. ca. 523) had noted that the Devil is wont to visit such emissions on priests during feast days in order to prevent their participation in communion as a result of ritual impurity. The *Vita S. Dioscori,* quoted by Yves of Chartres in his *Decretum,* notes that the saint instructed his monks not to worry if their emissions were not accompanied by unclean thoughts of women—they may simply be fulfilling a necessary bodily function. For a nocturnal emission could be regarded as either a venial or mortal sin, depending on the circumstances, e.g., whether it was caused directly by "unclean" thoughts. The *locus classicus* from which its definition comes, cited in all the major penitentials from Bede to Thomas of Chobham, was the *Epistles* of Gregory the Great, specifically the letter answering a question put to Pope Gregory by Augustine of Canterbury.[34] Gregory distinguished three kinds of emission. The first type is caused by a mere excess of fluid and such a discharge, unless accompanied by vile thoughts, is not regarded as sinful; however, if it should occur during waking hours, penance is required. Chobham notes that certain illnesses may also cause such involuntary emission.[35] On the other hand, some lascivious persons emit semen as a result of the slightest movement or casual friction, and their act is a mortal sin, unless they have attempted to frustrate this reaction by the use of cold baths and a hairshirt.

The second kind of emission noted by Gregory is caused by excessive eating and drinking, and this is a venial sin. If accompanied by vile thoughts, the sin is even greater. Gregory noted that a priest so polluted during the night must abstain from divine service on the following day, neither celebrating mass nor hearing confession. Thomas of Chobham, however, suggests that if it is a holiday and the church is filled with people, in the absence of another priest he ought to perform his duty after having undertaken some penance, for instance, a cold bath, fast, or use of a hairshirt.

The third and most serious type of emission cited by Gregory is the result of forethought, brought on by excessive contact with or thoughts of women, whose recollection returns at night. Such an emission is a mortal sin. To the extent that a man exercises his reason in deciding to eat and consort with women, both possible causes of the emission, and he exercises his reason in his sleep, a man may well be responsible for the emission. Burchard of Worms typically gives a regimen of psalms to be recited by those guilty of nocturnal emission, voluntary or involuntary, priest or layman. Peter Damian's biographer John of Lodi reports that when the saint was first subjected to carnal temptations in his youth, he would customarily get out of bed and throw himself nude into cold water in order to reduce his passions; when the diabolical urges had receded, he recited a series of psalms and was thereafter able to return to sleep.[36]

Aquinas likewise devoted considerable attention to the relative sinfulness of nocturnal emission, opting for the more liberal interpretation. For this was evidently a problem among the clergy, who were barred all conscious avenues of sexual expression and, unable to control their unconscious desires, suffered great pangs of guilt over nocturnal pollution. The most celebrated tale of such priestly guilt in the thirteenth century occurs in the *Autobiography* of Peter Celestine (Pope Celestine V, d. 1294), who was uncertain whether to celebrate mass following such an emission. His fellow monks were equally uncertain what to do (indicating perhaps the limited influence of scholastic philosophy among southern Italian monks). The following night he dreamed of a defecating donkey, whose slow, reluctant ascent of a mountain kept Peter from reaching a great palace peopled with Benedictine monks. An image of the Trinity, however, urged Peter not to be discouraged by the beast's unseemly act, for the creature had no choice. From this dream, Celestine concluded that his nocturnal emission, being the result of superfluous fluid rather than intoxication, was like the donkey's deed involuntary and therefore not sinful. He could thus perform the mass with a clear conscience. Since this biography was intended as a kind of testament to instruct Peter's eremitical followers, it seems obvious that such emissions were a commonplace among the cloistered, more so than other forms of lust or the sin against nature.[37]

## Indulgences

But while theologians developed a sophisticated theology of sin, classifying, defining, and clarifying the types of lust, reserving the most serious penance for sodomites, to what extent did the priestly physicians of the soul apply the prescriptions? For if the law had been carried out to the letter, Europe would have been transformed into one vast penal institution populated by millions of unwilling Christians restricted in diet and garb, excluded from communion and church services, condemned to a joyless life of fasts, prayers, and flagellation. Under such conditions, the church could hardly hope to compete with the promise of greater earthly pleasure that such sects as the Free Spirit, not to speak of Islam and Judaism, could offer. In order to mitigate the draconian punishments demanded since the Gregorian reform, several innovations developed rapidly in the twelfth century: reservation, dispensation, and indulgence.

As Thomas of Chobham noted:

> There are many cases that the local priest cannot dispose of in his own parish, but ought to be referred to his bishop or to the bishop's penitentiary, so that penance can be imposed. There are even certain crimes the bishop himself ought to hear in person, but because he is often prevented by the press of business he appoints vicars and penitentiaries under him in his episcopal see, and even archdeacons, lest the poor be worn down in the labor required to visit the bishop. And these vicars or penitentiaries hear the confessions the bishops ought to hear.

The number of sins thus referred to higher authority was considerable, including sodomy, bestiality, adultery, and rape, among the sins of lust.[38]

Such a hierarchical system of spiritual authority was easily abused. Just as the bishops had complained about the reduction of their privileges and the centralization at Rome evidenced by the continuous flow of papal emissaries, mendicants, and diplomats who superseded the local bishop, so also the parish clergy resented interference in its pastoral duties. Under an industrious and conscientious bishop like Eudes of Rouen, perhaps this system of reserved sins worked effectively. Too often, the low educational level of the clergy, the persistence of simony, vacant benefices, and disputed episcopal elections, all requiring time-consuming appeals to Rome, could permit the penitent to delay his case indefinitely. Episcopal visitations aimed at correcting such disorder in the parishes and monasteries were only just beginning to become a feature of church life.

While the power of reservation could effectively withdraw the penitent from the jurisdiction of the local clergy, the confessor himself possessed a tool that could also mitigate the rigors of the law: dispensation. If it were judged that the application of penance could create hardship for society or its members, the pastor could dispense with the observance of fasts and abstinence. The sinner could achieve at least partial redemption by fasts, for example, feeding the poor, genuflections, prayer, or participation in bridge or church building. For the confessor was frequently enjoined to take into consideration age, sex, handicaps, knowledge, length of time involved in sinning, and marks of contrition before imposing penance. Such exceptions could, according to the handbooks, remit penance of up to a year. If the confessor were a mendicant friar who would not remain to guarantee evidence of contrition, then the erring sinner might again avoid the full rigor of the law, unless his sin or crime were revealed to the secular authorities.

A third method of commuting penance was through an indulgence, a remission of punishment granted as a reward for acts of piety or charity acceptable as a substitute for the rigors of penance.[39] Such remissions, which could be granted by pope or bishop, became available from the eleventh century. Through the use of documents dispensing indulgences, Rome promoted such enterprises as the Crusades, the Jubilee of 1300, the building of new hospitals and leprosaria, and the canonization of new saints. An indulgence remitting part or all penance, might be granted to those who participated in or contributed to the dedication, ornamentation, or building of a new church; undertook a pilgrimage to Rome or Compostella; or simply attended church on certain holidays or feast days. As the number of such occasions multiplied, the church made sporadic attempts to halt the inflationary spiral; at Lateran IV, for example, Canon 62 provided that the dedication of a basilica could be accompanied by an indulgence of no more than a year and an anniversary of a dedication by an indulgence not exceeding forty days. The same statute prohibited the capricious exhibition of relics on less than solemn occasions, for the veneration of relics was another means whereby remission of sins might be secured. The statute aimed to curb clerics who displayed sacred relics in return for payment. In fact, as this canon suggests, unauthorized or even forged relics, which may have formed part of the booty brought from the East, had become the objects of veneration. Rome now undertook to become the final arbiter in the proclamation of saints' cults and the authentication of relics. But the increasing need for remission of penance is perhaps attested by the hundreds of saints' cults that received papal or episcopal authorization and by the new penitential orders linked to the mendicants that extended many of the restrictions of monastic life to the laity. Both of these institutions aided the alleviation of penance.

The dispensation of indulgences was thus mutually beneficial to both confessor and penitent. Churches, hospitals, orphanages, and monasteries were built with the contributions of the faithful; roads, lodging houses, and sacred shrines teemed with pilgrims; crusading armies in southern France, Spain, the Middle East, and eastern Europe were filled with recruits; and a host of new religious orders like the Cruciferians and Trinitarians found ready adherents. In return for support for the Church Militant, the sufferings of the Christian penitent were eased; how many former rapists, pimps, harlots, or indeed sodomites joined this throng of believers is impossible to estimate.

While the church always maintained that confession and genuine penitence must precede the granting of an indulgence—and theologians themselves were not united in accepting the effectiveness of the indulgence in remitting punishment for sin—abuse rapidly became widespread. By the thirteenth century, Parisian scholars like Hugh of St. Cher (fl. ca. 1230) had fully developed the theory that church authorities were the guardians of a treasury of merit and good works accumulated by Jesus, Mary, and the saints. As members of the same spiritual body, believers were entitled, through their confessors, to receive such grace for the remission of their own sins. Thus, paradoxically, while the thirteenth century witnessed a considerable refinement of the intellectual basis for repression of sexual nonconformity and a concomitant strengthening of penalties, there was a contrary tendency to mitigate the effects through a host of penitential variances. Indulgences, tertiary orders, and saints' cults all provided a means of easing the otherwise stringent penalties that rigorous application of canon law could exact—this despite the deep fear of sexuality and the "disorder of androgyny" that canon law and the penitentials expressed. Some writers, like William of Auvergne, had even emphasized the diseases, like leprosy, that resulted from overindulgence. Others had linked sexual freedom to paganism and the refinements of the nobility.

While relying on the same essential sources already cited by the twelfth-century theologians, the scholastic philosophers of the thirteenth century attempted to base their condemnation of sodomy on more rational grounds and attempted to fit their discussion into a systematic treatment of all the vices against nature. The main controversy revolved around the relative evil of the various crimes against nature—whether sodomy, incest, or bestiality should be regarded as the worst. The new *summae* also attempted a fuller integration of the literary traditions of canon law and scriptural commentary that until then had remained discrete; they also relied to a greater degree on the Roman law. It should not, however, be assumed that these theologians worked in an ivory tower. In fact, many of them were consulted in matters of legislation, and the thirteenth century witnessed a determined effort to make secular law conform to Christian morality. At the same time, various devices were conceived to soften the sometimes severe penalties required in canon law. As a result, many presumably escaped the full rigor of the law. The thirteenth century was a time of extremism, and the unique brilliance of the church was its ability to absorb and redirect the opposing forces within it that threatened to do the Devil's mischief and tear to shreds the seamless robe of Christ.

# V

## *Secular Law*

BY THE THIRTEENTH century, canon law and scholastic philosophy had undergone considerable refinement. From the ill-defined and localized concepts of the eleventh century, the new theologians forged a clear theory of sodomy as a sin comparable to homicide among the sins against nature, that is, contrary to reason and contrary to God's divine plan. The vague penances prescribed in the more primitive penitentials were replaced by well-organized confessional manuals that laid down the acceptable textual authorities and penances, considerably reducing the confessor's freedom to make ad hoc decisions. In canon law, sodomy became one of those infamous crimes that incurred the greatest dishonor and ill repute. For the cleric, this meant deprivation of his office and benefice; for the layman, the loss of all civil and political rights. Other crimes so designated included homicide, incest, sacrilege, perjury, adultery, apostasy, fornication, and heresy.[1]

In secular law, however, it was only the impact of Roman law that raised sodomy to the status of an infamous crime, calling forth the severest penalties inflicted by the state. Roman law was not applied with vigor until the late twelfth century when an aggressive group of jurists and lawyers centered around the developing university at Bologna began to revive and gloss the law. As we have seen, Gratian's *Decretum* (ca. 1140) did contain one passage, taken from the second-century jurist Paulus, condemning pederasty; and even the earlier canon law collection of Regino of Prüm contained a passage from Justinian's *Codex.* By the thirteenth century, however, the commentators on canon law commonly included citations from Roman law as confirmation of the increasingly stiff penalties imposed in canon law. The Dominican theologians, many of them trained at Bologna, in like manner began to incorporate citations from Roman law in their discussions of sodomy.

### Tribal Law

Until the twelfth century, tribal and common law predominated. This tradition characteristically treated sexual misdemeanors with relative lenience, often imposing fines related to social status and ability to pay rather than imposing capital punishment. In the early codes, homosexuality is in fact barely mentioned in comparison with such crimes as parricide, theft, incest, or rape.

The English, at least in their semifictionalized accounts of their prehistoric, pre-Christian ancestors, recognized the easier sexual environment that characterized the island before its conversion to Christianity. According to Ranulph Higden (d. 1364), Mempricius, the legendary fifth king of the Britons who allegedly ruled for twenty years in the time of King David, was known for his ferocity. When he left his wife and gave himself over to sodomy, his reward was to be devoured by wolves while hunting. Robert Manning of Brunne (ca. 1330) tells a similar story of Malgo, a sixth-century king of the Saxons, who in the third year of his reign took to sodomy, "a sinne against kynde"; as a result, he died suddenly in his bath at Winchester.[2]

The earliest Anglo-Saxon laws, dating from the seventh century, were still under the influence of the pre-Christian tradition, whereby each person's life was estimated in monetary terms (the *wergeld*) based upon his social status. In the event of inflicting death or other damage, the offender, rather than being imprisoned, was required to pay a sum to the victim or to the victim's kindred equivalent to the value of the life or limb lost. Moral offenses were likewise punished in monetary terms and were seen as a reflection on the clan of both the victim and the criminal. While incest, adultery, and rape, for example, were dealt with as violations of property law, subject to appropriate fines, no punishment is noted for homosexual offenses. The code of the Kentish king Ethelbert (early seventh century) dealt only with cases of rape, adultery, and incest, making no mention of sodomy. A law of King Withred of Kent (late seventh century) that betrayed the recent Anglo-Saxon conversion to Christianity excluded from communion all persons living in illicit unions (presumably in accordance with the rather restrictive Roman Catholic canons).[3]

The laws of Alfred the Great (d. 899), king of the West Saxons, indicate the continuing Christianization of European law and its impact on England. Whole passages are quoted from the Ten Commandments, Exodus, and the Acts of the Apostles; church councils and synods have already begun to provide punishments for a variety of unspecified crimes. On the other hand, in his introduction Alfred quotes the biblical passage imposing death on those who have relations with sheep (Lev. 20:15), but he makes no mention of homosexual offenses.[4] Despite this silence, however, it should be noted that the extant laws are not complete and frequently contain only the most recent enactments, not those of long standing. The nearly contemporary Lombard laws of Liutprand (733) exacted capital punishment from a man who allowed his wife to sleep with another and from the consenting wife; the husband was also required to pay a fine to the wife's family. In another highly elaborate Lombard law (731), punishment was exacted from a man who had "shamefully" conversed with another's wife or placed his hand on her bosom or elsewhere. Thus, although sexual life was controlled by law, homosexuality is again not mentioned. Other Lombard codes are even more reticent.[5]

The Visigothic kings of Spain, on the other hand, showed a singular zeal in punishing sexual offenders and eliciting episcopal cooperation in the creation of a theocratic kingship.[6] Their success was brief, for the Moslem conquest of the peninsula cut short their reign of terror against sexual and religious nonconformists and introduced a more liberal period. But while in power the Visigoths combined sexual, political, and religious repression. Their anti-Jewish legislation was the most severe ever enacted, in essence providing for forced conversion or exile, despite the considerable size of the Jewish minority. An edict of King Kindasvith (ca. 650) defined sodomy as a moral crime requiring the strictest punishment. Following trial by a secular court, both passive and active homosexuals were to be castrated. The offender was then taken to the local bishop, who imposed a religious penance; if the criminal had acted voluntarily, he could then avoid penance by admitting his act. If he had a wife and children, they had the right to claim his property and the wife could remarry. At the council of Toledo XVI (693), during his opening address King Egica urged the extirpation of homosexual acts; the council decided that clerics were to be degraded, perpetually exiled, and damned; others were to be punished in accordance with Kindasvith's earlier edict, excluded from communion, given one hundred stripes of the lash, shorn of their hair as a sign of disgrace, and perpetually exiled. Egica himself then added a further law, noting the church's responsibility to root out sins of the flesh. He nevertheless repealed the previous statute of Kindasvith and decreed that both laymen and clerics, of whatever class or origin, found guilty of *stuprum* (in this case, sodomy) were to be castrated and to undergo the most extreme punishment allowed by the law.

These precedents suggest that Germanic law was far from uniform in its treatment of sexual offenders; most of the codes are in fact silent about homosexuality. They display great concern for the regulation of marriage as an expression of property relations; far less interest is shown in specific sex acts as such. Adultery and rape, for example, are generally treated neither as sins nor as violations of the female's honor but rather as infringements on the traditional rights of her husband or father. Homosexuality, except insofar as it reflected on the honor of the clan, was a relatively innocuous crime, presumably not subject to severe penalties.

The laws of the Christianized Carolingian Empire, in contrast, reflect a determined attempt to realize the ideals of Old Testament kingship within a Christian framework. The coronation of Charlemagne by Pope Leo III in 800 A.D. was only one example of the cooperation between church and state that was to extend to morals legislation. The Carolingian rulers frequently used the episcopate as their local political representative in return for assistance in the spread of the faith, the foundation of monasteries, and the granting of lands to parish churches. Thus, it is not surprising that a 743 law of Carloman gave the bishops the right to try adulterous and incestuous persons.[7] Still, while laws against homosexuality do figure among the crimes, legislation against incest, adultery, rape, and clerical fornication (nothing is said of premarital sex among the laity) predominate (e.g., A.D. 789, 827, 838/39). In 789, the prohibition of the Council of Ancyra suggesting harsh penance for bestiality and sodomy was renewed, and bishops and priests were urged to impose stiff penalties for those evils. In 799, Charles likewise prohibited the wearing of men's garments by nuns; and in 802, among other abuses, he prohibited sodomy among monks. A further capitulary of Aachen in 803 (renewed in 814) listed sodomy with several other "abominable crimes," including adultery, fornication, incest, illicit marriage, homocide, perjury, and false testimony. All of these acts are defined as forms of sacrilege, subject to similar punishment. In 809, the council of Aachen warned bishops to protect students in their care from lust and drunkenness, but sodomy was not specifically mentioned. A monastic rule of Louis the Fat (817), perhaps with some concern for the sexual implications, prohibited the nude, public flagellation of wayward monks. In 826, the widespread existence of incest, parricide, and homicide was again noted; sodomy, however, the frequent companion of these vices, was not referred to. The most extended reference to the sodomitical vice comes from an 827 capitulary of Louis the Fat, whose citation of biblical precedents perhaps reflects the alleged Jewish influence during his administration.[8] The capitulary explains that both the Benjaminites and Sodomites were destroyed for such vices as sodomy and bestiality. Furthermore, like the practice of magic and other divining arts, sodomy is condemned in Leviticus. Consequently, the prohibition of Ancyra is renewed. All of this legislation, however, continues to treat sodomy as a religious crime, to be handled by the ecclesiastical authorities.

Because it is difficult to obtain reliable statistics for population or fertility during the early Middle Ages, it is difficult to relate these moral codes to social needs. Population density obviously varied greatly, and large areas of Europe were no doubt totally deserted and uncultivated. Only after the eleventh century did these regions acquire a stable, expanding population.[9] Certainly, there was no problem of overpopulation. But because the technological level was not yet capable of substantially increasing productivity and because arable land was limited, Europe could not successfully absorb any increase in population. Before the eleventh century, then, sexual behavior that might limit conception would not be regarded with the seriousness expressed after the twelfth century, when the expanding economy of Europe required a steady population growth. Famine, invasions, natural disasters, and a high infant mortality effectively reduced demographic pressures in the centuries before more efficient marshaling of resources, new settlements, and land clearance provided greater opportunities. The family was the center of rural life; the typical land division, the *mansus,* or hide, was capable of supporting a family, and taxes or penalties were levied on the group rather than the individual. Such crimes as sodomy or bestiality, it would seem, would have been less serious than rape, adultery, or incest and less likely to disrupt group solidarity. For a woman was regarded much as chattel, and the violation of her body was considered a violation of the property rights and productivity of the clan. The relative absence of legislation regulating homosexual acts in this period suggests two possibilities. Either homosexuality was not sufficiently widespread or disruptive to require attention or it was simply not regarded as an especially serious moral crime, unlike adultery, incest, or rape, which are dealt with at great length in these early law codes.

## Roman Law

Roman law deals with sodomy in a number of passages that unfortunately are rather obscure. Their impact on medieval law is thus uncertain. In 342, a statute of Constantine II and Constans[10] required "exquisite punishment" in cases of homosexuality, but this apparently applied only to passive sodomitical marriage and its enforcement may not have been carried out. In 390, a law of Valentinian II, Theodosius, and Arcadius[11] apparently prescribed public burning for passive sodomites. In the *Institutes* of Justinian (533),[12] homosexual acts were placed under the provisions of the *Lex julia de adulteriis.* More explicit legislation is found in the *Novellae* (538),[13] which legislated against homosexual acts and blasphemy. Here, the precedent comes from the Old Testament: acts contrary to nature are prohibited because they bring forth the wrath of God; the destruction of the five cities is the example presented. Such crimes, say the *Novellae,* result in famines, earthquakes, and pestilence. Such sinners are consequently admonished to cease their evil deeds rather than lose their immortal souls. Should they persist, they make themselves unworthy of God's mercy and subject to legal punishment. The prefect of the capital was ordered to arrest such blasphemous and lustful persons and to inflict extreme punishment on them, lest the city and state suffer harm. If, after sufficient warning, the wrongdoers persisted in their acts, they were to be condemned by God; should the prefect fail to act, he himself was to suffer God's judgment and "our" (i.e., the emperor's) indignation. A second even more verbose law dated 544[14] again proves the evils of sodomy with descriptions of the inextinguishable fire that consumed Sodom and with citations of the Pauline condemnation of unnatural sex acts. Such acts are so base, argues the law, that even brute beasts do not commit them; mankind too should abstain from these deeds. Those who have so sinned, should confess and do penance, especially during Easter season, lest they suffer more severe penalties, lose their salvation, and by their failure to repent bring ruin on all. Neither of these laws, however, seems very specific about the kind of punishment meted out to convicted sodomites. They do, nevertheless, emphasize that sodomy is not simply to be treated as a private act; the vice could do society irreparable harm by offending God and must therefore be decisively curbed by the state.

Azo's *Commentary on the Codex* (ca. 1230),[15] which refers to many of these passages, does not shed much light on any specific medieval interpretation. Azo does at least note the confusion between *stuprum,* or forcible deflowering of a virgin, and sodomy in Roman law. The very brevity of this discussion suggests that sodomy was not yet regarded as a sufficiently serious threat to warrant longer treatment. The commentary of Accursius (d. 1263) on the *Codex* is even more limited, merely noting that *stuprum* may refer to the rape of boys as well as to violation of virgins and widows; the same penalties apply in all cases.[16] It will be recalled that Accursius himself was accused of sodomy by Dante.

Despite the revival of Roman law studies, much of Europe still clung to traditional law; sodomy apparently remained a religious crime punished through a penitential discipline administered by the local priesthood. Toward the end of the twelfth century, however, such serious sins as heresy and sodomy were taken out of the hands of the local priesthood and made "reserved sins" that had to be referred to the bishop. Sodomy had already been for some time associated with heresy and this enhancement of episcopal power in the treatment of moral and theological nonconformity probably reflects the failure of the parish clergy, either through laxity, ignorance, corruption, or heretical sympathies, to deal adequately with the problem of heresy. The transfer of these sins to episcopal jurisdiction was itself short-lived, for the episcopate proved equally unwilling to apply the full rigor of the law, especially in such heresy-ridden areas as southern France. By the 1220s, the mendicant orders and the newly created papal Inquisition further reduced local responsibility for the treatment of sexual offenders. By the thirteenth century, some canonists, representing the centralizing tendencies within the church, even reserved such offenses to papal authority.[17]

A parallel, although somewhat more retarded, change occurred in secular law. The revival of Roman law, which tended to strengthen the pretensions of such centralizing rulers as the Holy Roman Emperor Frederick II, Louis IX of France, Edward I of England, and Alfonso X of Castile, played an increasing role in creating a national, nonlocal law and referring such capital crimes as sodomy to royal authority. The rise of heresy, with which sodomy had become irrevocably linked, also necessitated the enlistment of the stronger secular authorities on the side of Rome in the pursuit and prosecution of suspected heretics. In many instances, the use of the secular arm was necessary because the local population and government itself was infected with heresy and the local bishop loathe to act against his erring flock. At the Fourth Lateran Council of 1215, Rome was therefore obliged to call on the state to cooperate in the battle against heresy and to enact local legislation withdrawing political and civil rights from heretics and their allies.[18]



## Thirteenth-Century Reform

In English law, until the thirteenth century sexual morality fell under church authority and crimes against nature were identified with heresy. While both Glanville and Britton, the earliest collections of English law, make no reference to sodomy, *Fleta* (ca. 1290), a manual of English law published at the court of Edward I, in one passage condemned bestiality and sexual dealings with Jews and prescribed death by fire for sodomites caught in the act. The manual also noted that although sodomites were generally tried in church courts and the penalties imposed by secular tribunals, the king's court might also act independently.[19] A similar severity marked the otherwise enlightened legislation of Alfonso X of Castile (d. 1284), who provided castration followed by stoning to death for acts of sodomy (perhaps based on the Visigothic precedent). Alfonso's law, *Las Siete Partidas* (or The Book of the Laws, 1256/63), regarded sodomy as a form of infamy, bringing dishonor on the offender and his clan.[20]

French legislation, while also deferring to church authority, is somewhat fuller, although it is sometimes unclear whether the term *bougerie* means heresy or homosexuality. Phillippe de Baumanoir, in his *Les Coutumes de Beauvaisis,* noted that sodomites, because they erred against the Faith, were to be burned and their property confiscated. The *Coutumes de Touraine-Anjou* referred cases of sodomy to the bishops. If the case were proven, the accused was to be burned and his goods to be confiscated by the local baron. The *Établissements* of St. Louis provided a similar punishment, duly noting the accord with papal decretals. Another legal collection from Orléans (1260) produced during the reign of Louis IX provided mutilation for the first offense of sodomy, castration for the second, and burning for the third; women were likewise to lose a "member" for the first two offenses and were to be burned for the third. In addition, the goods of such felons were to be confiscated by the king.[21] In this intermediary phase, when sodomy was regarded as both a secular and a religious crime, there were bound to be jurisdictional disputes between lay and clerical authorities over adjudication of such cases. In 1261, for example, the bishop of Amiens undertook to try some alleged sodomites. A royal order demanded that such persons be handed over to the town government for adjudication. The charter of Amiens, however, granted by Philip Augustus in 1190, made no mention of the right of burghers to try such cases.[22] Evidently, although sodomy was technically a case reserved for ecclesiastical justice, a secular court was preferred to a religious court. But by the fourteenth century, under the influence of a ruler like Philip the Fair, sodomy had become a crime to be handled in the state courts. In 1310, a royal register notes that a certain Barthomaeus of Florence, evidently a banker for he is defined as a servant of the crown (*serviens noster*), was charged with sodomy in Bourges. An inquiry was ordered, but the evidence found was insufficient to support the charge.[23] In another case, in 1317 during the reign of Philip V, a certain Guiardus de Capis was accused by several persons, including a certain Coletanus, called Le Pele, of sodomy. The victim knew that Coletanus had been bribed by several inhabitants of the city to bring the charge. Fearful lest he be convicted on false testimony, Guiardus fled. But when he was called to the royal court, which apparently had a reputation for greater fairness, he returned—and was banished from France. After many later witnesses were called, however, the court discounted the false testimony and a royal pardon was granted.[24]

Both the French and English laws are in keeping with the general trend toward secularization of institutions and outlook that was to become increasingly evident, particularly in the more urbanized parts of Europe.[25] This tendency had already appeared in the eleventh century during the first stirrings of a mercantile economy, which was viewed with suspicion by the church, itself a great land-owner. The struggling communes often found their most strenuous opponents among the episcopate, which feared the erosion of its traditional rights of justice and taxation. Furthermore, Christian preaching continued to characterize the city as a center of greed, lust, ambition, and usury and to extol the pastoral virtues of solitude and country life. The rise of centralized monarchies and independent communes further exacerbated the conflict between the laity and clergy as the independent legal status of the church was diminished. Particularly in the thirteenth century, the state began to assume many of the burdens formerly reserved to the church. Charitable institutions, for example, were taken over by the municipal authorities and their clerical officials were transformed into state employees. Excommunicants, in addition to their religious liabilities, now suffered loss of property and civil rights if not reconciled to the church. The major precedent for this overlapping of spiritual and secular authority had in fact been the Inquisiton, which had so actively sought the cooperation of the state in the prosecution of heretics. By the 1240s, many states had invaded the moral sphere by enacting legislation against such strictly religious crimes as clerical concubinage and excessive display of wealth.

In Italy, the theoretical formulations of the Parisian scholars were soon to find more formal and effective expression in secular law under the influence of the evangelical mendicant orders that were rapidly replacing the more contemplative monastic orders as the militant representatives of Christianity. Both the Dominican and Franciscan orders actively sought, through example and word, to transform the secular world into a clearer reflection of the social gospel. While their rhetoric was religious, some considered their aims patently political: the brutal suppression of heresy, the extension of papal power, the reduction of episcopal privilege, and the protection of clerical rights. Despite their popularity and charitable enterprises, many states, particularly those allied to Emperor Frederick II and opposed to Rome, were at first suspicious of mendicant motives and, like Frederick, barred entry of the friars. This intense conflict was particularly sharp in the cities of northern and central Italy, where the mendicants were soon entangled in local politics, generally on the side of the *Popolani,* the republican, anti-imperial, and antiaristocratic party of the middle classes. The mendicant program, aside from its purely religious aspects, sought the following goals: an end to clan warfare in the cities; the active pursuit and persecution of heretics in accordance with papal instructions; the elimination of antiecclesiastical legislation; communal legislation against usury, imprisonment for debt and conspicuous consumption; and the realization of Christian morality in secular law through statutes against gambling, drinking, prostitution, abortion, and sodomy, among other vices.[26]

While already in the 1220s some aspects of this program had been enacted in the Guelph, or pro-papal, communes, the year 1233, the Great Alleluia, witnessed an unprecedented wave of religious enthusiasm that swept the crusading friars into positions of political power throughout Italy. Such friars as John of Vicenza, Bartholomew of Vicenza, and Gerard of Modena temporarily replaced the local podestà, and enacted legislation for the relief of the poor, the restoration of civil peace, and the expulsion or execution of heretics, sodomites, and other moral offenders. A wave of church building, feasts, processions, and preaching swept Italy. St. Dominic was raised to the honors of sainthood, miracles were performed, heretics were burned in great numbers, prisoners were released, and lay confraternities were created to seek out and punish heretics. A few voices, like that of the astrologer Guido Bonatto, were heard against the popular throng. For behind this enthusiasm, the directing hand of Rome was often visible. Indeed, the mendicant reformers' victory was short-lived; intracommunal strife soon broke out again, and in 1237 at the battle of Cortenuova, the pro-imperial Ghibelline party reestablished itself in northern Italy. The years to follow were years of political conflict. Only the death of Frederick II, the eventual extinction of the Hohenstaufens, and the collapse of the Ghibellines in 1266 enabled the earlier "puritanical" legislation to gain a permanent foothold. Many of the earlier statutes were reenacted or recodified in this period, although based on the halcyon days of 1233/34, when the mechanism of repression was first created.

The new statutes clearly indicate the connection between heresy and sodomy in the minds of the mendicant reformers and reveal the Inquisition as a tool of both political and sexual repression. The papal Inquisition now operated with a freer hand, despite isolated attempts, as at Milan and Genoa (Ghibelline towns), to frustrate the inquisitors' work. The heretics had long been suspected of sexual nonconformity because of their peculiar theological conceptions; the Ghibellines, often representing the interests of the older feudal aristocracy, were now easily branded sexual nonconformists because of the known disposition of the nobility for pederasty, adultery, and other sexual aberrations. The mendicants also aroused latent passions against usurers, Jews, and heretics, who had for some time been identified in the popular mind with the plutocracy. As Eric Erikson notes, those individuals or groups who see a danger to their socioeconomic status frequently tend to return to the more restricted, superstitious, and intolerant views of the past, regressing to earlier, dormant guilt feelings. Abhorrence of all things physical (i.e., sexual) is a frequent concomitant.[27] Italy in the thirteenth century was just then experiencing the increasing insecurity of urban life, a product of mini-industrialization, fed by the first signs of inflation, the ferment of new, unsatisfied social classes, guilds, and professions, and the pressures of an impoverished peasantry fleeing to the cities. This might well foster just such a reaction among the sons of the great merchant families who had formerly governed the cities and who often dominated the mendicant orders.[28] The kind of social ferment prevalent in the thirteenth century was as likely to breed the same kind of repressive mass movements so common to the twentieth century that direct much of their energies at the eradication of aberrant life-styles.

The effects of this reform program are most evident in the statutes of such cities as Perugia, Bologna, and Ancona. There, the new lay confraternities created by the reforming friars in 1233 were entrusted with the task of ensuring religious conformity and sexual orthodoxy, with specific attention to sodomy.[29] Soon after the founding of the Dominican and Franciscan orders, it had become clear that there were many men and women who, while sympathetic to the goals of the friars, were not prepared to abandon their families and professions to undertake the mendicant life. They preferred to adopt a life of simplicity and to provide political and moral support to the friars' programs while remaining at home and earning their own living. At first, such persons had gathered together in informal fellowship to partake of communion, confess, give alms, and abstain from worldly pleasures. The earliest rule, that of the Order of Penitents (1221), also known as the Franciscan Tertiaries, prohibited members from attending plays, gambling, bearing arms, and swearing; the demands of fasting, abstention, prayer, confession, and communion were considerably greater than those placed on the ordinary Christian. While such sympathetic popes as Gregory IX tried to free these penitents of all civic responsibilities, including military service, the Italian communes were not always willing to comply. Outside Italy, such figures as Louis IX of France and Ferdinand III of Castile joined the order, ensuring strong mendicant influence at court. In Italy, the surviving membership rolls indicate considerable influence among professionals and tradesmen.[30] These were the very same groups who were to take such a leading role in democratizing political life in the Italian communes, reducing the privileges of the aristocracy and enacting restrictive legislation. And it was only natural that the tertiaries themselves should assist in their enforcement; for in the absence of effective police forces, medieval law always placed far greater responsibility on the citizens themselves to bring criminals to book.

Simultaneously, the early thirteenth century in Italy was a period of profound social and political revolution during which the old communal oligarchies were replaced by a new regime of nouveaux riches and artisan guildsmen who destroyed the privileges of the nobility and considerably extended political rights. In such a democratized city as Bologna, center of the leading university specializing in canon and civil law and of the new Dominican order, an alliance of armed middle-class youth, parish associations, and guilds succeeded in imposing its will on the local podestà and installing a new constitution. Instead of the several hundred knights who had formerly controlled the communes, thousands of new men entered public life, excluding only the poor and unemployed, some lesser guildsmen, and feudal nobles. In short, a kind of middle-class revolution was achieved. With greater democratization came greater individual responsibility; the new party was generally anticlerical and antinoble but sympathetic to the reformism of the friars.[31] The statutes of Bologna (1245/67)[32] were introduced in 1265/66 by Loderingo d'Andalo, brother of Diana of Andalo, foundress of the order of Dominican nuns. They were promulgated at the behest of the popular, pro-Guelph (i.e., pro-papal) party. These laws provided that the Società beate Maria was to be vested with full authority to pursue heretics and sodomites and that the various organs of state were to assist them in the task. While these laws date from the 1260s, the statute notes that they were introduced by one brother Jacobinus; he may be either brother Jacobinus de Regio, active at Bologna during the Alleluia of 1233, or Jacobus de Boncambiis, who joined the Dominicans in 1233 (under miraculous circumstances) and later became bishop of Bologna. Evidence that the confraternity's antisodomitical activity predates this code, however, comes from a letter of 1255 addressed by the Dominican minister-general Humbert of Romans to the Bolognese brethren.[33] In it, Humbert notes that the confraternity should not only concern itself with the cult of the Virgin but also heresy and that "evil filth," sodomy. A similar letter, in somewhat abridged form, was addressed to the order at Mantua (1255) and Faenza (1261). While the statutes of these two towns do not specifically refer to the confraternity, presumably it functioned there and in other Italian communes in a manner similar to the group at Bologna. Essentially, the officials of the confraternity were the local agents of the Inquisition. These consisted of two captains from each of the three sectors of society: the people (i.e., shopkeepers, artisans, etc.), the *milites* (or knights of the commune), and the old nobility. The candidates were confirmed by the Dominicans, that is, the Inquisitor and his colleagues. A bull of Pope Innocent IV, *Ad extirpanda* (15 May 1252), had already established a rudimentary organization of laymen to assist in the extirpation of heresy; this body consisted of twelve men, two notaries, two servitors, and two Franciscan or Dominican friars.[34] Those brought before the inquisitorial court by the confraternity, if convicted of heresy, lost their property. The podestà was then instructed to establish procedures for the fulfillment of the ban on heretics. Presumably, the same code applied to sodomites and similar moral offenders. The Perugian (1342)[35] law code is particularly important, for this commune was the breeding ground of several lay confraternities, including the Flagellant movement. Its Society of the Virgin was founded as early as 1233 by Peter Martyr and was presumably early entrusted with the pursuit of sexual offenders and heretics. The law code provided that forty men were to be chosen, eight from each of the five quarters of the city, to investigate and denounce sodomites.

In the other communes, while the role of the confraternities as an instrument of repression is not explicitly mentioned, they probably played a role similar to that of the groups at Perugia or Bologna. Most of the statutes are in fact rather terse, merely providing the death penalty by burning for sodomites.[36] Often included was the provision that the family of the accused must withdraw from the place of execution (*antequam familia recedat de loco supplicii*) and that the accused's goods were to be confiscated.[37] In most instances, the podestà, and occasionally the captain of the people, was especially entrusted with the job of pursuing such offenders as parricides, heretics, incendiaries, rebels, adulterers, or poisoners. At Ascoli Piceno,[38] those who denounced heretics or sodomites received a bounty. Penalties were likewise provided for those who harbored sodomites: at Pisa a fine of 100 lire was exacted; at Bologna, whoever dwelt in a building where sodomy was practiced might be burned along with the house.[39]

The specific impact of religion on secular legislation dealing with moral offenders is apparent from the numerous references in secular law codes to the Church Fathers, Scripture, the *Decretum* of Gratian, and papal decretals. In most instances, this entailed a brief reference to the precedent of Sodom and Gomorrah as an example of God's wrath against sodomites.[40] Just as they were punished by a conflagration, it was alleged, so modern-day sodomites must suffer burning. In other instances, the legislation is described as a confirmation of "apostolic" (i.e., papal) decrees on the matter.[41] The Perugian legislation of 1342, on the other hand, contains rather extended references to Augustine, canon law, and papal decrees.[42]

Of all the Italian codes, the fullest clauses dealing with sodomy came from Florence, Perugia, and Siena. As Robert Davidsohn notes, the prevalence of pederasty at Florence led the Germans to dub pederasts "Florenzer" and their act "florenzen."[43] In 1305, the preacher Frà Giordano described the city as a veritable Sodom in which fathers encouraged their sons to vice for profit. The fifteenth-century chronicler Matteo Griffoni claimed that the destruction of one third of Florence by floods in 1333 was attributed by contemporaries to the sodomy practiced by its inhabitants. The 1325 statutes of the Florentine podestà provided a series of penalties that depended on the age of the offender and the frequency of the offense. Pederasty was punished by castration.[44] A boy under fourteen who voluntarily submitted to the act was beaten, driven through the city naked, or fined 50 lire; if he were between fourteen and eighteen, he paid a fine of 100 lire. A woman who permitted herself to be sodomized was punished as the underage boy. Such an act perpetrated by a panderer, his associate, or a perennial criminal resulted in a 500 lire fine; if the sum were not paid, his hand was cut off; if he had no hand, then his foot. A father who persuaded his son to commit such an act was punished in the same way.

The dwelling, field, or other building in which the act was committed (with the owner's consent) was destroyed or laid waste. Any man found in suspicious circumstances with a boy to whom he was not related was presumed guilty and dealt with in accordance with the law. Particularly severe punishment was exacted of "rogues," "imposters," and foreign criminals, of which Florence was notoriously full. Anyone convicted under this legislation was to be beaten and bruised by the populace with its bare hands and then led to the city prison; later the guilty party was burned at the stake. Two witnesses were sufficient for conviction, and the severest torture might be employed to elicit a confession. At Forlì, in contrast, only one witness was necessary in cases of sodomy, incendiarism, lese majesty, counterfeiting, or other public crimes, and extraordinary torture might be inflicted.[45]

The podestà, captains of the people, and other officials were given complete license to investigate, torture, and punish in any way they saw fit and to ban all suspects from the city. Accusations and denunciations were conducted in secret, and anyone might bring such an accusation. A penalty of 10 lire was further imposed for songs about sodomy or similar acts. None of these penalties could be mitigated or increased. Later, under Savonarola's regime in the 1490s, a new law against the "unmentionable vice" was passed, providing exposure on the wall of the Bargello for the first offense, fastening to a pillar for the second offense, and burning for the third.[46] The 1342 Perugian legislation had provided a fine of 200 lire for a first offense, 500 lire for a second, and burning for a third.

The two redactions of the Sienese code of 1262/70 differ somewhat in their treatment of sodomy.[47] The 1262 version lists sodomy under the penalties applied to heretics and "patarenes." Such an offender who did not confess within eight days following conviction by a bishop or chapter was permanently expelled from the jurisdiction of Siena, his goods were confiscated, half given to the poor and one half retained by the commune. Immediately after being accused, the suspect was expected to pay two lire deniers and he was suspended from office until his guilt or innocence could be established. On the first Sabbath of each month, heretics, patarenes, and sodomites were to be expelled from the city; and all those who aided or abetted such offenders were required to pay 100 lire deniers to the *militia*. Moreover, traitors and sodomites were prohibited from testifying in any court case. The 1309/10 redaction of the law merely prescribed a penalty for sodomy of 300 lire for a first offense by a sodomite or procurer; if this were not paid within a month, the criminal was suspended by his virile member in the Campo del Mercato.

While repressive, even barbaric, legislation against sexual offenders had everywhere become the norm, it is difficult to judge the degree of compliance, except in instances where charges of sexual immorality were linked with political nonconformity. One of the few known cases of an actual burning for sodomy comes from Ghent, perhaps the most radical commune of northern Europe. On 28 September 1292, a local villager named John, a maker of knives by trade, was sentenced to death by the local judge-administrators, the *scabini* of Ghent, for an act against nature ("detested by God") with a certain man. He was forthwith burned near the pillory of St. Peter of Ghent. This kind of extreme enforcement of morals legislation, apparently more characteristic of "popular" regimes, also extended to other offenses; the same document reports the banishment of a woman and the burning of her home to the ground for the sin of adultery.[48]

The persistence of antihomosexual feeling and the continuing impact of religious ideology on secular legislation is evident in the report of the Sienese city council discussions held on 13 September 1324. The council of nine provided for the appointment of men to pursue sodomites "in order to honor the Lord, ensure true peace, maintain the good morals and praiseworthy life of the people of Siena." Quoting Ephesians 5:6, the councillors voiced the fear that those whose crime was repellent to both God and the Devil and abhorrent to all peoples, unless prosecuted, would bring down the Lord's ire on the city. They hoped that Jesus and the Virgin Mary, the commune's special protectress, would remove the evil and that tranquillity and peace would be restored. The council voted 203 to 22 in favor of considering the measure and the proposal passed by a vote of 219 to 7.[49]

Despite their verbal identification with the laboring classes, the *fratres minores* and the Dominicans who initiated the repressive legislation of the thirteenth century were largely the sons of the merchant oligarchy that had dominated communal political life in the late twelfth and early thirteenth century. There is evidence, however, that as a result of the first industrial revolution and the admission of the rural nobility to the towns, the power of this class was under increasing attack. Furthermore, while the Peace of Constance (1183) had supposedly freed the cities of many of their feudal obligations to the Empire, beginning in the 1220s the emperor Frederick II had initiated a powerful coalition aimed at returning the independent city-states of Italy to imperial dependency. Frederick's Ghibelline supporters were drawn principally from the dispossessed lower middle class guildsmen and old feudal nobility, who formed a tacit alliance to destroy the merchant oligarchy and the alliance with Rome. How did the sons of the threatened merchant class react? Like many groups in a similar position. They attempted a return to older, more restrictive social values and they led a campaign of persecution against those elements perceived as destructive to the established social order. This phenomenon of reaction by an insecure middle class unable to handle the rapidly changing social reality and the imminent threat to its economic security has been observed elsewhere: more recently among the middle-class supporters of Nazism, the minions of the Silent Majority, and the Poujadist farmers of France. Likewise, in the thirteenth century, the conflict of classes, expressed in religious ideology, often resulted in sharp contrasts of sexual life-style: bishops like Henry of Basel (1215–1238), who sired twenty illegitimate children, and pious monks like Pope Celestine, who became frantic about one nocturnal emission, represent two such polar opposites.[50] The elements of this middle-class movement contain peculiar characteristics of both social reform and social reaction. Their program was highlighted by legislation against heretics, usurers, abortionists, pimps, prostitutes, sodomites, and conspicuous consumers.

By the middle of the thirteenth century, the instruments of sexual repression had clearly been established throughout much of Italy and northern Europe. The Inquisition and the lay confraternities associated with the mendicant orders became a means of persecuting not only heretics but also sodomites and other nonconformists. This development, in fact, particularly in Italy, paralleled a sharp movement toward political democratization whereby the old oligarchy was reduced and the social morality of the small bourgeoisie was written into law. In the popular mind sodomy became associated with the nobility and the clergy, and in northern Europe with Italian usurers and bankers. The antiaristocratic and antinoble bias of the lower middle class, in addition to limiting class privileges, resulted in organized attempts to impose a more rigid Christian morality as a means of purging the state of aristocratic influence. This repressive legislation, directed against gamblers, usurers, conspicuous consumers, prostitutes, adulterers, and sodomites among others, naturally took its justification from the prevailing Christian ideology that was characterized by a strong rejection of the pleasures of the flesh.

It had taken several hundred years for the theological views of the Gregorian reformers to achieve full realization in the secular law. The imposition of a specifically Christian sexual morality that saw in homosexual acts the greatest blasphemy against the natural order parallels the church's expansion of organizational and spiritual control over a sometimes recalcitrant, or even heretical, population. While the law itself was rigid, enforcement was not always effective and, like the prescriptions of penance, was intended more as a deterrent than as an effective tool of punishment.

The reintroduction of Roman law had slowly succeeded in creating a uniform system of criminal precedent throughout much of

Europe as well as reviving the harsh penalties against sex offenders that had been enacted by the Christian emperors. Particularly in the thirteenth century, a systematic uniformity began to enter European law, with little statutory difference in the treatment of sodomy in France or Italy. This change corresponded with political centralization, the reduction of local tradition, and the creation of a truly international culture under the leadership of the papacy, the mendicant orders, and the new universities. The new clerical elite, with some lay elements, moved freely between episcopal and secular chanceries, royal and papal diplomatic service, universities and monasteries. Thus, while many philosophers like Albertus Magnus or Alexander of Hales in their commentaries on Peter Lombard's *Sentences* might treat sodomy as a form of lust, their approaches differ little. Likewise, the jurists who comment on Roman antisodomy legislation, like Azo, Bartolus, or Accursius, generally cite the same sources or recommend the same punishment. And the numerous penitential manuals, from Alan of Lille to Raymund of Penyaforte or John of Freiburg, based as they are on the same authorities, differ more in nuance than substance.

The literary evidence further suggests that whatever may have occurred in the seclusion of an isolated field at nightfall or beneath the blankets of an army camp, homosexuality was regarded primarily as a vice of the church and the nobility. The growth of cities created a new locus, for the narrow streets and porticos and the transient population and crowded quarters offered more opportunity for anonymous or illicit sex than had existed previously; as a result, the image of the city as a center of sin and decay began to appear. Nevertheless, the reputation of the clergy and the old nobility for sexual nonconformity remained alive. In the late twelfth century, a movement to reduce clerical privilege and diminish the role of the old aristocracy gathered force. This anticlericalism expressed itself in the rise of antisacerdotal heretical sects, increasing attempts to tax the clergy and subject it to civil law, and an attack on papal authority. A parallel antiaristocratic reaction was to result in a veritable social revolution in the more economically advanced areas of Europe. The old landed aristocracy was expelled from the towns, its privileges reduced, and its place taken by a new aristocracy of wealth. In urban centers in northern Italy, the Rhine valley, Flanders, and northern France, by the early thirteenth century a new oligarchy of bankers, merchants, and manufacturers had succeeded in deposing the old ruling class and freeing itself from the commercial and legal impediments of feudalism. By mid-century, an even more radical alliance of small tradesmen, disaffected aristocrats, and mendicant reformers attempted to further transform the commune by extending the franchise and democratizing economic life. A secondary product of this attack on the clergy and nobility was a moral rigidity that persecuted all manner of social and sexual deviants, including gamblers, bigamists, adulterers, usurers, prostitutes, heretics, and sodomites. The laity thus undertook to continue the program outlined by the Gregorian reformers. Still, examples of persecution of homosexuals are rare, and the system of indulgences, remission, and penance offered the confessor an opportunity to temper the draconian punishment laid down by the law.

# Appendix

## The Trial of Arnold of Verniolle for Heresy and Sodomy

THE AREA OF southern France at the foot of the Pyrenées, largely contained within the county of Toulouse, had long been distinguished as the leading center of heresy in Europe, despite the bloody suppression of Catharism in the early thirteenth century and the establishment of the papal Inquisition.[1] In the mid-thirteenth century, however, under the rule of Louix IX of France, the old Cathar nobility received amnesty, regained much of its wealth, and took part in the later eastern Crusades. The area nonetheless continued to be politically fragmented into small but prosperous principalities like Foix, Urgel, Comminges, Béarn, and Couseran whose princes still often sheltered heretics. Despite the efforts of the pro-French bishop Bernard Saisset of Pamiers (1295–1312) to bring the area under tighter French control, a strong pro-Aragonese feeling remained; many a heretic found refuge in northern Spain, where the Inquisition did not operate. Although the center of Catharism had shifted to northern Italy, the late thirteenth century witnessed a revival of heresy during the reigns of Count Roger-Bernard of Foix and his daughter Marguerite of Béarn. As a result, an army of suppliants, notaries, judges, witnesses, and consultants entered the area to assist the inquisitors in their duties. In 1308/1309, as a result of the activities of the inquisitor Geoffrey d'Ablis in the Ariège region, both Sabartès and Montaillou, among other villages, experienced a wave of imprisonments, burnings, confiscations, and emigration. Under Bishop Jacques Fournier, a special prison, the Allemans, was built to house those accused before the Inquisition. While the chief victims of this revived antiheretical crusade were Albigensians and Waldensians who had escaped previous detection, a significant number of other criminals now peopled the Inquisition's prisons: judaizers, bigamists, sodomites, adulterers, lepers, and a host of others. The confessions extracted from these inmates were often elicited through the application of torture, in accordance with bulls issued by Innocent IV (1252), Alexander IV (1259), and Clement IV (1265). The techniques included the threat of death, the administration of a harsh imprisonment, and a visit by two friends of the suspect to convince him of the need to confess.[2]

One of the most active participants in this campaign against heresy was Bishop Jacques Fournier of Pamiers (1317–1326). Fournier had formerly served as a Cistercian at Boulbonne and as abbot of Frontfroide in the diocese of Narbonne. After completing his term at Pamiers, he was elevated to the see of Mirepoix (1326–1327) and then served as cardinal-bishop of St. Priscian until his election as Pope Benedict XII (1334–1342) to succeed John XXII. As bishop of Pamiers, under orders from Pope John, Fournier carried on a series of trials that provide one of the fullest records of mores and belief in the early fourteenth century. A host of defendants filed through his episcopal chambers—judaizers, Waldensians, Cathars, adulterers, sodomites, and others accused of lesser offenses. In many cases, Fournier demonstrated a remarkable concern for proper procedure and fairness, demanding corroboration by a number of witnesses before judgment. His inquisitorial register, which survives in 325 folio pages (*Vat. Lat.* 4030) written in four identifiable hands, may be supplemented by the nearly contemporary *Practica inquisitionis* by Bernard Gui, a manual of procedure for fellow inquisitors, and the unpublished register of the Carcassonne inquisitor Geoffrey d'Ablis.[3]

Among the defendants who appeared before the bishop was Arnold the Catalan of Verniolle, accused of acts of sodomy and heresy, the latter for illicitly hearing confessions. His trial began 9 June 1323 with testimony by Jean Ferrié (or Ferrier) of Bouriège. On June 13 and June 23, testimony was presented by Guillaume Roux (or Ros) of Ribouisse, aged 16, Guillaume Bernard of Gaudiès, aged 15, and Guillaume Boyer (or Bonier) of Plavilla, aged 18. On June 21, the court heard from Guillaume Pech (or Pecs) of Ribouisse, aged 19.[4] All of these witnesses were students at Pamiers.[5] On July 2, the Carmelite Peter Recort, Arnold's cellmate, who on 17 January 1329 was to be degraded and sentenced to life imprisonment at the Carmelite monastery of Toulouse, testified concerning his conversations with Arnold in the episcopal prison at Pamiers. On 23 and 28 June 1323 and on 1 August 1324, the defendant himself appeared and corroborated most of the previous testimony. Between 9 and 11 August 1324, Bishop Jacques Fournier of Pamiers, along with the chief inquisitor of Carcassonne, the Dominican Jean du Prat, held consultations with between twenty-seven and thirty-nine councillors in the episcopal palace of Pamiers concerning the fate of Arnold and the other prisoners held by the Inquisition. These judges included officials of the Inquisition, local canons, monks, friars, and *jurisperiti,* that is, lawyers and judges. In Arnold's case, Hugues de Brolio, a sacristan of Pamiers, Jacques de Glato, judge, and the Cistercians of Bonifont, Ademar de Montepasato and Raymond de Ferrariis, were added. They decided unanimously that Arnold should be bound in iron chains for life and fed a diet of bread and water without any possibility of amnesty. One of the Carmelites and all four of the Franciscans present, however, suggested that because he came of good family Arnold's punishment should be somewhat mitigated.[6] All of the others disagreed and sentenced him to degradation and life imprisonment. On 12 August 1324, the first half of the sentence was carried out, and Arnold, often described as a Franciscan apostate,[7] was deprived of all clerical privileges.



While many of those tried by Fournier were accused of moral crimes, it is clear that the inquisitor was more concerned with the defendants' supposed theological (i.e., heretical) transgressions than with their private behavior. No one was haled before the court for purely aberrant sexual behavior; in all cases, some religious unorthodoxy was sought. We have seen that by the fourteenth century the state, particularly in France, had begun to replace the church as the chief persecutor of such offenders of public morality as adulterers and sodomites. Clearly, private indiscretion was of far less interest to the church than heresy, which was often allied with political unorthodoxy. Although merely a subdeacon, Arnold had posed as a priest. The subdiaconate had undergone considerable change since its inception in the primitive church. It was only at the First Lateran Council (1123) that it had been recognized as a clerical order, obliged to practice "punctuality, vigilance, sobriety, and chastity." From the twelfth century onward, marriage of subdeacons was prohibited and chastity was to be observed on pain of the charge of sacrilege. While subdeacons were permitted to assist at the mass, Arnold had allegedly gone so far as to celebrate mass, hear confessions, and grant absolution, which were in themselves actionable offenses.[8] Furthermore, Arnold's commission of acts of sodomy was allegedly based on certain philosophical assumptions regarded as heretical. He believed that rape, the deflowering of a virgin, adultery, and incest were graver sins than sodomy and simple fornication, which were equal. This contradicted the accepted gradation of sins of lust enunciated in canon law. Arnold also argued that ejaculation of semen is demanded by nature and, even if the result of homosexual acts, a man is made healthier thereby.

The facts of Arnold's life and his homoerotic inclinations as elicited in sworn testimony before the inquisitors corroborate the sharp divergence between theory and practice characteristic of the Middle Ages. According to his own testimony, Arnold's first homosexual experience occurred in early adolescence before he had reached puberty when, crowded into one bed with his fellow students in grammar school, one of his comrades initiated him into the pleasures of the flesh. This confirms the fears voiced by monastic educators who, as we have seen, provided an elaborate set of rules in order to frustrate adolescent experimentation. Thereafter, despite his clerical status, Arnold had apparently indulged in sex with both men and women. In 1320, however, during the persecution carried out by Philip V against the lepers of France, he had suffered some sort of skin disorder soon after having sex with a prostitute. Lest he be associated with the hated lepers, Arnold decided to turn exclusively to boys for sex. Interestingly, while the prohibition on homosexuality had not impressed him, the theological identification of leprosy with sexual indulgence had. Thereafter, despite a few episodes of minor resistance, Arnold seemed to experience little difficulty in convincing a large number of local youths to frolic with him and satisfy his stated need for sexual gratification at least once every two weeks. These youths, despite their clerical background, were equally willing to express their sexual urges freely and a veritable lavender underground arose in the small village of Montaillou.

# AGAINST ARNOLD OF VERNIOLLE, SON OF WILLIAM OF VERNIOLLE OF THE LE MERCADAL PARISH OF PAMIERS, CONCERNING THE CRIME OF HERESY AND SODOMY

On the ninth day of June 1323, Jean Ferrié, son of Raymund Ferrié of Bouriège in the diocese of Alet, a student of liberal arts at Pamiers, came to our reverend father in Christ, Jacques, by the grace of God bishop of Pamiers, to reveal the following facts concerning the crime of heresy, recorded in his presence in the portico of the episcopal see of Pamiers. He swore on the Gospels to speak the whole truth and nothing but the truth concerning the crime of heresy, about himself and about all persons living and dead. After he took the oath, he spoke, confessed, and testified as follows:

He said that when he, in that same year during Holy Week, on a day in March, as he recalls, went to the Dominican monastery in Pamiers in order to confess to friar Bernard Scandala, he encountered Arnold of Verniolle of the Le Mercadal parish of Pamiers on the street near the convent. Arnold told him to accompany him, to bring a book to the market of Pamiers, and he would free him from his task.

He replied that he had to go to the Dominican house to confess his sins. Nevertheless, he went with Arnold, but he did not bring a book along. Along the way Arnold asked if he wanted to confess, and the speaker said he had already confessed to a certain Dominican, and wanted to confess only to him, because he had heard that one should confess all one's sins to only one priest and that if the penitent remembered something afterward, he should confess to the same priest.

Arnold said that it was just as valid to confess to him as to anyone else, "because I will as truly be your confessor as the other one was, because it is just as valid to confess to one man as to another."

When they approached the church of Le Mercadal, the speaker suggested they go in, and there Arnold could hear his confession. Arnold replied that he would not hear his confession in that church because if he entered many people would come to him to confess and he would have to linger there a long time. He would therefore hear Jean's confession in his own home, because it is just as pleasing to God as in a church.

The two of them then went to a house located near the church of Le Mercadal, sat down together at a table in the hall, and Arnold heard his confession. Among other things he confessed that he had once sworn falsely on the Gospels, and certain other mortal sins. Afterward Arnold absolved him and enjoined him to say, on bent and naked knees from then until the feast of All Saints, *Miserere mei Deus* once, *Paternoster* seven times, *Ave Maria* seven times, and *Laudatum*. He made the sign of the cross on the ground, kissed him, and said "In rememorationem. . . ."

After confession, the speaker asked Arnold to give him proof to show the parish priest that he had already confessed. Arnold replied that he would not give him such proof because it was enough for him to say that he had confessed to a chaplain and a Dominican. The speaker asked Arnold what his name was so that if he should remember any sin he could come back to confess to him. Arnold replied that his name was Arnold of Catalonia.

Afterward, the speaker confirmed that this same Arnold was named Arnold of Verniolle and that he was not a priest, because he had asked many people; and later, at Le Pomarol, Arnold told him that twelve students had already come to him to lighten their penance.

Asked if he had confessed anything else to Arnold, he replied that he had not. Asked if he knew or had heard that anyone else had confessed to Arnold, he replied that he had heard in school that some had confessed to Arnold, but he did not recall any of their names.

Arnold told him he had celebrated mass at the Dominican convent in Toulouse assisted by a certain student who at the time tutored Baudouin of Pamiers' sons.

He said nothing else pertinent. Asked if he had testified as a result of hatred, love, fear, instruction, or subornation by others, he replied in the negative, and that he had spoken only the truth.

He gave the aforesaid testimony in the presence of the lord bishop, on the year, date, and place noted above, in the presence of friars Galhard of Pomiès and Arnold of Le-Carla-le-Comte, Dominicans of Pamiers; brother Bernard de Taix, a Cistercian of Fontfroide; and of Master Jean Strabaud of Sautel, notary of the city and bishop of Pamiers, especially involved in cases before the Inquisition who, at the bishop's order, received the previous confession and deposition, on whose account, I, Jean Jabaud, clerk, faithfully transcribed and corrected the aforesaid from the original.

λ

On 13 June 1323, Guillaume Roux, son of Pierre Roux of Ribouisse in the diocese of Mirepoix, a student in the liberal arts at Pamiers, slightly over sixteen years of age, summoned by the reverend father in Christ Jacques, bishop of Pamiers by the grace of God . . . testified as follows:

He said that in that year, around the first day of Lent, on a Sunday between noon and three P.M. on a day and time not otherwise recalled, when the speaker was in the convent church of the Augustinians at Pamiers, he met Arnold of Verniolle who took him out of the church into the garden. Arnold told him that if he wanted to stay with a certain canon of St. Saturnin of Toulouse who had forty books and was prior of Lavelanet and [if he] would assist the canon by carrying his books to school, Arnold could secure the position for him and the canon would provide his needs, food, and clothing.

The speaker replied that he would willingly stay with the canon if he could study with him; the two of them then went to the Augustinian sacristy. Arnold made Guillaume swear on a missal that he would reveal to no one the canon's secrets and manner of living. Arnold then said that the canon frequently got drunk and in his drunkenness customarily assaulted others. If the speaker should see the canon drunk, it was advisable to put him to bed. He said the canon wanted women very much and usually either the speaker or any other servant who stayed with the canon would have to bring him women. If he wanted to stay, Guillaume should not reveal his knowledge of this to the canon.

The speaker promised Arnold to do this since Arnold told him it could be accomplished easily. He even told him that during the winter Guillaume would have to sleep in bed with the canon and that he ought to do whatever the canon wanted done; in the summer at midday, he is likely to rub the speaker's feet; but Arnold said he should tell no one about this.

When Guillaume said that it was sinful to bring such women to the canon, Arnold told him that it was not such a grave sin and that he would introduce him to some friars who would absolve him of any sin and impose a light penance.If he did the canon's bidding, he would make money and could give charity [as penance] from the canon's goods.

Arnold then suggested that Guillaume come to his house where he would show him books and he could stay. The two then went to Arnold's house and entered an upper room. When they were alone, Arnold showed him a book, saying it contained decretals, and after reading a bit told the speaker, "See what these decretals say here!" When the speaker said that he didn't understand the words of the decretals, Arnold told him in the vernacular [Provençal] that it was written that if a man plays with another, and because of the warmth of their bodies semen flows, it is not as grave a sin as if a man carnally knows a woman; because, so he said, nature demands this and a man is made healthier as a result. And, so he said, he himself could not stay with either a man or a woman, without semen flowing out.

When Guillaume said he didn't believe that it was a lesser sin to so behave with a man than to know a woman carnally, Arnold told him that it is a lesser sin and that the decretals said so. Arnold then threw the speaker down on the ground, placed his hands on his back, and lay on Guillaume. He then removed the speaker's clothes and told him to spread his thighs or some evil would befall him. The speaker then spread his thighs, and Arnold got completely undressed, embraced the naked youth, kissed him, placed his penis between Guillaume's buttocks, and, moving himself as with a woman, his semen flowed between the speaker's legs. When this was accomplished, Arnold told Guillaume to do likewise to him and that he could not leave the room until he had done so. Guillaume then likewise let his semen flow out between Arnold's buttocks, and Arnold then made a similar movement.

When this was over, Arnold said that they must mutually swear never to do this again, either with each other or with anyone else. They then swore on the Gospels.

When Guillaume said that he had committed a grave sin and heresy, Arnold said he would bring him to a Franciscan who would absolve him of this sin and impose a light penance. Arnold also gave him a book containing parchment folios which he kept in his home. Arnold said that if he wanted to stay in his home until the feast of the Nativity of John the Baptist and on some night play around with him, he would pay him. The speaker said he wouldn't do this and left Arnold's house while Arnold remained.

Afterward Arnold frequently met him in town, and when he encountered him he called Guillaume a heretic. Nevertheless, he did not bring him to that Franciscan to hear his confession concerning said sin, although Guillaume frequently asked him to do so.

Finally, about eight days later, Guillaume was with Arnold's illegitimate son in the furrier Tignol's workshop in the Villeneuve quarter of Pamiers. Arnold, who was also there, told the speaker to accompany him to a parcel of land which he owned in Le Pomarol where, so he said, there were some men. The speaker consented to join him and the two of them went to the field, but there was no one there. When they arrived, Arnold told him to undress and nap a bit because it was getting warm, and they could then carry on as they had done earlier in Arnold's house.

The speaker at first refused and fled; but Arnold pursued him and threw one of Guillaume's textbooks at him three times; as a result, its binding broke. Arnold then unsheathed a knife, pursued and assaulted him and brought him back to the field; with one hand he twisted the speaker's arm and in the other he held the unsheathed knife.

He then threw Guillaume on the ground and coiled his arms around his chest. He tried to lift him up and carry him to the spot where they had been, but when he couldn't, grabbing and pulling his hair, he dragged him there. While they were still dressed, Arnold threw him on the ground, and in the manner described earlier, thrust his penis between the speaker's thighs and, embracing and kissing him, released his semen. Both before and after perpetrating this sin, Arnold told him that this sin was less sinful than to know a woman carnally; and because Guillaume refused to commit this act with Arnold because of the oath he had sworn, and from which no one could absolve him, Arnold said he would absolve him. After it was over, Guillaume took his robe and left while Arnold remained in the field.

About eight days later, they met near the Carmelite house in Pamiers and Arnold asked Guillaume to join him to visit his son's fiancee and to give her a ring; after many stops, they came to Arnold's house and went to the aforementioned room. Arnold then closed the door and swore on the decretals and on his holy tonsure that they would not leave the room until they had again done what they had done before. Guillaume wanted to leave, but when he stepped on the doormat Arnold pulled it toward him and the speaker fell down. Arnold held his shinbone, dragged him to the bed, put him on it, and sodomized him in the manner noted above. When the deed was done, the speaker left the room and went away. Arnold also told him twice that if he wanted to carnally know his maidservant he would make sure he could have her.

Asked if Arnold had told him to confess to him and that he could as easily be absolved by him as by anyone else, he replied that he had not. But now Guillaume very much regretted what he had done, and he had never believed that it was less sinful to commit sodomy than to know a woman carnally. He offered to undergo the complete penance that the lord bishop wanted to impose upon him for the aforementioned acts. He said that he had heard in school, although he didn't remember by whom or about whom it was said, that some of the students had confessed to Arnold.

After perpetrating the last act, he told Arnold that the lord bishop would find out about it. Arnold responded by lifting something from the ground and saying that this object was as little value to him as if this deed would become known to the bishop [i.e., he didn't care]. He said nothing else pertinent.

Asked if he had testified as a result of hate, love, fear, instruction, or subornation, he said no, but that he had spoken the truth.

He further remembered that in addition to the instances already noted, in the same house, room, and bed, Arnold had twice committed sodomy with him; that on other days and times, at Arnold's instigation, in the same way Arnold committed sodomy with him and vice versa. He said he never did so with anyone else nor did anyone else solicit him to commit said crime. He added that Arnold promised to lend him his books and give him a knife if he would consent to commit this crime.

Arnold suggested to him that he could carnally know Jacoba, the
98 wife of Raymund Faur of the Loumet quarter of Pamiers, in whose house he dwelt and whose son he tutored. And although Arnold suggested that he have either Jacoba or her daughter, Bosaurs, the speaker himself never solicited either one.

On another occasion, in the portico connecting the dormitory and latrines of the Franciscan convent of Pamiers, to which he had come to confess about his aforementioned sins, Arnold solicited him to commit sodomy, telling him that he would introduce him to a friar of the same house who would lighten his penance and would absolve him of the oath they had sworn about not committing that crime. Arnold said that if they committed this act then Arnold would bring him the means of loosening his penance. Because Guillaume refused, Arnold would not introduce him to that friar. Asked if through hatred, etc. . . . as above, he said no.

λ

A year later, on 23 June [1324], Guillaume Roux again reported and came back to the lord bishop and in a court set up in his presence swore on the Gospels to tell the whole truth and nothing but the truth concerning himself and Arnold of Verniolle about the crimes of heresy and sodomy; after taking this oath, he said, confessed, and testified the following:

That same year, around the Feast of the Ascension on a rainy day between noon and three P.M., and on another day and time which he didn't recollect, when the speaker was at the school situated near the Carmelite house in Pamiers, Arnold of Verniolle came to him. He said that if Guillaume would come along with him, he would give him a writing tablet. The two of them came to a house situated near the home of the Minorissi family of Pamiers, although he didn't know whose house it was. In a box Arnold found four small tablets that he wanted to give to Guillaume and that Guillaume wanted to take, saying that they weren't particularly valuable. Next, Arnold shut the door, and on the ground floor room in which a bed was situated, Arnold lay down with his clothes on and asked Guillaume to lie down beside him. He did so and, in the manner described in the previous confession, Arnold committed sodomy on the speaker as they lay side by side. Arnold then told Guillaume to do the same to him, which he did. When that was done, they separated and Guillaume returned to school.

In Arnold's house, Arnold told him that he had committed the crime with only one other man. Asked if Arnold had admitted to having committed sodomy with a local squire or with someone else, Guillaume replied that he did not remember him saying so. He said that he had never committed this crime with anyone else nor had anyone ever solicited him to do it.

He said that Arnold told him that it was the right of priests to impose satisfaction on penitents after absolution because, if they wanted to, they could either bind or loose. But they imposed penitence or satisfaction so that men would be overcome by fear of penance, lest they readily return to their sins.

Arnold was especially friendly with Jean Scaunier, the tailor, who was living with the tailor de Calson in rue Romengos. He said nothing more of pertinence.

Asked if because of love, etc. . . . he said no.

Guillaume Roux made the preceding deposition and confessed in the presence of the lord bishop of Pamiers, on the year, date, and place cited above, in the presence of friars Galhard of Pomiès, Arnold of Le-Carla-le-Comte, Dominicans of Pamiers; Bernard de Taix, Cistercian monk of Fontfroide; and Master Jean Strabaud, curé of Sautel in the diocese of Pamiers, notary to the city and bishop of Pamiers, and especially in business of the Inquisition of depraved heresy, who at the order of the bishop received the preceding confession and deposition; which I, Jean Jabaud, clerk, faithfully transcribed and corrected from the original.

λ

On 13 June 1323, Guillaume Bernard, son of Jean Jeu of Gaudiès in the diocese of Mirepoix, student of the liberal arts at Pamiers, aged about fifteen and a half, was summoned by the reverend father in Christ lord Jacques, by the grace of God bishop of Pamiers, to testify about all crimes of which Arnold of Verniolle, clerk of Le Mercadal in Pamiers, stood accused, in the presence of the lord bishop, in the portico of the episcopal see of Pamiers. He swore on the Gospels to speak the whole truth and nothing but the truth about the crimes of heresy and sodomy denounced against Arnold, about himself and all others living and dead, and especially against Arnold, who had been detained under suspicion of such crimes; after taking this oath, he said, confessed, and made the following deposition:

In that same year, around the Feast of All Saints just past, one Sunday when Guillaume was at the Augustinian house of Pamiers, during mass after the elevation of the host Arnold met him and inquired where he had come from. Guillaume replied that he was from Gaudiès. Arnold said that he was acquainted with some people from Gaudiès who were staying in Toulouse, and among them was Bernard Faur, a student at Toulouse. The speaker said that this same Bernard was his second cousin. No other words were exchanged between them.

After lunch, Guillaume returned to the Augustinian convent to hear the sermon; when Arnold saw him in the church, he led him to the friars' refectory. There, he told Guillaume that if he wanted to lodge with a certain canon in Toulouse and bring his books back and forth from school for him, the canon would give him food and clothing; also, by staying with him, he could study with him. Guillaume replied that he would be willing to stay with the canon.

Arnold told him to swear never to reveal the canon's manner of living to anyone. He said he would willingly so swear, and he made this oath on a Bible in the refectory in which the friars gather to eat. After this oath, Arnold invited him to his home. There, in the south portico, Arnold asked if he would like to hear about the canon's mores and manner of living, and he said that he would. Arnold then took him to an upper chamber, and in the hall he saw Arnold's mother and nurse, although he did not know their names. When they were alone, Arnold closed the door and again asked if he wanted to hear about the canon. When he again replied yes, Arnold asked him to remove his overcoat and lie down on the bed, which he did. Arnold then lay down beside him, undressed both himself and Guillaume and spread his thighs; and the speaker did likewise at Arnold's order. Arnold then placed his penis between Guillaume's legs, embracing and kissing him, lying on his side, as his semen flowed between Guillaume's legs. Arnold afterward asked the speaker to do likewise to him, but Guillaume didn't want to. After the sin was perpetrated, Arnold said that the canon would carry on in the same way and that if Guillaume wanted to lodge with him he would have to do likewise, and that the canon would thus misuse him. When this was over, Guillaume left Arnold's house.

After Christmas, Bernard returned from Gaudiès and, on the feast of the Circumcision, he tarried in the sacristy of the Augustinian house, where Arnold met him and asked if he had spoken to his father about staying with the canon, and he said that he had.

One Sunday two weeks later, in the Augustinian church, Guillaume met Arnold, who asked him to come along with him. Arnold took him to the same house and same room, shut the door, embraced and kissed him. Despite Guillaume's reluctance, Arnold made him remove his overcoat, lie down on the bed, and committed the aforementioned crime on him again. Again, Arnold asked him to do likewise, but he said he didn't want to and left the house.

After Easter the speaker again returned from Gaudiès to Pamiers; when they met, Arnold asked why he hadn't come to his home. He then visited Arnold's house himself and they went to the same room. Arnold then closed the door and told Guillaume to undress completely, which he refused to do. Arnold told him to do it or some misfortune would befall him. The two of them undressed, lay down naked on the bed, and covered themselves with a blanket. Arnold lay on top of Guillaume and, placing his penis between his thighs and behaving as he would with a woman, performed sodomy on Guillaume. After this was over, Guillaume wanted to get out of bed, but at Arnold's instigation he likewise sodomized Arnold. When they had finished and had dressed, Arnold told the speaker that they should swear never to do this with anyone else. But when the speaker wanted to swear, Arnold told him not to swear, because afterward he couldn't commit sodomy with anyone else. Arnold then swore on his martyrology [*kalendarium*] not to commit sodomy with anyone else; when this was done, Guillaume left the room, and afterward they did not repeat these acts.



Asked if Arnold had told him that this sin was not as grave as carnal knowledge of women, he said no. Asked if Arnold asked him to confess to him, he said no. Asked if up to now he had confessed about this sin, or if Arnold had told him to confess to anyone about it, he said that he had not confessed, fearing that he would commit perjury during his confession, for Arnold had made him swear never to tell anyone about it. Arnold had not told him not to confess this sin to any priest. Asked if he had heard that Arnold committed the same sins with another man, or that he himself had done so, he said no. Asked if he knew anyone, or any youths, with whom Arnold was friendly, he said that Arnold was friendly with Guillaume Roux of Ribouisse; Guillaume Boyer, son of Bernard of Plavilla; and Guillaume Pech of Ribouisse. Asked if he had heard or knew that Arnold had heard anyone's confession, he said that a student from a village near Limoux told several people in school that he had confessed his sins to Arnold.

Arnold asked him frequently if he wanted to visit women with him, but he had replied no. He said nothing else pertinent, except that he was very sorry for what he had done and that he was prepared to undergo the penance imposed by the bishop.

Asked if because of hate, etc. . . . he said no.

He added further that around two weeks ago Arnold suggested that they go outside the city; and they came to a certain field in Le Pomerol belonging to Arnold; when they were there for some time, Arnold told him to remove his mantle, which he did. Arnold then took off his overcoat, lay on top of Guillaume, and placed his penis between Guillaume's legs. Kissing and embracing him, Arnold moved as he would with a woman and perpetrated the crime of sodomy on him.

λ

On 13 June 1323, Guillaume Boyer, son of Bernard Boyer of Plavilla in the diocese of Mirepoix, a student of the arts at Pamiers, aged about eighteen, summoned by the reverend father in Christ

Jacques, by the grace of God bishop of Pamiers, concerning those crimes denounced against Arnold of Verniolle, clerk of Le Mercadal in Pamiers, in a court set up in the presence of the lord bishop in the portico of the episcopal see of Pamiers, swore on the Gospels to speak the whole truth and nothing but the truth about the crimes of heresy and sodomy denounced against said Arnold, about himself and all persons living and dead, and especially against Arnold, who had been detained on suspicion of said crimes; after this oath, he said, confessed, and made the following deposition:

That same year, on the second day of Rogations [2 days before Ascension], Guillaume and Arnold went to the church of St. John the Martyr, to which Guillaume de Voisins' wife had come with some of her friends to hear mass. After they had witnessed communion, Guillaume and Arnold went out into the church cemetery and there Arnold asked him which woman he would prefer to have sex with. Guillaume replied that he preferred a girl who had come along with Voisins' wife. But he also told Arnold that it wasn't right to speak of such matters in a graveyard.

They then went to Arnold's house; on the way, Arnold asked, among other things, if he knew which sin was greater, sex between men or masturbation. He replied that he didn't know. Arnold then told him that these two sins were widespread among the religious [i.e., monks and friars]. Guillaume, surprised to hear this, said "Is that so?" And Arnold said that it was so. Afterward because they were near Arnold's house, they went in and went up to the upper chamber. In the hall they encountered the maid and another woman, with whom they had sex.

When they were in that room, Arnold took off his overcoat, sat down on a chair, and showed Guillaume his books; among other things, he asked Guillaume if he wanted him to write down a certain obsequy for the dead.

Afterward they returned toward the castle of Pamiers and when they were near the castle, Arnold said it would be fun to have sex with Gaillarda, Bartholomew of Rieu's maid, and Fina, Germani of Rieu's wife, in whose house Guillaume was then staying; that Guillaume ought to make an effort to know Gaillarda carnally; and that she was an animal who didn't know anything. It would also be good to have sex or stay with Fina, the speaker's mistress, who was Bartholomew of Rieu's widow. Guillaume said he didn't care about such things. They then had lunch at his house.

After lunch, although it was late, Arnold went to Fina's house, where Guillaume was staying. He asked the speaker to take a short walk with him. They then went to Arnold's field at Le Pomarol and sat down there. Arnold said, "If we were to get a hold of a woman here, what would you do with her?" Bernard said [he would do] nothing, and

Arnold embraced him and kissed his cheeks; the speaker told him to leave him alone. Afterward they got up and Arnold embraced him again, but they didn't touch each other in any other way. 

When they walked through that field, Arnold asked Guillaume whom he had confessed to this year and he said he had confessed to the Franciscan friar Arnold Marti, who had refused to absolve him on the first day of his confession. Arnold asked him which sins the friar had refused to absolve; but the speaker said he wouldn't do this since it is forbidden to reveal such things. Arnold then said: "Do you want to confess to me?" But Bernard replied that he didn't because he had already confessed this year and because Arnold wasn't even a priest. Arnold then said that there was a certain Dominican friar who had heard confessions this year and had asked Arnold what penance was suitable to impose for certain sins. There were then no other words between Guillaume and Arnold concerning this matter.

About two weeks ago, a certain boy in school said that Arnold had heard his confession this year. When Guillaume [the speaker] and Raymund, the rector of Artix's nephew, met Arnold near the parish church of Le Mercadal, they told him that a boy in school had reported that Arnold had heard his confession; but Arnold said the youth didn't know what he was talking about and turned red with embarrassment. The same day, Arnold went to the workroom in Guillaume's house and asked who had told him that he had heard his confession. Guillaume reported that it was a boy from the area of Limoux and added, "How can you hear confessions, since you're not a priest?" Arnold replied that he did not proceed in the manner of a priest. When Guillaume behaved as if to make an obscene gesture, Arnold said, "Because you're so talkative, I'll give you a slap."[9] Nevertheless, he didn't do so and they exchanged no more words concerning this matter, nor did they discuss anything else, as he testified above.

Asked if Arnold solicited him to commit sodomy, or he committed sodomy with him, he said not except the time referred to above. Arnold had afterward made the preceding remarks about the sins of sodomy and masturbation and made the speaker swear by God and the Blessed Mary not to reveal their past or future conversations because none of their friends should find out what he had seen him do or heard him say. For evil might result because of this from this friend; because this friend could not approve of the pain that his friend [i.e., Guillaume] might sustain because of revealing it to his friend.[10] He said nothing more of pertinence after diligent inquiry. Asked if from hate, etc. . . . he said no.

The aforementioned confessions and depositions were made in the presence of . . . , which I, Jean Jabaud, clerk, faithfully transcribed and corrected from the original.

λ

In June 1323, Guillaume Pech, son of Fabri Pech of Ribouisse in the diocese of Mirepoix, a student of the arts [*grammaticalibus* ] in Pamiers, aged about nineteen, summoned before the lord bishop . . . swore, said, confessed, and testified:[11]

That same year, in the week of the Feast of the Ascension, on a day he did not recall, as the speaker and Arnold of Verniolle were approaching the church of Pamiers, Arnold told him that he had gotten him a place with the canon of St. Saturnin in Toulouse (which, he said, was in the home of Master Hugues Artaudi, prior of Pradières, canon of Pamiers) in return for bringing the canon's books back and forth to school. When they neared the Carmelite house, among other things, Arnold said that he was a priest and had celebrated mass many times and that he wanted the speaker to have a bit of the wafer Arnold had consecrated. And he added that after he had celebrated mass for the first time, he had not accepted donations; for neither he, nor an acquaintance of his whose name he did not mention, accepted contributions. For, he said, if a man like himself has as much as he has, he ought not to burden his indigent friends by accepting contributions during his first mass.

Arnold asked the speaker if he would know how to assist him to say mass, and he replied that he did because he had stood by his own priest. The speaker surmised that Arnold wanted to celebrate mass at either the Dominican or Augustinian house, but he didn't do this at that time; he only said the litany of the mass of the Blessed Virgin as they passed through the street toward Mas-S. Antoine.

During the vigils of the Pentecost just past, he and Arnold came to Arnold's field in Le Pomarol, and Arnold asked him if he had confessed during Lent and if he would afterward confess because it was Pentecost. Guillaume replied that he would confess during Lent. Arnold said: "Why don't you confess to your close friend; it is just as valid and even more so to confess to your friend as to someone else." He added: "Today I heard many confessions." Among the people he named was Guillaume de Maseriis who was lodging with Master Pierre, his mother's physician from Pamiers; and another Guillaume who was lodging in the home of Martin de Berliffiaco of Le Mercadal, saying that they had confessed to him that day.

Finally, turning to speak to Guillaume, he said: "You ought to confess to your close friend, because it is just as valid as if you were to confess to a stranger." From the sign which Arnold made, Guillaume understood that Arnold wanted him to confess to him. But Guillaume didn't want to do this, although Arnold repeated it to him several times.

Asked if he had ever solicited him to commit sodomy, he said no. 105

Asked if he knew anyone whose confession had been heard by Arnold, he said no, except as noted above. He said nothing else pertinent.

Asked if because of hate, etc. . . . he said no.

Guillaume made the previous deposition . . . which I, Jean Jabaud, clerk, faithfully transcribed and corrected from the original.

λ

In the same year, on June second, friar Pierre Recort[12] of the Carmelite order, who had stayed in Arnold's cell for several days and who had heard him speak about the crimes of heresy and sodomy, came before the lord bishop of Pamiers to reveal these matters . . . after taking his oath, he said, confessed, and made the following deposition:

During the feast of St. Barnabas the Apostle just past, Arnold of Verniolle was incarcerated along with the speaker and Raymund Bar of Montaillou. Arnold pulled the speaker to one side and asked why he had been imprisoned. Pierre likewise asked why Arnold had been imprisoned. He replied that he had been accused of committing the crime of sodomy with three youths, one from Gaudiès and the other two from Ribouisse. He was also accused of posing as a priest, of hearing confessions, and of absolving penitents of their sins.

Pierre asked: "Did you indeed commit these crimes?" Arnold replied that he had. He [Arnold] said that because they wanted him to write some parables or verses for them, Arnold used to go with one or another of the aforementioned youths, bringing along some wine, silver cups, and food to a field that is situated opposite the leprosary of Pamiers. When they were there, they sometimes used to spread out a robe, dance, and wrestle, and afterward commit sodomy with each other. The boys would even come to his home and there, in an upper chamber, which was his study, they committed sodomy with him and he with them. And in that way one day the three youths fooled around with Arnold, lying down together on the bed, one of them committing sodomy with the other as the third watched. Because one of them already knew about it, they were all fired up about this sin. Arnold started to do this on the feast of All Saints last year and frequently committed that crime with the three boys.

He told Pierre that he believed that sodomy is a mortal sin, although it is equal to simple fornication or fornication with prostitutes. Although he had heard that sodomy is a graver sin than simple fornication, he didn't believe it was, unless a man lay on top of another man like a woman or committed the sin through the rear. When Pierre asked why he had carried on in this way with youths when he could have had enough women, Arnold told him that during the period that they were burning lepers, he was in Toulouse and had sex with a prostitute. After perpetrating that sin, his face swelled up and as a result he was afraid of becoming a leper. He therefore swore from then on not to know women carnally; and, in order to keep that oath, he carried on in the above manner with those youths.[13]

Arnold told him that when he was caught, he came back from Toulouse with a certain youth of Moissac, of good family; during the journey Arnold committed sodomy with him. The youth promised never to reveal anything about the crime, even if he knew that because of it he would be flayed [i.e., tortured]. Arnold was very much afraid that the youth would be captured by the lord bishop along with Arnold's nephew, his illegitimate sister's son, named Estaunié. He said that he had, however, not committed sodomy with his nephew. Arnold said that the fellow knew his secrets well and he feared that if they were captured he would reveal all.

Arnold told him that even before he had become a Franciscan, Arnold had committed that sin. Because of that same sin, a certain Franciscan friar of Toulouse, either the son or nephew of Raymund of Gaudiès, had left the order. He was his friend in the order and maligned the friars because of this sin.

When he was a student at Toulouse, Arnold lodged in rue Agulhieras, near a canonry. At that time, a certain woman sent her son Arnold Refectorarii, who could already recite seven psalms, to receive instruction from Arnold. Arnold carried on with the boy, committing sodomy with him. Arnold did not tell Pierre about committing sodomy with the boy at any other time.

Arnold had said that the bishop would have enough on his hands if he were to apprehend everyone in Pamiers who had been infected with that crime because there were more than three thousand persons. But he did not name anyone whom Pierre could recall.

Arnold told him in the cell that while he was a student at the Franciscan convent of Bordeaux friar Bernard Raynier had been accused of seducing the niece of the former bishop of Toulouse, Gaillard de Preyssac,[14] and was incarcerated at the Franciscan convent of Mirepoix. Arnold was placed in the same prison and the two of them used to discuss their incarceration and what they would do, that is, how they would live, outside the prison. Among other things, Bernard told Arnold how they would hear confessions when they got out, while Arnold told him how he would absolve penitents: "May the Lord take pity on you and relieve you of your sins, and may he lead you to eternal life"; and he would add, "May God absolve you of your sins." But he did not say "I absolve you."

Arnold said that when more intelligent folk came to him to confess, he would not apply that kind of absolution but would send them to Bernard to receive absolution. Arnold told Pierre that Bernard had instructed him that if he had absolved penitents in the aforesaid manner, they were absolved. When Arnold and Bernard left prison, they went to different places and churches and Arnold heard the confessions of many and diverse persons and absolved them in this way. Arnold did not, however, reveal to Pierre either the persons or the places.

Finally, Arnold separated from Bernard and went to Rome alone and somehow he earned his needs along the way. But he never told Pierre that he heard confessions along the way, nor did he say that he believed that penitents were absolved in this way, that although he was a subdeacon they were absolved.

Arnold said that some of the aforementioned youths confessed to him that year and he absolved them in the same way and told many that he was a priest, although this was not true.

Arnold told him that he went to the baths of Ax-les-Thermes with a certain Raymund, whose name he didn't recall, although Arnold said his name was Raymund. At Tarascon, they went to the church of the Blessed Virgin of Sabartès, where they met two bell-ringers commonly called nuns; Arnold told them that out of devotion to that church, he wanted to celebrate his first mass secretly, so that none of his friends would know and so that he could celebrate it that much more devoutly. When he entered the church, Arnold donned priestly garments and celebrated the mass. Afterward, the two nuns who took part in the mass along with Raymund, told Arnold that if he wanted to eat with them, they should bring food from Sabartès and they would be happy to join them. But Arnold did not tell Pierre whether he ate with the nuns.

After brother Gaillard de Pomiès[15] had told Arnold that among other things he had gravely erred by celebrating mass and hearing confessions, Arnold wanted to cancel what he had said about the mass; that because there were no wafers in the church, he had not celebrated the mass. He sometimes even told the speaker that what he had said about celebrating the mass was out of stupidity and foolishness.

Arnold told him that he frequently spoke with the Waldensian Raymund de Costa,[16] who was staying in Pamiers, whom Arnold commended for his knowledge of literature; Pierre did not recall what else touching heresy had been said by Arnold.

Pierre said that about a year ago Arnold Maury of Montaillou stayed with brother Pierre Geniès, a monk of Fontfroide, a penitent of the bishop, in a room situated beside the tower where the speaker was staying. Among other things Arnold told him on that day was that he had a brother who had fled from the kingdom of France because of heresy.[17] And the brother, who was his fourth, came to the hospice of St. Susanna (Hospitallet); but because he dared not proceed further, he sent for Arnold to bring him an alb [a liturgical garment]. Arnold brought the brother said alb, finding him beside the hospice. Afterward the fugitive, after taking counsel with them, left with the aforementioned three men in the direction of Catalonia. Arnold did not tell him the names of the brother's three friends.

On another day, when the speaker had cried out about the length of his incarceration and because he could not go to church, as consolation Arnold told him what is written in Scripture: "I send you forth as lambs among wolves" [Luke 10:3]. And he added that the speaker [Pierre] said that he would not be able to go to church because he was of low moral standing, that that church is good in which the souls of good people are found.

Arnold spoke to him of the human soul, but Pierre didn't remember what he said; but it seems that he held erroneous views in this area. He said nothing more of pertinence regarding Arnold.

Asked if because of hatred, etc. . . . he said no.

Friar Pierre testified the preceding in the presence of the lord bishop, on the day and place noted above, in the presence of the Dominican friar Gaillard de Pomiès; brother David de Savardun, a Cistercian of Fontfroide; and Guillaume Petri of Barthe, rector of Vira, notary of the bishop in cases pertaining to the Inquisition concerned with the investigation of heresy; and of Master Jean Straubaud. I, Jean Jabaud, clerk, faithfully transcribed and corrected the aforesaid from the original.

λ

## Confession of Arnold of Verniolle, Son of the Subdeacon Guillaume of Verniolle of the Le Mercadal Quarter of Pamiers, concerning the Crimes of Heresy and Sodomy

On 23 June 1323, Arnold of Verniolle, son of the subdeacon Guillaume of Verniolle of the Le Mercadal quarter of Pamiers, an apostate from the Franciscan order, strongly suspected and accused of the crimes of heresy and sodomy, was arrested and, at the order of the reverend father in Christ, the lord Jacques, by the grace of God bishop of Pamiers, was bound over in prison at the order of the aforesaid lord bishop and was led into the bishop's presence to the upper gallery of the episocopal see at Pamiers, to a court set up in his presence. He swore on the Gospels that he would speak the whole truth and nothing but the truth concerning said crimes and others touching upon the Catholic faith and the office of the Inquisition touching depraved heresy, both about himself and about all others living and dead; after taking this oath, he said, confessed, and made a deposition as follows:

That same year, during Lent, although he doesn't remember whether it was the seventh day or some other, he was at the Augustinian church in Pamiers. While he was there a large number of people wanted to confess, including a student aged between sixteen and eighteen, whose name he didn't know, dressed in blue and not from Pamiers. The youth came to him and asked if he were a priest, because he wanted to confess. Arnold said that he was a priest and was willing to hear his confession. They then prostrated themselves in the church and prayed and he heard the student's confession. 109

Among other things, he [the student] confessed about the sin of fornication with public prostitutes, the theft of fruit, grain, or herbs from the fields, and similar deeds. He [Arnold] did not recall what other kinds of mortal sins the student confessed to.

After the confession, Arnold told him to say the *Confiteor*. The student did so and Arnold said: "May the Omnipotent Lord take pity on you and wash away your sins; may he grant you eternal life." Then he added, "May the Omnipotent God grant you absolution and remission of all your sins." He then placed his hands on the penitent's head and recalls saying: "By the authority of God I absolve you of your sins." But he does not recall completely if he said this or not. Finally, he imposed the following penance upon him: every day until the feast of the Nativity of John the Baptist he must say five *Paternosters,* seven *Ave Marias,* and *Miserere mei Deus.* He then prayed on bared knees. But he did not impose upon him any penitence nor grant him satisfaction. He told him that before he went to communion, should he remember any sin, he should come back to confess that sin. He said that his name was Arnold of Catalonia. But the student did not come back to confess, for he [Arnold] saw him going into town.

He said nothing to him about these matters.

Finally, after several days, although he doesn't remember when exactly, at about three o'clock, the speaker and a student, not from Pamiers (he doesn't know either his name or place of origin), aged between sixteen and eighteen and a half, went to the street where the Dominicans are situated, opposite the former home of Raymund de Surp. The student asked Arnold if he were a priest, because he wanted to confess. He said that he was and would hear his confession if the youth so desired. They went to Raymond de Surp's house; in the hallway, the speaker sat down on the bench beside the head of the dining table and the student either sat down or bent down on the ground beside Arnold (he does not recall if he bent his knees or sat down). Arnold, holding a cowl over his head, heard the student's confession; among other things, he confessed that he had stolen fruit from someone and had sworn falsely. About the other kinds of sins confessed, Arnold did not recall.

110 When the confession was completed, Arnold told the student to say his *Confiteor,* absolving him in the manner described above, and imposed a similar penance. He didn't recall if he told the youth that he was named Arnold of Catalonia or that should he remember any other sins he should return.

Asked if he had heard anyone else's confession or had absolved anyone else in a similar way, he said that he had not.

Asked if he had spoken to someone else or suggested to anyone else that they ought to confess to him, he replied that this year during Easter, while he and a certain student who was lodging with either Pierre or Jean Rieux of Le Mercadal, whose name he didn't recall, were going to or leaving Arnold's field at Le Pomarol, the student told Arnold that he had confessed to friar Arnold Martini, a Franciscan of Pamiers; the youth had noted that after confession he remembered another sin and wanted to go back to the friar to confess it. Arnold thereupon told the youth to confess the sin to him and he would absolve him, because he was a priest. But the student replied that he could not give him solace and hear his confession, since he well knew that he wasn't a priest. He did not recall whether he had said similar things to anyone else.

Asked if he had celebrated mass or masses or had worn holy garments as a subdeacon in the church of the Evangelists, he replied that he had not. Asked if he had told anyone that he was a priest, he said he had so told the three aforementioned students. He told a certain student who stayed with Jacques of Paris, a dyer of Le Camp in Pamiers, that he was a priest and had celebrated mass. But he didn't tell him where he had celebrated mass.

He recalled further that after he had for the first time heard the second student's confession at the home of Raymund de Surp, the next day the two of them crossed the city and passed beside the church of Le Mercadal in Pamiers. The student said that he had just then recalled some sins which he wanted to confess and they entered the church. The two of them prostrated themselves on the steps before the altar of St. Bartholomew and the student confessed again. And Arnold absolved him of these sins in the aforementioned way and imposed a penance similar to the first.

Asked if he had later told those students who in his guise as a priest had confessed to him that he was not a priest, he said that he had not, although he frequently saw and greeted them. Asked if at that time when he had heard these students' confessions as a priest and absolved them as a priest he believed before or after or now believed that he could hear anyone's sacramental confession or absolve anyone of sin,

especially mortal sins, so that they were truly absolved of sin, he replied
that he had not; nevertheless, he had heard their confessions, wanting
to know their consciences, and what sins they had committed. After- 111
ward, he didn't tell them that he wasn't a priest, having told them
earlier that he was.

He was asked why, when he heard the confessions of these students in order to know their consciences and what sins they had committed, although he did not believe he could absolve them, he absolved them of their sins, even though he didn't believe he had the power to do so. He replied that he had at first said that he was a priest and had heard confessions as a priest but was afterward embarrassed to say he wasn't a priest and couldn't absolve them. Because of this embarrassment, he absolved these students, although he didn't believe this absolution was valid.

Asked if anyone had taught him that he could pose as a priest and hear anyone's confession and absolve them, he replied in the negative; nor did he know anyone else who, although not a priest, had dared to hear confessions as he did.

He further recalled that during the same year at Easter, although he didn't recall the time or day nor whether it was before or after the preceding events occurred, he was in the Dominican chapel where at about three he was accustomed to read theology. A student, not from Pamiers, dressed in a brown mantle, about twenty years old, came in and said he was looking for a Dominican to confess to. The two of them sat down at the foot of the pulpit and as they spoke the student said, among other things, "Are you a priest?" Arnold said that he was. The student said he would prefer to confess to Arnold more than to anyone else, while Arnold said he would be pleased to hear his confession. The two of them prostrated themselves on the stairs where they were and the student confessed his sins. Among other things, he confessed that he had committed fornication with prostitutes and solicited both married and unmarried women to commit that vice; that he was sometimes drunk and frequently considered how he could commit that sin; he had also stolen some fruit and other things. He likewise spoke about other kinds of sins, which Arnold didn't recall.

After the student had confessed his sins, Arnold absolved him and imposed a certain penitence as satisfaction. But he did not recall which penitence he had imposed. Afterward he never saw the student again.

He [Arnold] said and confessed the following regarding the sin of sodomy:

About twenty years ago, although he doesn't remember when, when he was about ten or twelve, his father sent him to study grammar in Pamiers, at Master Poncius de Massabucci's place in the Borayria district of Pamiers. Poncius later became a Dominican. At this school he

boarded with Master Poncius; Pierre Illat of Montsegut; Bernard Balessa of Le Mercadal; Arnold Auriol, son of Pierre, a knight near
112 Bastide de Serou, who already shaved his beard and is now a priest;
Bernard ofVerniolle, the speaker's brother; and other students, whose names he did not recall.

And while Arnold lodged in that room with these students, for about six weeks he shared a bed with Arnold Auriol. After they had been together for about two or three nights and Arnold Auriol thought that Arnold was asleep, he started to kiss the speaker and placed himself over Arnold's thighs. He then placed his penis between Arnold's thighs and moving himself about as with a woman, he ejaculated between Arnold's thighs. He continued this sin all night, as long as the speaker slept with Arnold Auriol. Because Arnold was still a boy, this act was displeasing to him; but because of shame, he didn't dare to reveal it to anyone. At that time, he didn't even have the will or desire to commit that sin, for, so he said, he did not yet have such desires. After six weeks, the speaker, along with Master Poncius, Arnold Auriol, the speaker's brother Bernard of Verniolle, and a certain Theobald of Cintegabelle, who already shaved his beard, moved to another house near Pont de Lasclades. This house now belongs to the Salvetati family. Arnold slept there in one bed with his brother and Master Poncius, who solicited Arnold to commit that vice.

At that time Arnold Auriol slept with Theobald and did not commit sodomy with Arnold nor discuss it with him.

He said that about a month ago a certain youth, aged about eighteen, whose name he didn't know, came to Pamiers to stay with Bartholomew of Auterive, a shoemaker of Le Mercadal, from whom Arnold customarily purchased his shoes. Since Arnold knew him from Toulouse, the youth came and told him that he no longer had a place to stay; Arnold therefore asked if he would like to lodge with him. The youth therefore came to Arnold's house and in a room adjacent to the hall spent one night naked in bed with Arnold. And when the two of them were in bed together naked, Arnold embraced and kissed the youth and asked if he would like Arnold to put his penis between the boy's thighs. The youth replied that he could do as he wanted. Arnold, putting his penis between the boy's thighs, as they stood [sic] side by side ejaculated semen and committed sodomy with the youth twice that night, behaving as described above. The youth, however, did not sodomize Arnold, nor did Arnold ask him to do so. The next morning when they got up, Arnold told the youth not to tell anyone what had happened that night, for, he said, "if anyone should find out, I'll get in trouble." Nevertheless, he didn't ask the boy to swear not to reveal these events to anyone. Nor did Arnold give him anything except food; nor did he commit that sin with him afterward, although he spoke with him frequently thereafter.

He said that the same year around last Christmas on a day which he didn't recall Guillaume Roux of Ribouisse in the diocese of Mirepoix, a student at Pamiers and tutor to the sons of Raymund Faur also called Recurul of the Loumet quarter of Pamiers, came to Arnold's house and asked if he knew a cleric whom he could serve and who would be willing to hear his lessons, because his brother didn't want to provide for his studies. Arnold replied that master Maurand, prior of Lavelanet and canon of St. Saturnin of Toulouse, was looking for a cleric like him to bring his books back and forth for him to school. Arnold made this Guillaume swear on a martyrology [*kalendarium*] or liturgical book [*collectarium*] not to reveal, even to the canon, the things that Arnold would tell him about this canon.



After Guillaume had so sworn, Arnold told him that he had heard that the canon sometimes kissed and embraced youths and afterward he would put his penis between their thighs and perpetrate that sin, "and if, by chance, you lodge with him, you'll have to allow him to do likewise with you if he so desires."

Guillaume answered that he was willing; Arnold then asked if he had already committed this sin with someone else. Guillaume replied that he had done so with a certain squire of his country, who had shared his bed; he added that he knew well how to commit that crime, and even told Arnold the squire's name, although he [Arnold] didn't recall it. This conversation took place in the upper chamber of Arnold's house, in which there was a bed. Arnold thereupon said to Guillaume, "Do you want me to demonstrate that act to you, and will you show me how the squire acted with you?" Guillaume replied that he was willing. They then undressed, lay down nude on the bed and, in the aforementioned way, first one and then the other committed sodomy; they then swore on the Gospels never to reveal anything about this sin to anyone. Arnold then borrowed from Guillaume a book by Ovid, whose title he didn't know.[18] Guillaume then asked Arnold to give him a knife which he carried with his knives[19] but Arnold refused, and said he would give him a different one.

Asked who told him that master Maurand committed such acts, he said that around the feast of the Nativity of John the Baptist last year, when he was studying in Toulouse, a book porter who lodged with Maurand told Arnold on rue Agulhieras that he would willingly leave his master. This is because he didn't like Maurand's habits, that when he was in bed he made him rub his feet; when he was warm, he embraced and kissed him and put him to bed. Arnold surmised from this statement that the canon carried on that vice and the porter explicitly admitted it when asked. It seems to the speaker that the porter's name was Gerald and he was from either Limoges or Cahors; and he told Arnold that he lived with the canon for a year.

Arnold said that afterward he and Guillaume Roux committed

sodomy with each other in the same room and bed, on different occasions, two or three times. The speaker likewise committed that sin
114 with Guillaume Roux in the same way, except that they only lay down on the bed naked the first time. Guillaume often even committed the crime with the speaker, and it seems that he enjoyed it as much as Arnold did, to tell from his words and deeds. On the last occasion that they did this, they swore on the Gospels not to do so with anyone else. Guillaume excepted the canon, since he was going to lodge with him. They swore otherwise not to commit the sin again with each other.

After this oath, about eight days later, Arnold and Guillaume Roux went to Arnold's brother Guillaume's field at Le Pomarol. When they got there, Arnold told Guillaume Roux that they should remove their mantles and commit sodomy as they had done before. Guillaume said that he wouldn't do so. Arnold said that if they committed sodomy after having sworn not to do so again, the Franciscan lector of Pamiers, who had power over such things, would absolve them. Guillaume refused to consent to this; but because Arnold still wanted to commit sodomy with him, he made certain signs, embraced him, wrestled him down to the ground, and turned Guillaume over, as if to commit sodomy. But this didn't happen; he had only acted to test and tempt Guillaume to see if he wanted to commit that sin or not; but at that time the speaker did not commit sodomy with Guillaume, nor Guillaume with him.

Asked if he had solicited Guillaume to commit sodomy in the Franciscan house at Pamiers, he replied that he was not sure if he had or not. He said that in various places he and Guillaume had discussed committing that sin.

Asked if he had sometimes told Guillaume or anyone else that sodomy was a lesser sin than carnal knowledge of women, he replied that he had so told Guillaume Roux but did not recall where or when. He had said that he believed that simple fornication and sodomy were equal sins; he said that he truly believed that sodomy and simple fornication were equal sins and that rape, deflowering of a virgin, adultery, and incest were greater and graver sins than sodomy. He said that he maintained this belief from the feast of All Saints until very recently. But he always believed that sodomy and simple fornication were mortal sins.

The speaker even told Guillaume Bernardi, son of Jean Jeu of Gaudiès, that sodomy and simple fornication were equal sins. He had said this to both Guillaume Roux and Guillaume Bernardi because they had asked him if said sin of sodomy, which he had committed with them, was a sin of heresy. He answered them that said sin was not a sin of heresy but was rather equal to carnal knowledge of women or prostitutes.

Asked if he had told these people that sodomy and fornication were equal in order to induce them to commit sodomy, he replied that he had not, since they had both voluntarily committed the act with him, and the speaker with them, as it appeared to him from their words and deeds. For Guillaume Roux had told Arnold in his house when they discussed the matter, "Do you want me to show you what a man can do when he wants to have sex with another man but doesn't have the chance, so that he can satisfy his lust?" Guillaume then added that he frequently took his penis in his own hand and rubbed it in order to satisfy his lust; he also told Arnold that he would show him how to do it if he wanted him to; Arnold had said that he wasn't interested because he would never do it.



Asked if anyone had told him that sodomy and simple fornication were equally blameworthy, or if he had heard the contrary preached in church or had read it somewhere, or if anyone had told him that sodomy is graver than any other type of lust [*luxuria*], with the exception of bestiality, he replied in the negative; except that he well knew that the rectors of churches and chaplains could not commonly absolve penitents of sodomy, but only bishops or those so licensed by bishops could absolve sodomites. On the other hand simple rectors and chaplains could absolve penitents guilty of simple fornication and adultery without special permission from the bishop.

Asked if he had told any of the above persons, showing or pointing out in a book of decretals that it was so written, that sodomy is a lesser sin or equal to fornication, he replied that he had not. But he had told Guillaume Roux that in some men nature demands that they perform that act or know women carnally; and, he said that he very much felt in himself that his body would suffer if he should abstain for more than eight or fifteen days if he did not have sex with a woman or didn't commit that crime with a man. Nor, he said, did he believe that he committed a greater sin by committing sodomy with a man than by knowing a woman carnally.

Last year, around the feast of All Saints just past, at the Augustinian house in Pamiers, Arnold encountered Guillaume Bernardi, a student from Gaudiès. He said that if he wanted to lodge with a certain canon of St. Saturnin of Toulouse who was also prior of Lavelanet, in return for which he would carry the prior's books back and forth from school for him, Arnold would get him the position. Guillaume asked about the canon's manner of living and habits; Arnold made Guillaume swear on a book never to disclose or reveal to anyone what he would tell him about the canon's manner of living. Arnold did not recall where that oath was made, but it was either in the Augustinian house or in Arnold's house. After the oath was made, Arnold told Guillaume that the canon occasionally drank wine and afterward had his servant rub his feet and then kissed and embraced the servant, so he had heard. But he didn't know if he did something afterward with the servant. But when Guillaume Bernardi asked Arnold what the canon had done, Arnold told him that the canon put his penis between the servant's thighs and satisfied his lust; and the speaker believes that he also added, "Have you occasionally done this?" Guillaume Bernardi replied embarrassedly that he knew what it was and said, "Do you want me to show you?" Arnold replied that he would. These last words were exchanged in the upper chamber of Arnold's and his brother Guillaume of Verniolle's home. Arnold then said to Guillaume, "Should we do it naked or dressed?" Guillaume replied that they should do it in whatever fashion Arnold preferred; the speaker replied that they should undress and lie down naked on the bed, which they did. There, in the same manner in which he committed sodomy with Guillaume Roux, Arnold committed sodomy with Guillaume Bernardi, and Guillaume with him. After this, Arnold committed sodomy with Guillaume three or four times thereafter, at different times, during different holidays, but in the same room and bed. But they only lay down nude the first time.

Asked if he committed sodomy anywhere else with Guillaume Bernardi, he replied in the negative.

Asked if he had instigated Guillaume to commit sodomy with the speaker, he said that he had and that Guillaume had committed sodomy in the same way with the speaker three or four times.

Asked about how old Guillaume was, Arnold replied that he didn't know for sure, but he seemed to be between sixteen and eighteen years old.

Asked if he had made Guillaume swear never to commit sodomy with anyone else or even with Arnold, or if he himself had so sworn, he replied in the negative.

Asked if he told Guillaume or made him swear never to reveal that vice which they had committed nor even to confess about that sin, he replied that he had not, except as stated above.

He said that on the feast of Pentecost just past, but at a time he didn't recall, on a certain holiday after vespers, Arnold went to a garden belonging to Germanus Fromagerii, situated at the far end of Las Gransas; he was followed by an eighteen-year-old youth of Mirepoix, whose name he didn't recall, an apprentice to the shoemaker Bernard of Toulouse of Le Mercadal in Pamiers. They went together to the garden; along the way the youth told Arnold that he couldn't earn enough as a shoemaker and would willingly serve another master, asking if he could find him one. Arnold replied that he believed that Master Bernard Saisset, canon of Pamiers, needed such a servant and that Arnold was willing to ask if he was interested in the youth's services. The youth replied that if Arnold should secure the position for him, he would get Arnold some good-looking women he knew. Arnold replied, "If you could procure such women for me, I would be very pleased, and you would have done well." As they spoke of such matters, they entered the garden and lay down on a mound of dirt. Arnold removed his mantle because he was warm. When they sat down, the youth told Arnold that he would tell him how he satisfied his lust when he had no women. Arnold asked him about this method; the youth then embraced him and put Arnold under himself, saying that he would demonstrate the aforementioned technique. Arnold told him that he knew well how to do it and put the youth under himself. But neither he nor the youth did anything.

Finally, the youth told Arnold that he would teach him another method, that is, that while they were standing side by side he would place his penis between Arnold's legs in order to commit sodomy and that they should get ready to do it that way. But Arnold didn't want to do this and said that he knew that method well. The youth told him that many good men did this, and Arnold replied that it was so, as he heard said, even the religious [priests and monks]. The youth asked if the canon did such things and Arnold replied that he didn't believe so, since he was an upright man.

Asked if he had committed sodomy with anyone else, or anyone had solicited him to commit that crime, he replied in the negative.

Asked if he had confessed to any priest or religious about that crime which he had committed, he replied that he had not; and he had also not confessed during Lent that year, nor since the feast of St. Luke; but when he was sick he had confessed to a certain Carmelite lector.

Asked if he had taken communion during Easter, he replied that he had not, nor for the past twelve years since he left the Franciscan order. He had refused to take communion for the past twelve years or to confess his sins during last Lent because every day he resolved to enter a new religious order. Then he would confess his sins and he would begin to do what he ought to do in order to be a good man and he would cease his sins.

Asked if he had absolved anyone who had confessed to him of sodomy, he replied that he hadn't.

Asked if he had told anyone with whom he had committed sodomy or whom he had solicited to commit that crime that he would take them to a religious who would absolve them of that sin and would impose a light penance, he said that he had not.

Asked if he had heard the confessions of many others aside from those mentioned above, or had solicited others to confess to him, he replied that he had not. Asked if when he absolved penitents in the above manner he believed that he could in fact absolve and that they were completely absolved of their sins, he replied in the negative. Nevertheless, he had not told those who confessed to him and were absolved in the above manner, and to whom he said he was a priest, that they ought to confess to another priest since they were not absolved because he wasn't a priest.

Asked if he believed or had ever believed that any man not ordained as a priest could absolve a penitent of his sins through penance in a sacramental manner, he replied in the negative.

Asked why, although he did not believe that he who was not a priest could not absolve anyone of their sins, did he so frequently hear so many people's confessions as a priest, telling them that he was a priest; and why he had absolved them in the above manner, although he believed that this absolution was not valid; and why, before they had completed their confession he had not told them to confess to another priest who could absolve them of their sins, he replied that he had wanted to hear many people's confessions in order to know what sins they had committed, if they had committed the same sins he had committed, and how. He had begun to hear confessions that year during Lent, and before that he never heard confessions. He said that those persons who had confessed to him he had absolved of their sins although he believed that his absolution had no validity. But when he told them that he was a priest and had heard their confessions, he was embarrassed not to absolve them of their sins. Although one of them, who had confessed to him, after confession and absolution wanted to receive communion from him, Arnold did not tell him that he should not receive communion until he had confessed to another priest and was absolved by him since Arnold didn't have such power. Rather he said that he should take communion in the name of the Lord because, so he said, he was embarrassed to tell this person then that he couldn't grant communion because Arnold wasn't a priest, since he had already told him that he was.

Asked if anyone had taught him that he ought to hear or could hear confessions and absolve of sin, or knew that anyone not a priest heard confession and absolved of sin, or heard this said about anyone, he replied in the negative.

Asked if he told anyone that he was a priest and had celebrated mass, he replied that he had, but he didn't remember to whom, except as stated above.

Asked if he had ever celebrated mass or masses anywhere, he replied in the negative.

Asked why he had said that he was a priest and had celebrated mass when he wasn't a priest and hadn't celebrated mass, he replied that he didn't know, except that he had said this to some people in order to hear their confessions.

Asked if he knew anyone not ordained as a priest who celebrated mass and said he was a priest, he replied that he didn't.

Asked if he believed or had ever believed that one not ordained a 119
priest could celebrate mass so that during this mass the body and blood of Christ were created, he said that he had not.

Asked if he had administered any sacrament aside from confession to anyone, he replied that he had not.

After diligent examination, he said nothing else pertinent.

Because, following the deposition of witnesses in the court set up in judgment against Arnold by the lord bishop, it did not seem to the lord bishop that Arnold had fully confessed the truth about himself and others, but rather that he had concealed a great many grave matters despite his oath, the bishop therefore admonished and warned him according to the law to confess the truth about both himself and others. He bound him over until the following Monday, which will be the twenty-eighth day of the present month [June]; in the meantime, the lord bishop wanted to inform himself and inquire about Arnold more fully and completely concerning those crimes and other matters touching the Catholic faith.

Arnold of Verniolle confessed and testified the preceding in the presence of the lord bishop, in a place, year, and day noted above, in the presence of the friars Gaillard of Pomiès and Arnold of Carla, Dominicans of Pamiers; Bernard de Taix, a Cistercian of Fontfroide; of Master Guillaume Nadini of Carcassonne, notary of the king of France and of the lord bishop in cases relating to the Inquisition touching the investigation of heresy; and of Jean Strabaud of Sautel, notary of the city of Pamiers, who at the bishop's order received the preceding confession, which I, Jean Jabaud, clerk, faithfully transcribed and corrected from the original.

On 28 June, which day in the preceding acts had been set aside for Arnold of Verniolle's full confession to testify about himself and others about the crime of heresy, of sodomy, and other things of which he was very much suspected and about which he had not yet, so it appeared, fully confessed, he was led to the presence of the lord bishop in an upper chamber of the episcopal see of Pamiers and in a court established there swore again to tell the whole truth and nothing but the truth concerning the aforementioned crimes relating to the office and business of the investigation of heresy, about himself and all others living and dead. After this oath, he was asked if he wanted to confess more fully and completely and to reveal the truth about himself and others regarding those matters touching the office and business of the Inquisition involved in the investigation of heresy; he replied in the negative, because he knew nothing more, so he said.

The lord bishop then ordered that Arnold should be taken to and placed in the prison of the castle of Pamiers.

120 These acts were set down on the year, day, and place noted above, in the presence of the lord bishop, the Dominican friars Gaillard of Pomiès and Arnold of Carla, of the monastery of Pamiers; Bernard of Taix, Cistercian of Fontfroide; and Master Jean Strabaud of Sautel, notary, which I, John Jabaud, faithfully transcribed and corrected from the original.

A year later, on 1 August 1324, Arnold of Verniolle, taken from the prison in the tower of Les Allemans, and brought before the lord bishop in an upper chamber of the episcopal see of Pamiers, in a court set up in the bishop's presence, swore again to tell the whole truth and nothing but the truth concerning heresy and sodomy, about himself and all persons living and dead; when this oath was completed, he was asked if what he had confessed to the bishop on 23 June 1323 was full and complete and true. When this was read to Arnold, the bishop suggested that he consider whether he did not remember his confession. Arnold replied that everything in his confession was true and complete and that it was entirely factual and that he needn't read the confession since he remembered it.

Asked if he wanted to add or subtract anything in his confession, concerning himself or others living or dead, he replied in the negative.

Asked if he ever told anyone or he believed that sodomy with men was a lesser sin than simple fornication with a prostitute, and especially if he had shown anyone that this was written in a book of decretals, he replied in the negative.

Asked if he told anyone or believed that because his nature required him to satisfy his lust either with a man or a woman it is not sinful to have relations with men or women, or that these may be minor or venial sins, he replied that he believed that his nature inclined him to commit sodomy, although he always believed that sodomy is a mortal sin. Nevertheless, he held that sodomy is as sinful as simple fornication and that illicit deflowering of a virgin and incest may be graver sins, and in any case the same as men carnally knowing other men. And he had indeed told this to Guillaume Roux, son of Pierre Roux of Ribouisse, and Guillaume Bernardi, son of Jean Ioc of Gaudiès in Mirepoix, with whom he committed sodomy. But he had not told them this in order to induce them to consent to perpetrate that sin with him lest they not do it. He told Guillaume Roux that the sin of masturbation by rubbing the penis or some other movement is equal to the sin of simple fornication and to the sin of sodomy. They were equal, so he said (and, so he said, he had believed this in his heart at that time, from the feast of All Saints just past until he confessed) even if that sin of masturbation was committed on purpose and deliberately.

Asked if he had told anyone or believed that he, a subdeacon, could sacramentally absolve penitents of mortal sin so that they were completely absolved by him of all their sins and that it was not necessary 121
for them to again confess to another priest, he replied that he had indeed told others that he could absolve them of their sins, and he even absolved as he said above; when he had heard them confess sacramentally even mortal sins, he did not, however, say to any of them that they should go to confess these sins to another priest, although he knew that some, after such confession, said they wanted to take communion, and he said that they could take communion. But he never believed that although not a priest he could absolve them of mortal sins confessed to him sacramentally. He believed that those who confessed their sins and were absolved by him ought to confess their sins to another priest and be absolved by them; nevertheless he had told them the preceding things and had heard confessions in order to know the penitents' sins, although he had sinned mortally by hearing confessions and saying that he could absolve them of their sins.

Asked if he told anyone or believed that the imposition of satisfaction for sins confessed was not necessary in order to free one of the punishment owed for sin, but that such satisfaction may be imposed only ad hoc so that, fearful of punishment, they may be held back from subsequent sins, he replied in the negative.

Asked if he told anyone that he had celebrated mass or if he had really celebrated mass or wore clerical vestments in order to celebrate mass, and if he believed that in celebrating mass he could create the body and blood of Christ, he replied that he had indeed told some people that he had celebrated mass and that he was a priest. But he had not in fact done so, nor worn clerical vestments, nor did he believe that someone who was not a priest could create the body and blood of Christ.

Asked if he had committed the crime of sodomy with anyone else, or with the aforementioned persons or others in other places, except as described above, he replied in the negative.

Asked if he had committed any other heretical acts, or knew anyone who had, he replied in the negative.

He said nothing else pertinent, after diligent inquiry.

Asked if he were penitent for having believed and uttered the above errors and for the fact that he taught them, initiating others into error, and if he wanted to turn back from those errors, he replied in the affirmative and he said that he was prepared to undergo that penance which the lord bishop would impose on him for the aforesaid. After the abjuration for heresy was received and in accord with the vow herein written, the lord bishop would absolve him in accordance with the rules of the church from the sentences which he had incurred for the crimes of heresy and sodomy, provided he had made full confession and was penitent concerning the preceding. Otherwise, it was not the bishop's intention, so he said, to absolve him from the preceding sentences. But it was reserved to said Arnold that if he should in the end recall something about said crimes, such confession about himself and all others living and dead would be accepted.

The tenor of his abjuration and oath was as follows: "I, Arnold, in a court set up in the presence of your reverend father in Christ, lord Jacques, by the grace of God bishop of Pamiers, do abjure in my heart every heresy raised up against the faith of our Lord Jesus Christ and the Holy Roman Church and every heretical belief of every sect damned by the Roman Church, under the pain which by law those who relapse into heresy suffer. I swear and promise to pursue heretics to the best of my ability and even those whom I know and believe are fugitives because of the crime of heresy; to have them captured and brought back to the best of my ability to the lord bishop and his successors and inquisitors of depraved heresy, whomever they are, and wherever I know them to be.

"I swear and promise to keep, serve, and defend the Catholic faith which the holy Roman Church observes and preaches.

"I swear and promise to obey and comply with the orders of the Church and of said Lord bishop and inquisitors and to appear before them any day or any place, whenever and as often as I may be called or required to do so, summoned by messenger, letters, or in some other way; and never to flee nor knowingly absent myself contumaciously; and to undertake and complete, to the best of my abilty, the punishment or penitence which he may impose upon me. And to this end I bind both myself and my goods."

The preceding acts, in the preceding fashion, said Arnold abjured and swore in the bishop's presence on the aforesaid year, day, and place in the presence and by the testimony of friars Gaillard de Pomiès, Arnold de Carla, Dominicans; the most distinguished men Master Arnold Docesii, an official of Pamiers; Bernard Faix, the bishop's vicar; and Master Jean Strabaud of Sautel, notary who received this testimony at the bishop's order; on whose account I, Jean Jabaud, clerk of Toulouse, faithfully transcribed and corrected from the original.

λ

In the name of Our Lord Jesus Christ, Amen.[20] It has been established as a result of written confessions made in court before us, the bishop and inquisitor, that Arnold of Verniolle, subdeacon of the city of Pamiers, apostate from the Franciscan order, whom we have first decreed must be deposed from orders as subdeacon and cleric, from every tonsure and clerical privilege, and degraded on this day and place, in order to receive penance from us and hear the definitive sentence peremptorily imposed upon him, must undergo the salutary penance of life imprisonment. . . .

You, Arnold of Verniolle, have fallen into the horrible and damnable crime of sodomy, as is noted above in your full confession, and because of which you are to be gravely and harshly punished . . . You should therefore be degraded and placed in iron chains in the strictest prison, to be fed a diet of bread and water for life . . . so that no one may grant you grace in future, neither the bishops nor inquisitors who succeed us. . . .

After this, the lord bishop, dressed in his pontifical robes with his pastoral staff and his cap without a mitre, deposed the aforesaid Arnold of Verniolle, a subdeacon dressed in his subdeacon's garb, from his office, degrading, stripping, and depriving him of his position [there follows an elaborate description of the ceremony of clerical degradation, etc.].

# *Notes*

## Introduction

1. See, e.g., Henricus de Segusio, *Summa aurea*, ed. Nicholas Soranza (Lyons, 1537), fols. 244v, 283r; Terence McLaughlin, ed., *The Summa Parisiensis on the Decretum Gratiani* (Toronto, 1952), C.32, q.5. c.10.
2. John Peckham, *Divinarum sententiarum* (Paris, 1513), fols. 48v–49r.
3. H. Montgomery Hyde, *The Love That Dared Not Speak Its Name* (Boston, 1970), pp. 27–59; Arno Karlen, *Sexuality and Homosexuality* (New York, 1971), 66 ff.
4. Derrick S. Bailey, *Homosexuality and the Western Christian Tradition* (London, 1955), 127 ff; Marcel Eck, *Sodome, essai sur l'homosexualité* (Paris, 1966), 71 ff; Thorkild Vanggaard, *Phallòs* (New York, 1972), p. 59.
5. James D. Steakley, *The Homosexual Emancipation Movement in Germany* (New York, 1975), is the best treatment of this movement. For a more general survey, see John Lauritsen and David Thorstad, *The Early Homosexual Rights Movement (1864–1935)* (New York, 1974). In another work, *Religious Roots of the Taboo on Homosexuality* (New York, 1974), Lauritsen lays the entire blame for homosexual oppression at the doorstep of religion.
6. See Numa Praetorius, "Die strafrechtlichen Bestimmung gegen den gleichgeschlechtlichen Verkehr," *Jahrbuch für sexuelle Zwischenstufen* 1 (1899): 97–158; *idem*, "Ein homosexueller Ritter des 15. Jahrhunderts," *Jahrbuch für sexuelle Zwischenstufen* 12 (1912): 207–30.
7. For a brief biographical sketch reprinted from the *Enciclopedia séxualis*, ed. Victor Robinson (New York, 1936), pp. 317–21, see *A Homosexual Emancipation Miscellany* (New York, 1975).
8. See Iwan Bloch, *Die Prostitution*, 2 vols. (Berlin, 1912), 1:791 ff, on the Middle Ages; for Linsert, see Jonathan Katz, ed., *Documents of the Homosexual Rights Movement in Germany, 1836–1927* (New York, 1975), pp. 281–302.
9. See James Cleugh, *Love Locked Out: A Survey of Love, License, and Restriction in the Middle Ages* (London, 1963), 89 ff; Bailey, *Homosexuality;* Gordon Westwood, *Society and the Homosexual* (London, 1952), pp. 79–82. For earlier work, see Geoffrey May, *Social Control of Sexual Expression* (London, 1930), p. 47; D. Stanley-Jones, "Sexual Perversion and the English Law," *Medical Press Circular* 215 (1946): 391–98, who suggests that the introduction of Aristotle to the curriculum at Paris somehow veiled a battle over homosexuality.
10. J. M. Livingood, ed., *National Institute of Mental Health Task Force on Homosexuality: Final Report and Background Papers* (Rockville, Md., 1972).
11. Vern L. Bullough, *Sexual Variance in Society and History* (New York, 1976), 372 ff.; *idem*, "Heresy, Witchcraft, and Sexuality," *Journal of Homosexuality* 1(1974): 183–201.
12. Cleugh, *Love Locked Out*, p. 298.
13. E. William Monter, "La Sodomie à l'époque moderne en Suisse romande," *Annales. Sociétés, économies, civilisations* 29 (1974): 1023–33.
14. G. Ruggiero, "Sexual Criminality in the Early Renaissance: Venice 1338–1358," *Journal of Social History* 8 (1975): 18–37.

15. J. L. Flandrin, "Mariage tardif et vie sexuelle: Discussions et hypothèses de recherche," *Annales. Sociétés, économies, civilisations* 27 (1972): 1351–78; *idem,* "Contraception, mariage et relations amoureuses dans l'Occident chrétien," *Annales. Sociétés, économies, civilisations* 27 (1972): 1351–78. For a more general work, see his *L'Église et le contrôle des naissances* (Paris, 1970).

# Chapter I

1. Roswitha of Gandersheim, *Passio metrica S. Pelagii,* in *PL* 137:1093–1102; for a translation, see *The Sufferings of Pelagius,* in *The Non-Dramatic Works of Hrosvitha,* ed. M. Gonsalva Wiegand (St. Louis, 1936), pp. 128–57; Karl Müllenhoff and Wilhelm Scherer, *Denkmäler deutschen Poesie und Prosa aus dem viii-xii Jahrhundert,* 2 vols. (Berlin, 1892), vol. 1, n. 23; W. Leonhardt, "Die Homosexualität in der altesten deutschen Dichtkunst," *Jahrbuch für sexuelle Zwischenstufen* 12 (1912): 153–65.

2. For accusations against the Provençal nobility, see Ralph Glaber, *Historiae sui temporis,* in *Recueil des historiens des Gaules et de la France,* 24 vols. (Paris, 1738–1905), 10:42; on Moslem attitudes toward sex, see Vern Bullough, *Sexual Variance in Society and History* (New York, 1976), pp. 205–44.

3. Quoted in Paul Lacroix, *Histoire de la prostitution,* 6 vols. (Brussels, 1851–1853), 3:263.

4. Augustin Fliche, *La Réforme Grégorienne et la réconquête chrétienne (1057–1123)* (Paris, 1950), 462 ff., on the "moral disorder" of the period.

5. Guillaume de Nangis, *Chronique latine,* ed. P. Geraud, 2 vols. (Paris, 1843), 1:11; Henry of Huntingdon, *Historia anglicana,* ed. T. Arnold, Rolls Series, vol. 73 (London, 1879), p. 242; Gervase of Canterbury, *Chronica,* ed. W. Stubbs, Rolls Series, vol. 73 (London, 1880), pp. 93–94; Orderic Vitalis, *Historia ecclesiastica,* ed. Augustin Le Prévost, 5 vols. (Paris, 1838–1855), 3:324; Eadmer, *Vita Anselmi,* ed. M. Rule, Rolls Series, vol. 81 (London, 1884), 359 ff; John of Salisbury, *Frivolities . . . ,* ed. and trans. J. B. Pike (Minneapolis, 1938), p. 200.

6. Duncan Grinnell-Milne, *The Killing of William Rufus* (Newton Abbott, 1968), pp. 40–41; Austin Lane Poole, *From Domesday Book to Magna Carta, 1087–1216* (Oxford, 1958), p. 99; Jack Lindsay, *The Normans and Their World* (New York, 1974), p. 412; John Graham, *The Homosexual Kings of England* (London, 1968), p. 14, alleges, without a shred of evidence, that Rufus was killed in a jealous rage by his lover William Tirel, earl of Poix.

7. P. Delhaye, "Deux adaptations du 'De amicitia' de Cicéron du xiie siècle," *Recherches de théologie ancienne et mediévale* 15 (1948): 304–31; E. R. Curtius, *European Literature and the Latin Middle Ages,* trans. W. R. Trask (New York, 1963), notes that this treatise was part of the standard twelfth-century school curriculum.

8. For the life of Aelred, see *DHGE,* 1:1165–67; cf. Walter Daniel, *Life of Aelred of Rievaulx,* ed. F. M. Powicke (London, 1963), p. 40; Aelred of Rievaulx, *De spirituali amicitia,* in PL 1:38–41 and 1:57–60; and *idem, Speculum caritatis,* in *idem, Opera omnia ascetica,* ed. A. Hoste and C. H. Talbot, *Corpus christianorum continuatio mediaevalia* (Tournhout, 1971), 1:79–80.

9. Leopold Delisle, "Notes sur les poésies de Baudri, Abbé de Bourgeuil," *Romania* 1 (1872): 23–50; for texts, see *PL* 146:1181–1208; on Baudri, see *DHGE* 6:1434–37; on Marbod, see *LTK* 6:864; for texts, *PL* 171:1465–1780; for Hilary, see *PL* 171:1381–1463. A general discussion of this period is found in Helen Waddell, *The Wandering Scholars* (London, 1927). Ernst R. Curtius, *European Literature and the Latin Middle Ages,* trans. W. Trask (New York, 1963), pp. 113–18, contains a discussion of sodomy in twelfth-century poetry. See D. Duemmler, "Zur Sittengeschichte des Mittelalters," *Zeitschrift für deutsches Altertum* 22 (1878): 256–58, which gives some examples of sodomy in Latin poetry and notes a twelfth-century poem, *De Sodomita prelato,* which I have not seen.

10. Guibert of Nogent, *Self and Society in Medieval France: The Memoirs of Guibert of*

*Nogent (1064?–c.1125),* ed. John F. Benton, trans. C. C. Swinton Bland (New York, 1970), pp. 51, 82, 87, 94.

11. R. Lavaud, "Éclaircissements sur la vie et l'oeuvre d'Arnaut Daniel," *Annales du midi* 23 (1911): 5–31; cf. Denis de Rougement, *Love in the Western World,* trans. Montgomery Belgion (New York, 1974), pp. 98–99; R. Lavaud, "Les Poésies d'Arnaut Daniel: Texte d'après Canello," *Annales du midi* 22 (1910): 21-25; Rene Nelli, *L'Érotique des troubadours* (Toulouse, 1963); R. S. Briffault, *The Troubadours,* trans. L. F. Koons (Bloomington, 1965).

12. Mansi, 19:741; Guibert of Nogent, *Memoirs,* pp. 18, 212.

13. Bernard of Clairvaux, *Sermones in Cantica,* c. 66, in *PL* 183:1095.

14. Christine Thouzellier, *Catharisme et Valdéisme en Languedoc à la fin du xii*[e] *et au début du xiii*[e] *siècle,* 2d rev. ed. (Louvain, 1969), pp. 81–92; Rene Nelli, *La Vie quotidienne des Cathares du Languedoc au xii*[e] *siècle* (Paris, 1969), pp. 60–62; Arno Borst, *Les Cathares,* trans. Ch. Roy (Paris, 1974), 150 ff; M.-H. Vicaire, "Les Cathares albigeois vus par les polémistes," in *Cathares en Languedoc: Cahiers de Fanjeaux,* vol. 3 (Toulouse, 1968), p. 125.

15. *Tractatus de hereticis,* c. 1, in A. Dondaine, "La Hiérarchie cathare en Italie," *Archivum fratrum praedicatorum* 20 (1950):310; Peter of Vaux-de-Cernay, *Hystoria albigensis,* ed. P. Guebin and E. Lyon, 3 vols. (Paris, 1926–1939), 1:1–3.

16. Étienne de Fougères, *Le Livre de manières,* in Ch. V. Langlois, *La Vie en France au moyen âge de la fin du xii*[e] *au milieu du xiv*[e] *siècle,* 4 vols. (Paris, 1924), 2:10; P. Viollet, ed., *Les Établissements de Saint Louis,* 4 vols. (Paris, 1881–1886), 2:50; Matthew Paris, *Chronica majora,* ed. H. R. Luard, 7 vols., Rolls Series, vol. 57 (London, 1857), 5:513; for further linguistic examples, see Fréderic Godefroy, *Dictionnaire de l'ancienne langue française,* 10 vols. (Paris 1880–1902), 4:465 (*herite*), 1:698 (*bougeron*); *Oxford English Dictionary,* 13 vols. (Oxford, 1933–1970), 1:1160.

17. Gordon Leff, *Heresy in the Later Middle Ages,* 2 vols. (Manchester, 1967), 2:714, 721; Robert E. Lerner, *The Heresy of the Free Spirit in the Later Middle Ages* (Berkeley, 1972), p. 117; A. Segarizzi, ed., *Historia fratris Dulcini heresiarche,* in *RIS,* vol. 9, pt. 5, p. 53; Salimbene de Adam, *Cronica,* ed. O. Holder-Egger, in *MGHS* 32:287.

18. Edmond Martène and Ursinus Durand, eds., *Veterum scriptorum et monumentorum . . . collectio,* 9 vols. (Paris, 1724), 9:950; Ignaz von Dollinger, ed., *Beiträge zur Sektengeschichte des Mittelalters,* 2 vols. (Munich 1890), 2:206, 371–372; Henry Charles Lea, *A History of the Inquisition of the Middle Ages,* 3 vols. (London, 1963), 1:9, 2:335.

19. Quoted in John H. Mundy, *Europe in the High Middle Ages 1150–1309* (London, 1973), p. 24; cf. also Alexander of Roes, *Schriften,* ed. H. Grundmann and H. Heimpel (Stuttgart, 1958), pp. 160–161; A. de Montaiglon and G. Raynaud, eds., *Recueil général et complet des fabliaux des xiii*[e] *et xiv*[e] *siècles,* 6 vols. (Paris, 1872–1890), 2:81.

20. Walter Mapes, *De Nugis curialium,* ed. Thomas Wright, Cambridge Society Publications, vol. 50 (London 1850), p. 33.

21. James of Vitry, *Historia orientalis* (Douai, 1597), p. 278.

22. Antonio Beccadelli [Panormita], *Hermaphroditus* (Coburg, 1824), 2:6; Iwan Bloch, *Die Prostitution,* 2 vols. (Berlin, 1912), 1:798 ff.

23. Mansi, 27:683 ff; Pierre de Langtoft, *Chronicle,* ed. Thomas Wright, 2 pts., Rolls Series, vol. 47 (London, 1866–1868), 1:347, on Boniface VIII.

24. J. R. Maddicott, *Thomas of Lancaster, 1307–1322* (Oxford, 1970), p. 83; Chalfont Robinson, "Was Edward II a Degenerate?" *American Journal of Insanity,* 66 (1910):445–65; George L. Haskins, ed., "A Chronicle of the Civil War of Edward II," *Speculum* 14 (1939): 73–81; N. Denholm-Young, ed., *Vita Edwardi secundi* (London, 1957), pp. 1, 2, 27–28.

25. Cited in Anonymous Norwegian scholar, "Spuren von Kontrarsexualität bei den alten Skandinaviern," *Jahrbuch für sexuelle Zwischenstufen* 4 (1902):245.

26. Eletto Palandri, "Andrea de' Mozzi nella storia e nella leggenda," *Giornale dan-*

*tesco* 32 (1929): 93–118; P. Fiorelli, "Accorso," *Dizionario biografico degli italiani,* 17 vols. (Rome, 1960–1974), 1:116–120; A. d'Addario, "Adimari Tegghiaio," *Dizionario biografico degli italiani, 17* vols. (Rome, 1960), 1:281; Undine Freiin von Verschuer, "Die Homosexuellen in Dantes *Gottlicher Komodie," Jahrbuch für sexuelle Zwischenstufen* 8 (1906): 353–63. The persons punished for sodomy by Dante are the Guelph politicians Count Guido Guerra, Tegghiaio Aldobrandi di Adimari, and Jacopo Rusticucci, who had a reputation for being married to a shrewish wife; the poets Priscian, Brunetto Latini, Arnaut Daniel, and Guido Guinicelli; the bishop of Florence Andrea dei Mozzi; and the jurist Accursius. Richard Kay, "The Sin of Brunetto Latini," *Medieval Studies* 31 (1969): 262–86, argues convincingly that these people are not being punished for sodomy but rather for acts against nature by serving themselves rather than God's natural scheme. For, in fact, no other source links any of these figures with sodomy.

27. The material on the Templars is overwhelming and continues to be produced. I have relied on George Lizerand, ed., *Le Dossier de l'affaire des Templiers* (Paris, 1964), which contains a good introduction and selection of the most important contemporary documents.

28. Lodovico Frati, *La Vita privata di Bologna dal secolo xiii al xvii* (Bologna, 1900), pp. 81–82.

29. G. Ruggiero, "Sexual Criminality in the Early Renaissance: Venice 1338–1358," *Journal of Social History* 8 (1975): 18–37, while concentrating on rape cases, which were not handled severely and resulted in lower penalties for the nobility, gives several examples of indictment for sodomy. See also Antonio Lombardo, ed., "Le Deliberazione del consiglio del XL della repubblica di Venezia," *Deputazione di storia partria per le Venezie* 9 (1957): 13–14, for trials; cf. also Stanley Chojnacki, "Crime, Punishment, and the Trecento Venetian State," in *Violence and Civil Disorder in Italian Cities,* ed. Lauro Martines, (Berkeley, 1972), pp. 184–228.

30. Bloch, *Die Prostitution,* 1:794–804, contains an excellent summary of the laws and trials for sodomy in Venice in the fifteenth century.

31. Justus Hashagen, "Aus Kölner Prozessakten: Beiträge zur Geschichte der Sittenzustände in Koln im 15. und 16. Jahrhundert," *Archiv für Kulturgeschichte* 3 (1905): 301–21, for reports of the Cologne clergy. The nearly contemporary case of Richard Puller of Hohenburg, accused of sodomy and heresy in the late fifteenth century, is documented in Karl Heinrich Ulrichs, "Ein homosexueller Ritter des 15. Jahrhunderts," *Jahrbuch für sexuelle Zwischenstufen* 12 (1912), 207–30.

32. Louis Crompton, *Gay Genocide: From Leviticus to Hitler,* forthcoming (in *The Gay Academic*).

33. James A. Brundage, "Prostitution in the Medieval Canon Law," *Signs* 1 (1976): 825–45; *idem,* "Concubinage and Marriage in Medieval Canon Law," *Journal of Medieval History* 1 (1975):1–17; Barbara Kellum, "Infanticide in England in the Later Middle Ages," *History of Childhood Quarterly* 1 (1973): 367–88.

34. William Saffady, "Fears of Sexual License during the English Reformation," *History of Childhood Quarterly* 1 (1973): 89–97.

35. Emmanuel Le Roy Ladurie, *Montaillou, village occitan de 1294 à 1324* (Paris, 1975), pp. 209–41.

36. Otloh of St. Emmeram, *Liber de cursu spirituali,* p. 232; *idem, Liber de suis tentationibus . . . ,* in *PL* 146: 47–50; v. Jean Leclercq, "Modern Psychology and the Interpretation of Medieval Texts," *Speculum* 48 (1973), 476–90.

37. On Equitius, see *DHGE* 25:659; *AS,* 7 March 1:647–50.

38. John of Lodi, *Vita Petri Damiani,* in *AS,* 23 February 3:424.

39. Peter the Venerable, *De Miraculis* 1:4, in *PL* 189:80.

40. *PL* 215:189.

41. Ilene Forsyth, "Children in Early Medieval Art: Ninth through Twelfth Cen-

tury," *The Journal of Psychohistory* 4 (1976): 31–70.

42. *PL* 150:939 ff; Edmond Martène, ed., *De Antiquis monachorum ritibus* (Bassano, 1788), p. 230.

43. Eadmer, *Vita sancti Anselmi,* ed. and trans. R. W. Southern (London, 1962), pp. 37–40.

44. Bonaventure, *Regula novitiorum,* 7:1, in *Opera omnia,* ed. PP. Collegii S. Bonaventurae, 10 vols. (Quaracchi, 1948), 8:483.

45. John of Lodi, *Vita Petri Damiani.*

46. The following is based largely on Robert Bultot, *La Doctrine du mépris du monde,* 6 vols. (Louvain, 1963), 4:1, 100–110; see also Mary McLaughlin, "Survivors and Surrogates: Children and Parents from the Ninth to the Thirteenth Centuries," in *The History of Childhood,* ed. Lloyd de Mause (New York, 1974), pp. 103–04.

47. Philip E. Slater, *Microcosm* (New York, 1966), 7 ff; Ray E. Helfer and C. Henry Kempe, eds., *The Battered Child* (Chicago, 1968).

48. Georges Duby, "Structure de parenté et noblesse dans la France du Nord aux xi$^{e}$ et xii$^{e}$ siècles," in *Hommes et structures du moyen âge* (Paris, 1973), pp. 267–85; *idem, Rural Economy and Country Life in the Medieval West,* trans. C. Postan (London, 1968); B. H. Slicher van Bath, *The Agrarian History of Western Europe,* trans. O. Ordish (London, 1963), 78 ff; Josiah C. Russell, *Late Ancient and Medieval Population* (Philadelphia, 1958), 125 ff., on France.

49. On the introduction of primogeniture and its effects on the family, see Robert Boutruche, *Seigneurie et féodalité,* 2 vols. (Paris, 1970), 2:224–34; F. Pollock and F. W. Maitland, *The History of English Law before the Time of Edward I,* 2nd ed., 2 vols. (Cambridge, 1968), 2:262–74; Ranulf de Glanvill, *Tractatus de legibus consuetudinibus regni Angliae,* ed. G. D. Hall (London, 1965), p. 75; K. Schmid, "Zur Problematik von Familie, Sippe, und Geschlecht: Haus und Dynastie beim mittelalterlichen Adel," *Zeitschrift für die Geschichte des Oberrheins* 107 (1957): 1–62; L. Lancaster, "Kinship in Anglo-Saxon England," *British Journal of Sociology* 8 (1958): 230–50, 359–77.

50. For the creation of youth groups, see G. Duby, *The Early Growth of the European Economy,* ed. and trans. H.B. Clark (London, 1973), pp. 36, 79, 171, 184–85, and *idem,* "In Northwestern France: The Youth in Twelfth-Century Aristocratic Society," in *Lordship and Community in Medieval Europe,* ed. Frederic L. Cheyette, (New York, 1968), 198–209. For valuable material describing the ethos that pervaded these youthful bands, drawn from medieval French romances, see P. Guilhermoz, *Essai sur l'origine de la noblesse en France au moyen âge* (Paris, 1902), pp. 242–48, 471.

51. Lawrence Stone, *The Crisis of the Aristocracy* (Oxford, 1965), p. 669, notes the shift away from parental authority in late sixteenth- and early seventeenth-century England; p. 666 notes the prevalence of homosexuality at the Tudor and Stuart courts; 66 ff. notes the vast increase in the number of peers, reduction of land holdings, the high fertility, and high rate of land turnover. Cf. also Jane K. Breitscher, "'As a Twig Is Bent . . .': Children and Their Parents in an Aristocratic Society," *Journal of Medieval History* 2 (1976): 181–91.

52. Orderic Vitalis, *Historia ecclesiastica,* 6; Guibert of Nogent, *Memoirs,* pp. 146–50, on the adulterous, amoral group surrounding Enguerrand of Boves; Paul Meyer, ed., *Histoire de Guillaume le Maréchal,* 3 vols. (Paris, 1891–1901).

# Chapter II

1. On the debasement of the clergy, see Émile Amann and Auguste Dumas, *L'Église au pouvoir des laïques (888–1057)* (Paris, 1948), 476 ff; for attacks on clerical mores, see Gabriel Le Bras, *Institutions écclésiastiques de la Chrétienté mediévale,* 2 pts. (Paris, 1959), 1:163 ff; Augustin Fliche, *La Réforme grégorienne et la réconquête chrétienne (1057–1123)* (Paris, 1950).

2. Philip Jaffé, ed., *Bibliotheca rerum germanicarum,* 6 vols. (Berlin, 1869), 5:114–22, for text; cf. Fliche, *La Réforme grégorienne,* pp. 29–30, 102.

3. On the canons, see Le Bras, *Institutions écclésiastiques,* 1:179; Ch. Dereine, "Chanoines," *DHGE* 12:353–405; P. Torquebiau, "Chapitres des chanoines," *DDC* 3:530–95; *idem,* "Chanoines," *DDC* 3:471–88.

4. Henry Charles Lea, *A History of the Inquisition of the Middle Ages,* 3 vols. (London, 1963), 1:31.

5. Anselm of Lucca, *Collectio canonum,* ed. F. Thaner (Innsbruck, 1906), bks. 10, 11; Fliche, *La Réforme grégorienne,* 462 ff.

6. On Regino, see R. Naz, "Reginon de Prüm," *DDC* 7:533–36; for the text of his work, see Regino of Prüm, *Reginonsis libri duo de synodalibus causis et disciplinis ecclesiasticis,* in *PL* 132:175–400 (331 ff. on sodomy); for another edition, see J. F. Schannat and J. Hartzheim, eds., *Concilia germaniae,* 3 vols. (Cologne, 1760), 2:438–532.

7. Cuthbert H. Turner, ed., *Ecclesiae occidentalis monumenta juris antiquissima,* 2 vols. (Oxford, 1899–1939), 2:19; Mansi, 2:526.

8. Mansi, 2:16.

9. *Codex Theod.* IX. 7. 6. (For the manner of citing Roman law, V. G. Mollat, "Corpus iuris civilis," *DDC* 4:680–81.)

10. For such earlier penitentials, see, e.g., F. W. H. Wasserschleben, ed., *Die Buss-ordnungen der abendländischen Kirche* (Dublin, 1963), which contains most of the earlier material. V. also John T. Noonan, Jr., *Contraception* (Cambridge, Mass., 1966), 152 ff., which contains a wealth of information on sexual mores and theory in the Middle Ages; John T. McNeill and Helena M. Gamer, *Medieval Handbooks of Penance* (New York, 1938), contains translations of some of the penitential material.

11. *MGH. Leges,* 1:61 (Regino 2:257, 258).

12. *MGH. Leges,* 2:259 (Isidore of Seville, *Excerpta canonum. V. De diversitatibus nuptiarum et scelere flagitiorum,* Tit. xiii & Tit. xiv, in *PL* 84:76).

13. R. Naz, "Droit germanique," *DDC* 4:1495–1502; and *idem,* "Droit romaine," *DDC* 4:1502–14, on the unique legal situation that characterized the ninth, tenth, and eleventh centuries.

14. On Burchard, see G. Allemang, "Burchard de Worms," *DHGE* 10:1245–47; J. Petraux, "Burchard de Worms," *DDC* 2:1141–57; P. Fournier and G. Le Bras, *Histoire des collections canoniques en occident depuis les Fausses Décretales jusqu'au Décret de Gratien,* 2 vols. (Paris, 1931–1932), 1:365–431; for the text, see Burchard of Worms, *Decretum,* in *PL* 140:537 ff. Burchard provides the following penalties (cols. 924–33): 1) lesbian acts: three years for use of a dildo, seven years for two nuns, three years for two women; 2) anal intercourse: fifteen years if under twenty, twenty-five years if over twenty and married, until death if over fifty and married; 3) interfemoral: from one to three years, depending on frequency; 4) two brothers: fifteen years and abstention from meat; 5) oral intercourse: seven years or until end of life; 6) boys: ten days to two years, depending on offense. In addition, Burchard includes some vaguer prescriptions, one providing a

three-year penance for sodomy in general, another leaving the penalties to the discretion of the confessor.



15. See G. Bareille, "Saint Pierre Damien," *DTC* 4. 1:40–54; *AS* 23 February 3: 412–33.

16. *PL* 142:1411; Mansi, 19:737–39.

17. For the text, see Peter Damian, *Liber Gomorrhianus*, in *PL* 145:160–90. For epistles between the pope and Peter, see *PL* 145:150–55; *PL* 144:208–09; Mansi, 19:685–86. The sources used by Peter are discussed in J. Joseph Ryan, *Saint Peter Damian and His Canonical Sources* (Toronto, 1956), pp. 28–31. Ten or twelve years after the composition of the *Liber Gomorrhianus*, Peter addressed a letter to cardinals Hildebrand (later Gregory VII) and Stephen, asking them to intervene for the return of a certain manuscript still in the hands of Pope Alexander II, who had a rather liberal record in the treatment of sexual offenders. Quoting Suetonius's description of the immoralities of Tiberius Caesar, he charges that this work had been taken from him under false pretenses (see *PL* 114:270–72, *Epist.* 2.6). H. C. Lea, *A History of Sacerdotal Celibacy in the Christian Church*, 3d rev. ed., 2 vols. (New York, 1907), 1:219, suggests that the manuscript here referred to is the *Liber Gomorrhianus*, whose contents might cause grave scandal to the church.

18. E. Amann and L. Guizard, "Yves de Chartres," *DTC* 16.2:3626–40; Yves de Chartres, *Correspondance*, ed. J. Leclercq, 2 vols. (Paris, 1949), 1:290–97.

19. Yves de Chartres, *Decretum*, in *PL* 161:47–1022 (681–88 on sodomy).

20. *Ibid.*, 685–88.

21. For a general, but quite thorough, discussion of canon law, see "Corpus iuris canonici," *DDC* 4:610–43, which also explains the method of citation. On Gratian, see J. de Ghellinck, "Gratien," *DTC* 6.2:1731–51; J.-Fr. von Schulte, *Die Geschichte der Quellen und der Literatur des kanonischen Rechts von Gratian auf die Gegenwart*, 3 vols. (Stuttgart, 1875–1880), vols. 1 and 2, for the period up to and including Gratian; Fournier and Le Bras, *Histoire des collections canoniques*, vol., 2; for a good discussion of the sources, see the standard edition by Emil Friedberg and Emil Richter, eds., *Corpus juris canonici*, 2 vols. (Graz, 1959), vol. 1, *Prolegomena*.

22. C.32, q.7. c.11; Augustine, *De Adulterinis conjugiis*, I.9, in *idem*, *Oeuvres complètes*, ed. G. Combès, 37 vols. (Paris, 1960), 2:124 ff; also *De Bono conjugali*, pp 8–11, in *ibid.*, 40 ff; Yves of Chartres, *Decretum*, 9:110; Peter Lombard, *Sententiarum libri quattuor*, ed. PP. Collegii S. Bonaventurae, 2 vols. (Quaracchi, 1916), 4.38.

23. C.32, q.7. c.13; Augustine, *Confessions*, 3:8, in *PL* 32:689; Yves of Chartres, *Decretum*, 9:105; Peter Lombard, *Sententiarum libri quattuor*, 3. 16 (17). 3.

24. C.32, q.7. c.14; Augustine, *De Bono conjugali*, 8, in *PL* 40:379; Yves of Chartres, *Decretum*, 9:106; Peter Lombard, *Sententiarum libri quattuor*, 2. 16 (17). 31.

25. C.32, q.7. c.12; Ambrose, *Liber de Abrahamo*, 1:.6. 12, in *idem*, *Opera*, ed. C. Schenkel, *CSEL*, vol. 32, pt. 1, p. 537; Yves of Chartres, *Decretum*, 9:115.

26. *De Penitentia*. D.1, c.15; Peter Lombard, *Sententiarum libri quattuor*, 4. 14; *Digest* XIV. 11. 1. 2. ("Qui puero stuprum abducto ab eo vel corrupto comite persuaserit . . . punitur capite").

27. Peter Lombard, *Sententiarum libri quattuor*, 4. 39. 4; 4. 41. 4; on Peter, see J. de Ghellinck, "Pierre le Lombard," *DTC* 12.2:1941–2091; for another edition, see *PL* 192:519–964.

28. Alexander of Hales, *Glossa in quattuor libros Sententiarum Petri Lombardi*, 4 vols. (Quaracchi, 1930–1951), 4.38.16. His texts come from Augustine, *De Adulterinis conjugiis*, 1.9 (C.32, q.7. c.13) and Jerome, *Ad Amandum presbyterum*, Epist. 55.3, in *PL* 22:563

29. Alan of Lille, *De Planctu naturae*, in *PL* 210:431–82; V. also *idem*, *Anticlaudianus*, ed. R. Bossuat (Paris, 1955). On Alan, see M. Jacquin, "Alain de Lille," *DHGE* 1:1299–1304.

30. D. Duemmler, "Zur Sittengeschichte des Mittelalters," *Zeitschrift für deutsches Altertum* 22 (1878): 256–58.
31. I have used *Graz U.B.* 620, 180–234 (fols. 184r–184v on sodomy).
32. Alan of Lille, *Liber poenitentialis,* ed. Jean Longère, 2 vols. (Louvain, 1965), 2:110–11; *idem,* "Liber poenitentialis . . .," *Archives d'histoire doctrinale et littéraire du moyen âge* 32 (1965): 169–242; cf. also Odon Lottin, "Le Traité d'Alain de Lille sur les vertus, les vices, et les dons du Saint Esprit," *Medieval Studies* 11 (1950): 20–56 (p. 45 on the sin against nature).
33. For the text of Bartholomew's penitential, see A. Morey, *Bartholomew of Exeter, Bishop and Canonist* (Cambridge, 1937), pp. 235–237. His citations include the council of Ancyra statute (Yves of Chartres, *Decretum*, 9:88), and selections from Basil (Yves of Chartres, *Decretum,* 9:93), the *Roman Penitential* (Burchard of Worms, *Decretum,* 17:56) and the canons of Pope Martin on bestiality (Burchard of Worms, *Decretum,* 17:38, Yves of Chartres, *Decretum,* 9:109).
34. Beryl Smalley, *The Study of the Bible in the Middle Ages* (Oxford, 1952), 46 ff; G. W. H. Lampe, *The Cambridge History of the Bible,* 3 vols. (Cambridge 1969), 2:294 ff; An edition of Anselm of Laon's work, ascribed to Walafrid Strabo, appears in *PL* 113 and 114.
35. On Nicholas, see F. Vernet, "Lyre (Nicolas de)," *DTC* 9:1410–22; P. Glorieux, *Répertoire des maîtres en théologie de Paris au xiii*[e] *siècle,* 2 vols. (Paris, 1933, 1934), 2:215–31; Nicholas's work has been published in numerous editions. I have used Nicolas of Lyre, *Postilla super totam Bibliam,* 4 vols. (Strassbourg, 1492). The best edition of Nicholas and Anselm combined is Léandre de Saint Martin, ed., *Biblia sacra cum glossis ordinaria,* 6 vols. (Antwerp, 1634).
36. Derrick S. Bailey, *Homosexuality and the Western Christian Tradition* (London, 1955), 9 ff.
37. Gregory I, the Great, *Moralia,* 33:13, in *PL* 76:688; Augustine, *Quaestionum in Heptateuchem,* 1:42, in *PL* 36:559.
38. Gregory I the Great, *Liber regulae pastoralis,* 3:27, in *PL* 77:102–03.
39. Alcuin of York, *Interrogationes et responsiones in Genesem,* Inter. 183, in *PL* 100:541.
40. Bailey, *Homosexuality,* 53 ff.
41. Augustine, *De Civitate Dei,* 18:34, in *PL* 76:688.
42. Josephus, *Jewish Antiquities,* trans. and ed. H. St. J. Thackeray and Ralph Marcus, 9 vols. (London, 1966), 5:144.
43. Jerome, *Commentarium in Ezechiel,* 5:16, in *PL* 25:155; cf. also Rabanus Maurus, *Commentarium in Ezechiel,* 7:15, in *PL* 110:690–92.
44. In Wisdom 19:8, the Egyptians are also likened to the people of Sodom; Wisdom 10:8–9 describes the deceptive foliage of the Dead Sea, which was to become a metaphor for the vices of *luxuria.*
45. Rabanus Maurus, *Commentarium in Ecclesiasticum,* 4:2 ff., in *PL* 109:866 ff.
46. Augustine, *De Gratia et libero arbitrio,* 21, in *PL* 44:909; *idem, Contra Iulianum Pelagianum libri sex,* 3:20, in *PL* 44:722.

## Chapter III

1. Anselm of Canterbury, *Opera omnia,* ed. F. S. Schmitt, 6 vols. (Stuttgart, 1968), 3:169, 4:257, 365; William of Malmesbury, *Gesta pontificum anglorum,* ed. N. E. S. A. Hamilton, Rolls Series, vol. 52, (London, 1857), p. 120; Mansi, 20:1152; Augustin Fliche, *La Réforme grégorienne et la réconquête chrétienne (1057–1123)* (Paris, 1950), p. 340.
2. Reinhold Rohricht, *Regesta regni Hierosolymita mxcvii-mccxci* (Innsbruck, 1893–1904), p. 20; Mansi, 21:261-65.
3. M. le Comte Beugnot, ed., *Assizes de Jérusalem,* 2 vols., in *Historiens des croisades,* vols. 1 and 2 (Paris, 1841–1843), 1:210.
4. For text, see Joseph Alberigo et al., eds., *Conciliorum oecumenicorum decreta,* 3d ed. (Bologna, 1973), p. 191 (c. 7); Fliche, *La Réforme grégorienne,* pp. 390–93.
5. Alberigo, *Decreta,* pp. 198 (c. 7), 201 (c. 17). Cf. also Augustin Fliche, R. Foreville, and J. Rousset, *Du Premier concile du Latran à l'avènement d'Innocent III,* 2 pts. (Paris, 1948–1953) 1:69–71, 137–38.
6. Alberigo, *Decreta,* p. 217 (c. 11); Fliche et al., *Du Premier concile,* 2:156–74; X. V. 31. 4; C.32, q.7. c.13; X. III. 1. 8.
7. X. V. 31. 4.
8. *Decretales Gregorii Noni cum glossis edita ultima* (Venice, 15––), 1782–83; on Bernard, see Paul Ourliac, "Bernard de Parme ou de Botone," *DDC* 2:781–82.
9. Alberigo, *Decreta,* p. 242; X. III. 1. 13; Fliche, *La Réforme grégorienne,* pp. 199, 205.
10. This refers to the *Novellae* 77 and 141, in *Corpus iuris civilis,* Theodore Mommsen and Paul Krüger, eds., 3 vols. (Berlin, 1908–1914).
11. Marion Gibbs and Jane Lang, *Bishops and Reform 1215–1272* (Oxford, 1934), p. 159, on unsuccessful efforts to impose celibacy.
12. Mansi, 22:705, for Odo's statutes (1196); Odette Pontal, ed., *Les Statuts synodaux français du xiii*[e] *siècle. I. Les statuts de Paris et de l'Ouest (xiii*[e] *siècle)* (Paris, 1971), p. 62; *PL* 215:1433.
13. Pontal, *Les Statuts synodaux,* p. 62.
14. F. M. Powicke and C. R. Cheney, eds., *Councils and synods . . . ,* 2 vols. (Oxford, 1964.
15. Eudes of Rouen, *Register,* ed. J. F. O'Sullivan, trans. S. M. Brown (New York, 1964), p. 3.
16. Mansi, 22:910.
17. Edmond Martène and Ursinus Durand, eds., *Thesaurus novus anecdotorum,* 5 vols. (Paris, 1717), 4:380a; Pontal, *Les Statuts synodaux,* pp. 254, 208, 224.
18. D. S. Bailey, *Homosexuality and the Western Christian Tradition* (London, 1955), 97, on reserved sins. For a list of the reserved cases in the thirteenth century, see Pontal, *Les Statuts synodaux,* pp. 62, 224.
19. Ralph B. Pugh, *Imprisonment in Medieval England* (Cambridge, 1968), pp. 376–67, 381.
20. *Pentateuch with Targum Onkeles, Hapthorath, and Rashi's Commentary,* ed. and trans. M. Rosenbaum and M. Silberman, 5 vols. (New York, 1929–1934), Gen. 18:20 ff.
21. Louis M. Epstein, *Sex Laws and Culture in Judaism* (New York, 1948), pp. 64–67, 135; I. J., "Homosexuality," *Encyclopedia judaica,* 16 vols. (New York, 1971–1972), 8:961–62; cf. Harry Sperling and Maurice Simon, eds. and trans., *The Zohar,* 5 vols. (London, 1931), 1:344 ff.; Louis Ginzberg, *The Legends of the Jews,* trans. Henrietta Szold, 7 vols. (Philadelphia, 1910), *passim,* is filled with references to the Talmudic material.

22. Moses Maimonides, *Code. Book 5. The Book of Holiness,* trans. Louis Rabinowitz and Philip Grossman (New Haven, 1965), pp. 10, 13–15, 135, 145, 141–42.
23. Moses Maimonides, *Guide to the Perplexed,* trans. S. Pines, (Chicago, 1963), 3.49; *idem, Medical Aphorisms,* trans. Fred Rosner and Suessman Monter, 2 vols. (New York, 1970), *passim.*
24. Fred Rosner, *Sex Ethics in the Writings of Moses Maimonides* (New York, 1974), pp. 115, 122.
25. Abraham Hacohen of Lunel, *Orchoth Hayim* (Berlin, 1902), p. 106 [in Hebrew].
26. *Sefer Ha-hinukh,* ed. Aharon Halevi (Jerusalem, 1912), n. 209 [in Hebrew].

# Chapter IV

1. Augustin Fliche et al., *La Chrétienté romaine (1198–1274)* (Paris, 1950), 139 ff; A. Luchaire, *Innocent III,* 6 vols. (Paris, 1905–1908), vol. 6, on the council. For the text of conciliar decisions, see Joseph Alberigo et al., eds., *Conciliorum oecumenicorum decreta,* 3d ed. (Bologna, 1973), pp. 230–271; for a translation, see Harry Rothwell, ed., *Historical Documents, 1189–1327* (London, 1975), pp. 643–676.
2. Henri Maisonneuve, *Études sur les origines de l'Inquisition* (Paris, 1960), 229 ff., on early attempts to suppress heresy.
3. D. W. Robertson, "Frequency of Preaching in Thirteenth-Century England," *Speculum* 24 (1949): 376–88; Fliche, *La Chrétienté romaine,* pp. 203–04. In a letter of 18 January 1221, Honorius III noted that "the Lord has raised up the Dominican order so that they might evangelize the word of God, in the degradation of voluntary poverty, against destructive heresies and other fatal plagues" (Maisonneuve, *Études,* p. 246). This may be taken to include such crimes as sodomy and incest, which had already been defined as "fatal."
4. X. III. 1. 13.
5. X. III. 41. g; Fliche, *La Chrétienté romaine,* pp. 205–06.
6. *PL* 215:189.
7. For a general discussion of the *summa,* see P. Glorieux, "Sommes théologiques," *DTC* 14.2:2341–64. On the more specific *summae* on penitence, see P. Michaud-Quantin, "À propos des premiers *Summae confessorum,*" *Recherches de théologie ancienne et mediévale* 26 (1959): 264–306; P. Mandonnet, "Frères prêcheurs," *DTC,* 6.1:902; J. Dietterle, "Die *Summae confessorum* von ihren Anfänger an bis zu Silvester Prierias," *Zeitschrift für Kirchengeschichte* 24 (1903): 353–74, 520–48; 25 (1904): 248–72; 26 (1905): 59–81, 350–64; 27 (1906): 70–79, 166–88, 296–310, 431–42; 28 (1907): 401–31; P. Anciaux, *La Théologie du sacrement de pénitence aux laïques* (Louvain, 1949); A. Teetaert, *La Confession aux laïques dans l'Église latine depuis le vii^e siècle jusqu'au xiv^e siècle* (Paris, 1926).
8. Maisonneuve, *Études,* 248 ff., on the use of Dominicans in the Inquisition.
9. G. C. Capelle, *Autour du décret de 1210. III. Amaury de Bène* (Paris, 1932).
10. Caesarius of Heisterbach, *Dialogus de miraculorum,* ed. J. C. Strange, 2 vols. (Cologne, 1851), 1:304–307.
11. Peter Cantor, *Summa de sacramentis et animae consiliis,* ed. J. A. Dugauquier, in *Analecta mediaevalia namurcensia,* vols. 4, 7, 11, 16, 21 (Louvain, 1954–1967); Peter Cantor, *Verbum abbreviatum,* chap. 138, in *PL* 205:333–35; see also John W. Baldwin, *Masters, Princes, and Merchants: The Social Views of Peter the Chanter and His Circle,* 2 vols. (Princeton, 1970), 1:339, 2:229, on Raoul Ardent.
12. V. L. Kennedy, "The Handbook of Master Peter, Chancellor of Chartres," *Medieval Studies* 5 (1943): 1–38.
13. For the relevant texts, see *B. N. Nouv. Acq.* 232, fols. 137v, 146v, 139v, 155v. The treatise also includes the same definition of *luxuria,* including sodomy, found in earlier such manuals (see fol. 163r). Another member of Peter the Cantor's circle, Robert of Courson, notes that the church still permitted the elevation of sodomists to higher office. See V. L. Kennedy, "The Contents of Courson's *Summa,*" *Medieval Studies* 9 (1947): 81–107.
14. Robert of Flamborough, *Liber poenitentialis,* ed. J. J. Francis Firth (Toronto, 1971), 272 ff.
15. *Ibid.,* pp. 195–96.

16. *Ibid.*, p. 298; for Gregory the Great, *PL* 161:170–72.
17. Thomas of Chobham, *Summa confessorum*, ed. F. Broomfield (Louvain, 1968), pp. 398–403. Thomas's condemnatory citations are drawn from C.32, q.7 and Peter Lombard, *Libri IV Sententiarum*, 4. 38. 2. He also draws on Yves of Chartres, Bartholomew of Exeter, and Robert of Flamborough for his specific punishments.
18. *Ibid.*, p. 298.
19. Paul of Hungary, *Liber de poenitentia*, in *Bibliotheca casiniensis*, vol. 4 (Monte Cassino, 1880), pp. 191–215; see also R. Chabanne, "Paulus Hungarus," *DDC* 6:1270–76; Teetaert, *La Confession aux laïques*, p. 351.
20. Alan of Lille, *Anticlaudianus*, ed. R. Bossuat (Paris, 1955), 3:122 ff.
21. C.32, q.7. c.11–12.
22. C.24, q.1. c.21.
23. *Codex*. 9. 9. 30; *De poenit.* D.1, c.15; X. III. 2.
24. Paul here relies upon the *Glossa ordinaria* treatment of these passages in Ezekiel and Romans, which is the source of numerous quotations from Ambrose, Gregory, and other commentators. The four great vices are found in Genesis 19, Genesis 4, Ecclesiastes 25, and James 5.
25. On William, see *LTK* 10:890–91; *DTC* 6.2:1967–76; P. Anciaux, "Le Sacrement de pénitence chez Guillaume d'Auvergne," *Ephemerides theologicae lovaniensis* 24 (1948): 98–118. The relevant texts are found in William of Auvergne, *De Poenitentia* 19 and *De Legibus* 13, in *idem*, *Opera omnia*, 2 vols. (Paris, 1674), 2:232, 1:44.
26. Gregory the Great, *Moralia*, 33.13, in *PL* 76:688; *Glossa ordinaria*, in *PL* 112:128.
27. Thomas Aquinas, *Summa theologiae*, ed. Dominicans of Blackfriars, 60 vols. (Cambridge, 1964–1966), 2a.2ae.154.11–12.
28. Duns Scotus, *Commentarium super IV libros Sententiarum*, 2.7.1, in *Opera omnia*, ed. L. Wadding, 11 vols. (Lyons, 1639); Raymund of Penyaforte, *Summa de poenitentia* (Verona, 1744), p. 439; Alexander of Hales, *Glossa in quattuor libros Senteniarum Petri Lombardi*, 4 vols. (Quaracchi, 1930–1951), 4.38.16; Vincent of Beauvais, *Speculum maius*, 4 vols. (Douai, 1624), 2:916–917, 3:1372. As the most readily available encyclopedia of the period, Vincent's work was an effective means of transmitting scholastic philosophy to a wider audience.
29. William Peraldus, *Summa de virtutibus et vitiis*, 2 vols. (Lyons, 1668), 1:21–22.
30. John of Freiburg, *Summa confessorum* (Augsburg, 1476), 4:34; see *DTC* 8.1:761–62, on John. Another widely disseminated *Summa confessorum* in alphabetical order was composed by Bartholomaeus of Pisa. Sodomy is treated under *luxuria*, which contains the standard gradation of sins, and under *sodomia*, which defines the vice and provides appropriate penance. Cf. Nicolaus de Ausmo, *Supplementum Summae Pisanellae* (Nuremburg, 1478), fols. 164v–165v, 270r.
31. *Sefer Ha-hinukh*, ed. Aharon Halevi (Jerusalem, 1912), cc. 200, 201.
32. Thomas of Chobham, *Summa confessorum*, pp. 401–03; cf. Robert of Flamborough, *Liber poenitentialis*, pp. 229–31; Bartholomew of Exeter, *Liber poenitentialis*, pp. 235–36; Yves of Chartres, *Decretum*, 9:88, 90, 107, 108, in *PL* 161:681, 686; Burchard of Worms, *Decretum*, 17:38 in *PL* 140:926.
33. Burchard of Worms, *Decretum*, vol. 17, cc. 40, 41, 43.
34. Gregory the Great, *Epist.* 11.4.64, in *PL* 77:1198–1200.
35. Thomas of Chobham, *Summa confessorum*, pp. 330–33; Bartholomew of Exeter, *Liber poenitentialis*, p. 269; Bede, *Historia ecclesiastica*, 11.14, in *PL* 95:66–68; Gratian, *Decretum*, D.6, c.1; Yves of Chartres, *Decretum*, cc. 111, 113; Peter Celestine, "L 'Autobiografia' di Pietro Celestino," in *Celestiniana*, ed. Arsenio Frugoni (Rome, 1954), pp. 62–63.
36. Burchard of Worms, *Decretum*, cc. 40–41; John of Lodi, *Vita Petri Damiani*, in *AS*, 23 February 3:424.
37. Thomas Aquinas, *Summa theologiae*, 2a.2ae.154.5; Peter Celestine, "L 'Autobiografia' di Pietro Celestino," pp. 62–63.

38. Thomas of Chobham, *Summa confessorum,* pp. 212–218; cf. Alan of Lille, *Liber poenitentialis,* in *PL* 210:245.

39. Hippolyte Delehaye, "Les Lettres d'indulgence collectives," *Analecta Bollandiana* 44 (1926):342–79, 45 (1927): 97–123, 323–44, 46 (1928): 149–57, 287–343; E. Jombart, "Indulgences," *DDC* 5:1331–52; Thomas P. Oakley, "Alleviations of Penance in the Continental Penitentials," *Speculum* 12 (1937): 488–502; for the penitential prescriptions, see Robert of Flamborough, *Liber poenitentialis,* pp. 375–77; see also R. Naz, "Dispense," *DDC* 4:1284-96.

# Chapter V

1. Peter Landau, *Die Entstehung des kanonischen Infamiebegriffs von Gratian bis zur Glossa ordinaria* (Cologne, 1966), 48 ff.
2. Ranulf Higden, *Polychronicon*, ed. J. R. Lumby, 9 vols., Rolls Series, vol. 41 (London, 1869), 3:4–5; Robert Manning of Brunne, *The Story of England*, ed. F. J. Furnivall, 2 vols., Rolls Series, vol. 87 (London, 1887), 2:500.
3. F. L. Attenborough, ed., *The Laws of the Earliest English Kings* (Cambridge, 1922), *passim*.
4. F. Liebermann, ed., *Die Gesetze der Angelsachsen*, 3 vols. (Halle, 1903–1916), 1:39.
5. Katherine F. Drew, ed. and trans., *The Lombard Laws* (Philadelphia, 1973), 197–98, 201–02; *MGH. Leges*, 4:158.
6. P. D. King, *Law and Society in the Visigothic Kingdom* (Cambridge, 1972), 122 ff., on legislation.
7. *MGH. Leges*, 1:61, 78–79, 203, 160–61, 201, 255; Mansi, 17:368, 526.
8. Mansi, 17:1101, 1143–44.
9. M. M. Postan, ed., *Cambridge Economic History of Europe. I. The Agrarian Life of the Middle Ages* (Cambridge, 1966), 69 ff.
10. *Cod. Theod.* IX. 7. 3. (*Cod. Just.* IX. 9. 31).
11. *Cod. Theod.* IV. 18. 4.
12. *Inst.* IV. 18. 4.
13. *Novellae* 77.
14. *Novellae* 141.
15. Azo, *Lectura super Codicem*, in *Corpus glossatorum juris civilis*, ed. M. Viora, 10 vols. (Turin, 1966–1969), 3:691.
16. Accursius, *Glossa in Digestum novum*, in *Corpus glossatorum juris civilis*, ed. M. Viora, 10 vols. (Turin, 1968), 9:430.
17. Landau, *Die Entstehung*, p. 139, for Huguccio's opinion.
18. Henri Maisonneuve, *Études sur les origines de l'Inquisition* (Paris, 1960), 233 ff.
19. F. Pollock and F. W. Maitland, *The History of English Law before the Time of Edward I*, 2d ed., 2 vols. (Cambridge, 1968), 2:556, 543.
20. A. Duboys, *Du Droit criminel de l'Espagne* (Paris, 1870), p. 43; Julio Caro Baroja, "Honour and the Devil," in J. G. Peristany, ed., *Honour and Shame: The Values of Mediterranean Society* (Chicago, 1970), pp. 79–137, discusses the disabilities suffered by perpetrators of infamous crimes like sodomy.
21. P. Viollet, ed., *Les Établissements de Saint Louis*, 4 vols. (Paris, 1881–1886), 3:50, 2:147; P. N. Rapetti, ed., *Li Livres de jostice et de plet* (Paris, 1850), pp. 12–13, 215–16; Phillippe de Beaumanoir, *Les Coutumes de Beauvaisis*, ed. A. Salmon, 2 vols. (Paris, 1970), 1:431.
22. M. le Comte Beugnot, ed., *Les Olim ou Régistres des arrêts rendus par la cour du roi*, in *Documnets in édits* . . ., ser. 1, vol. 28 (Paris, 1839), pt. 1, pp. 988–989; pt. 3, p. 572.
23. *Ibid.*, pt. 1, p. 136.
24. *Ibid.*, pt. 8, pp. 1202–04.
25. G. de Lagarde, *La Naissance de l'esprit laïque*, 5 vols. (Louvain, 1956), 1:174–83.
26. A. Vauchez, "Une Campagne de pacification en Lombardie autour de 1233," *Mélanges d'archéologie et d'histoire* 78 (1966): 503–49.
27. Eric Erikson, "Ego Development and Historical Change," *Psychoanalytic Development of the Child* 9 (1946): 369.

28. See my "A Profile of Thirteenth-Century Sainthood," *Comparative Studies in Society and History* 18 (1976): 429–37, for a prosopographical study of leading thirteenth-century mendicant figures.
29. G. G. Meersseman, "Études sur les anciennes confréries dominicaines," *Archivum fratrum praedicatorum* 20 (1950): 5–115; 21 (1951): 51–196; 22 (1952): 5–176.
30. John R. H. Moorman, *A History of the Franciscan Order* (Oxford, 1968), pp. 40–45, 216–25.
31. J. K. Hyde, *Society and Politics in Medieval Italy* (London, 1973), pp. 104–18.
32. C. Fasoli and P. Sella, eds., *Statuti di Bologna dell' anno 1288,* 2 vols., in *Studi e testi,* vols. 73 and 85 (Rome, 1937–1939), 2:195; L. Frati, ed., *Statuti di Bologna dell' anno 1245 all' anno 1267,* 3 vols. (Bologna, 1869–1877), 3:408, 447; see also L. Frati, *La Vita privata di Bologna dal secolo xiii al xvii* (Bologna, 1900), pp. 81–82, which notes that burning was the punishment for sodomy, rape, infanticide, and heresy.
33. Meersseman, "Études," 22 (1952):90.
34. Mansi, 18:569.
35. G. Degli Azzi, ed., *Statuti di Perugia dell' anno mccxlii,* in *CSI,* vols. 4 and 9 (Rome, 1914–1916), 9:79–80.
36. G. Dahm, *Das Strafrecht Italiens im ausgehenden Mittelalter* (Berlin, 1931), p. 439.
37. *Statuta civitatis Cremonae* (Cremona, 1578), p. 31; *Statuta urbis Ferrarae* (Ferrara, 1567), fol. 151v; E. Anderloni and P. Sella, eds., *Statuti del Lago Maggiore . . .,* in *CSI,* vol. 6, 2 pts. (Rome, 1914), 2:125.
38. L. Zdekauer and P. Sella, eds., *Statuti di Ascoli Piceno dell' anno mcclxxvii* (Rome, 1910), p. 88.
39. F. Bonaini, ed., *Statuti inediti della città di Pisa dal xii al xiv secolo,* 3 vols. (Florence, 1854–1870), 1:384; Fasoli, *Bologna,* 2:196.
40. *Statutorum magnificae civitatis Paduae libri sex,* 2 vols. (Venice, 1767), 2:204; Dahm, *Das Strafrecht Italiens,* p. 440: *Statuto del commune di Lucca dell' anno mcccvii* (Lucca, 1867), p. 230; E. Rinaldi, ed., *Statuti di Forlì dell' anno mcclix con le modificazioni del mcclxxiii,* in *CSI,* vol. 5 (Rome, 1913), p. 208.
41. Bonaini, *Pisa,* 1:364.
42. Degli Azzi, *Perugia,* 2:79–80.
43. R. Davidsohn, *Geschichte von Florenz,* 4 vols. (Berlin, 1896–1927), vol. 4, pt. 3, p. 320.
44. R. Caggese, ed., *Statuti della Repubblica florentina: Statuto del podestà dell' anno 1325* (Florence, 1921), pp. 218–219; Matthaeus de Griffonibus, *Memoriale historicum de rebus Bononensium,* ed. L. Frati and A. Sorbelli, in *RIS,* vol. 18, pt. 2 (Citta di Castello, 1902), p. 42.
45. Rinaldi, *Forlì,* pp. 208, 222.
46. L. Landucci, *A Florentine Diary,* ed. and trans. A. Jervis (London, 1927), pp. 77, 201, 218.
47. L. Zdekauer, ed., *Il Constituto del Commune di Siena dell' anno 1262* (Milan, 1897), pp. 52, 251; *idem,* "Il Frammento degli ultimi due libri del più antico constituto senese (1262–1270)," *Bulletino senese di storia patria* 3 (1896): 86; see also William Bowsky, "The Medieval Commune and Internal Violence: Police Power and Public Safety in Siena, 1287–1355," *American Historical Review* 73 (1967): 1–17.
48. Leopold August Warnkönig, *Flandrische Staats- und Rechtsgeschichte bis zum Jahr 1305,* 3 vols. (Tübingen, 1839), vol. 3, pt. 2, pp. 76–77.
49. See Siena, *Archivio di Stato,* CG. 101, fols. 84r–91v; *Statuti,* Siena. 23, fols. 116r–120r.
50. M. Mollat and P. Wolff, *The Popular Revolutions of the Late Middle Ages,* trans. A. L. Lytton-Sells (London, 1973), *passim.*

# Appendix

1. On the Inquisition at Pamiers, see Jean Duvernoy, *Inquisition à Pamiers* (Toulouse, 1966); J.-M. Vidal, *Le Tribunal d'Inquisition de Pamiers* (Toulouse, 1906).
2. R. Chevalier, "Torture," *DDC* 7:1293–1314.
3. On Fournier, see J.-M. Vidal, ed., *Bullaire de l'Inquisition française au xiv*[e] *siècle* (Paris, 1913), p. 54; *DTC* 2:542-703.
4. The text of Arnold's trial comes from Jean Duvernoy, ed., *Le Régistre d'Inquisition de Jacques Fournier, évêque de Pamiers,* 3 vols. (Toulouse, 1965–1966), 3:14–50.
5. Heinrich Denifle, *Die Entstehung der Universitäten des Mittelalters bis 1400* (Berlin, 1885), pp. 638–639, on the University of Pamiers, which was confirmed as a *studium generale* 18 December 1295 by Pope Boniface VIII.
6. For the text of this discussion, see C. Douais, *L'Inquisition, ses origines—sa procedure* (Paris, 1906), pp. 294–307.
7. Thomas Aquinas notes that apostasy, or backsliding from God, in addition to rejection of the faith itself, may also involve withdrawal from the religious life to which one is bound by profession or from the holy orders that one has received. Because Arnold had apparently at one time been a member of the Franciscan order, he was called an apostate. See Thomas Aquinas, *Summa theologiae,* 2a.2ae.12.1.
8. A. Michel, "Sous-Diacre," *DTC* 14.2:2459–66.
9. The phrase here used, *ponere aliquid,* strictly means "to place a bet." But in this context, the above translation seems more plausible.
10. This passage is rather confusing. The scribe, because he was writing in the third person and using indirect discourse, appears to have had some difficulty separating one "he" from another.
11. The text gives the year 1321. Since all of the other testimony was given in June 1323, I presume this is a scribal error.
12. Pierre Recort, after ten years' detention, was condemned on 27 January 1329 to life imprisonment in irons, on a diet of bread and water, in the Carmelite monastery of Toulouse on charges of having seduced three women and on suspicion of sorcery. Fournier himself did not complete the case and seems to have been unsure about the man's guilt. It remained for his successor as bishop of Pamiers, Dominic Grima (1326–1348), and the inquisitors Henry de Chamay and Pierre Brun to complete the trial. See Vidal, *Bullaire,* pp. 53–54.
13. For a discussion of the sources relating to the antileper campaign, see J.-M. Vidal, *La Poursuite des lépreux en 1321,* 2 vols. (Toulouse, 1899–1900). This fantastic episode in the annals of obscurantist persecution is unraveled in the testimony of Guillaume Agassa before Fournier's court. In 1321, Agassa was accused of having taken part in the alleged plot by the king of Granada and the sultan of "Babylon," using the Jews as intermediaries, to get lepers to poison the wells of Christendom. As a result, a massacre of lepers was carried out throughout France. See Vidal, *Bullaire,* p. 53; Duvernoy, *Régistre,* 2:135–47, for Agassa testimony; Henry C. Lea, *A History of the Inquisition of the Middle Ages,* 3 vols. (London, 1963), 2:380.
14. Gaillard de Preyssac, bishop of Toulouse (1306–1317), subsequently served at Riez, Maguelonne, and Arles before his death in 1327. He was also a nephew of Pope Clement V.
15. Gaillard de Pomiès served as vicar or lieutenant to the bishop in matters pertaining to the Inquisition. See Vidal, *Inquisition,* pp. 74, 84.

16. For the trial of Raymund de Costa (or de la Cote-Saint-André) on charges of Waldensianism, see Duvernoy, *Registre,* 1: 40–122.

17. Since the term *frater* is used rather than *germanus,* and Arnold was formerly a Franciscan, it is not clear whether the brother here referred to is a biological relation or merely another member of the order.

18. For the popularity of Ovid's work in the Middle Ages, see Ernst R. Curtius, *European Literature and the Latin Middle Ages,* trans. W. Trask (New York, 1963); J. de Ghellinck, *L'Éssor de la littérature latine au xii$^{e}$ siècle,* 2 vols. (Paris, 1946).

19. *Cum glaubiis* ("with little balls") makes no sense. Perhaps this is a misspelling for *glaviis* ("knives").

20. Taken from *B.N.* Doat. 28, fols. 71r–76v.

# *Bibliography*

## Manuscripts

Alan of Lille. *Sermones de peccatis capitalibus.* Graz. U.B. 620, fols. 180–234.

Peter of Chartres. *Manuale de mysteriis.* Bibliothèque Nationale. Nouv. Acq., 232.

Siena. Archivio di Stato. *Statuti,* Siena. 23, fols. 116r–120r.

———. CG.101, fols. 84r–91v.

Bibliothèque Nationale. Fonds latins, Doat. 28, fols. 71r–76v.

## Primary Sources

Abraham Hacohen of Lunel. *Orchoth Chayim.* Berlin, 1902 [in Hebrew].

Accursius. *Glossa in Digestum novum.* In *Corpus glossatorum juris civilis,* ed. M. Viora, vol. 9. Turin, 1968.

Aelred of Rievaulx. *Opera omnia ascetica.* In *Corpus christianorum continuatio mediaevalia,* ed. A. Hoste and C. H. Talbot, vol. 1. Tournhout, Belgium, 1971.

———. *Speculum caritatis.* In *PL* 195:501–621.

———. *De spirituali amicitia.* In *PL* 195:659-702.

Aharon Halevi, ed. *Sefer Ha-Hinukh.* Jerusalem, 1912 [in Hebrew].

Alan of Lille. *Anticlaudianus.* Ed. R. Bossuat. Paris, 1955.

———. *The Complaint of Nature.* Trans. D. M. Moffat. New York, 1908.

———. *De Planctu naturae.* In *PL* 210:431–82.

———. "Liber poenitentialis." Ed. J Longpère. In *Archives d'histoire doctrinale et littéraire du moyen âge* 32 (1965):169–242.

———. *Liber poenitentialis.* Ed. J. Longpère. 2 vols. Louvain, 1965.

Alberigo, Joseph, et al., eds. *Conciliorum oecumenicorum decreta.* 3d ed. Bologna, 1973.

Alcuin. *Interrogationes et responsiones in Genesem.* In *PL* 100:515–66.

Alexander of Hales. *Glossa in quattuor libros Sententiarum Petri Lombardi.* 4 vols. Quaracchi, 1930–1951.

Alexander of Roes. *Schriften.* Ed. H. Grundmann and H. Heimpel. Stuttgart, 1958.

Ambrose. *Opera.* Ed. C. Schenkl. In *CSEL,* vol. 32, pt.1. New York, 1962.

Anderloni, E., and Sella, P., eds. *Statuti del Lago Maggiore . . .* 2 parts. In *CSI,* vol. 6. Rome, 1914.

Anselm of Canterbury. *Opera omnia.* Ed. F. S. Schmitt. 6 vols. Stuttgart, 1968.

Anselm of Laon. *Glossa ordinaria.* In *PL* 113, 114.

Anselm of Lucca. *Collectio canonum.* Ed. F. Thaner. Innsbruck, 1915.



Aquinas, Thomas. *Summa theologiae.* 42 vols. London, 1963–1974.

———. *Summa theologiae.* Ed. Dominicans of Blackfriars. 60 vols. Cambridge, 1964–1966).

Attenborough, F. L., ed. *The Laws of the Earliest English Kings.* Cambridge, 1922.

Augustine. *De Bono conjugali.* In *PL* 40:373–96.

———. *De Civitate Dei.* In *PL* 76:13–804.

———. *Confessiones.* In *PL* 32:659–868.

———. *Contra Iulianum Pelagianum libri sex.* In *PL* 44:641–874.

———. *De Gratia et libero arbitrio.* In *PL* 44:881–912.

———. *Oeuvres complètes.* Ed. G. Combès. 37 vols. Paris, 1960.

———. *Quaestionum in Heptateuchem.* In *PL* 34:547–824.

Azo. *Lectura super Codicem.* In *Corpus glossatorum juris civilis,* ed. M. Viora, vol. 3. Turin, 1968.

degli Azzi, G., ed. *Statuti di Perugia dell anno MCCCXLII.* In *CSI,* vols. 4, 9. Rome, 1914–1916.

Bartholomew of Exeter. *Liber Poenitentialis.* In *Bartholomew of Exeter, Bishop and Canonist,* ed. A. Morey, pp. 175–300. Cambridge, 1937.

Baudri de Bourgeuil. *Carmina.* In *PL* 166:1181–1208.

Beccadelli, Antonio [Panormita]. *Hermaphroditus.* Coburg, 1824.

Bede. *Historia ecclesiastica.* In *PL* 95:23–290.

Bernard of Clairvaux. *Sermones in Cantica.* In *PL* 183:785–1198.

Beugnot, M. le Comte, ed. *Assises de Jérusalem.* 2 vols. Paris, 1843.

———. *Les Olim ou Régistres des arrêts rendus par la cour du roi.* 3 vols. In *Documents inédits sur l'histoire de France,* vol. 28. Paris, 1839.

Bonaini, F., ed. *Statuti inediti della città di Pisa dal XII al XIV secolo.* 3 vols. Florence, 1854–1870.

Bonaventure. *Opera omnia.* Ed. PP. Collegii S. Bonaventurae. 10 vols. Quaracchi, 1968.

Bouquet, M., ed. *Recueil des historiens des Gaules et de la France.* 24 vols. Paris, 1738–1904.

Burchard of Worms. *Decretum libri XX.* In *PL* 140:537–1058.

Caesarius of Heisterbach. *Dialogus de miraculorum.* Ed. J. C. Strange. 2 vols. Cologne, 1851.

Caggese, R., ed. *Statuti della Repubblica fiorentina: Statuto del podestà dell' anno 1325.* Florence, 1921.

Capelle, G. C. *Autour du décret de 1210. III. Amaury de Bène.* Paris, 1932.

*Corpus glossatorum iuris civilis.* Ed. M. Viora et al. 10 vols. Turin, 1966–1969.

*Corpus iuris civilis.* Ed Theodore Mommsen and Paul Krüger. 3 vols. Berlin, 1908–1914.

———. Ed. and trans. S. P. Scott. 17 vols. Cincinnati, 1932.

*Corpus scriptorum ecclesiasticorum Latinorum.* 56 vols. Vienna, 1866–1932.

*Corpus statutorum italicorum.* Ed. Pietro Sella. 22 vols. Milan, 1912–1946.

Daniel, Walter. *The Life of Ailred of Rievaulx.* Ed. F. M. Powicke. London, 1963.

Dante Alighieri. *La Divina commedia.* Ed. C. H. Grandgent. Cambridge, Mass., 1972.

*Decretales Gregorii Noni cum glossis edita ultima.* Venice, 15––.

Denholm-Young, N., ed. *Vita Edwardi secundi.* London, 1957.

von Döllinger, I., ed. *Beiträge zur Sektengeschichte des Mittelalters.* 2 vols. Munich, 1890.

Dondaine, A. "La Hiérarchie cathare en Italie." *Archivum fratrum praedicatorum* 20 (1950):234–324.

Drew, K. F., ed. and trans. *The Lombard Laws.* Philadelphia, 1973.

Duns Scotus, John. *Opera omnia.* Ed. F.Lychetus. 11 vols. Lyons, 1639.

Duvernoy, J., ed. *Le Régistre d'Inquisition de Jacques Fournier.* 3 vols. Toulouse, 1965.

Eadmer. *Vita Anselmi,* ed. M. Rule. Rolls Series, vol. 81. London, 1884.

———. *Vita sancti Anselmi.* Ed. and trans. R. W. Southern. London, 1962.

Eudes of Rouen. *Register.* Ed. J. O'Sullivan, trans. Sidney Brown. New York, 1964.

Fasoli, G., and Sella, P., eds. *Statuti di Bologna dell' anno 1288.* 2 vols. Rome, 1937–1939.

Frati, L., ed. *Statuti di Bologna dell' anno 1245 all' anno 1267.* 3 vols. Bologna, 1869–1877.

Friedberg, Emil, and Richter, Emil, eds. *Corpus iuris canonici.* 2 vols. Leipzig, 1879–1881.

Gervase of Canterbury. *Chronica.* Ed. W. Stubbs. Rolls Series, vol. 73. London, 1880.

Glaber, Ralph. *Historiae sui temporis.* In *Recueil des historiens des Gaules et de la France,* vol. 10. Paris, 1738–1905.

Gratianus. *Decretum cum glossis.* Lyon, 1584.

Gregory the Great. *Epistolae.* In *PL* 77:441–1352.

Gregory the Great. *Liber regulae pastoralis.* In *PL* 77:9–126.

———. *Moralia.* In *PL* 75:509–1162, 76:9–782.

Guibert of Nogent. *Self and Society in Medieval France: The Memoirs of Abbot Guibert of Nogent (1064?–c. 1125).* Ed. John F. Benton. Trans. C. C. Swinton Bland. New York, 1970.

Guillaume de Nangis. *Chronique latine.* Ed. P. Gérard. 2 vols. Paris, 1843.

Hashagen, Justus. "Aus Kölner Prozessakten: Beiträge zur Geschichte der Sittenzustände in Köln im 15. und 16. Jahrhundert." *Archiv für Kulturgeschichte* 3 (1905):301–21.

Henricus de Segusio [Hostiensis]. *Summa aurea.* Ed. Nicolas Soranza. Lyon, 1537.

Henry of Huntingdon. *Historia anglorum.* Ed. T. Arnold. Rolls Series, vol. 74. London, 1879.

Hilary of Tours. *Carmina.* In *PL* 171:1381–1463.

Innocent III. *Opera omnia.* In *PL* 214–217.

Isidore of Seville. *Excerpta canonum.* In *PL* 84:25–92.

Jaffé, Philip, ed. *Bibliotheca rerum germanicarum.* 6 vols. Berlin, 1869.

James of Vitry. *Historia orientalis.* Douai, 1597.

Jerome. *Ad Amandum presbyterum.* In *PL* 22:560–65.

———. *Commentarium in Ezechiel.* In *PL* 25:15–490.

John of Freiburg. *Summa confessorum.* Augsburg, 1476.

John of Lodi. *Vita Petri Damiani.* In *AS,* 23 February 3:422–33.

John of Salisbury. *Frivolities . . .* Ed. J. B. Pike. Minneapolis, 1938.

Josephus. *Jewish Antiquities.* Trans. and ed. H. St. J. Thackeray and Ralph Marcus. 9 vols. London, 1966.

Kuhn, K. H., ed. and trans. *Pseudo-Shenorite on Christian Behavior.* In *Corpus christianorum orientalium,* vol. 207. Louvain, 1960.

Landucci, L. *A Florentine Diary.* Ed. A. Jervis. London, 1927.

Lizerand, Georges, ed. *Le Dossier de l'affaire des Templiers.* Paris, 1964.

Lavaud, R. "Les Poèsies d'Arnaut Daniel: Text d'après Canello." *Annales du midi* 22 (1910):20–55.

Liebermann, F., ed. *Die Gesetze der Angelsachsen.* 3 vols. Halle, 1903–1916.

Lombardo, Antonio, ed. "Le Deliberazione del consiglio del XL della repubblica di Venezia." *Deputazione di storia patria per le Venezie* 9 (1957):1–50.

Lottin, O. "Le Traité d'Alain de Lille sur les vertus, les vices, et les dons du Saint-Esprit." *Medieval Studies* 12 (1950):20–56.

Maimonides, Moses. *Code.* Ed. and trans. L. Rabinowitz and P. Grossman. 10 vols. New Haven, 1951–1965.

———. *Guide to the Perplexed.* Trans. S. Pines. Chicago, 1963.

———. *Medical Aphorisms.* Ed. and trans. Fred Rosner and S. Muntner. 2 vols. New York, 1970.

Mansi, G.D., ed. *Sacrorum conciliorum nova et amplissima collectio.* 59 vols. Florence, 1759–1767.

Mapes, Walter. *De Nugis curialium.* Ed. T. Wright. Camden Society, vol. 50. London, 1850.

Marbod of Rennes. *Carmina.* In *PL* 171:1465–1780.

Martène, Edmond, ed. *De Antiquis monachorum ritibus.* Bassano, 1788.

———, and Durand, V., eds. *Thesaurus novus anecdotorum.* 5 vols. Paris, 1717.

———. *Veterum scriptorum et monumentorum . . . collectio.* 9 vols. Paris, 1724.

Matthaeus de Griffonibus. *Memoriale historicum de rebus Bononensium.* Ed. L. Frati and A. Sorbelli. In *RIS,* vol. 18, pt. 2. Città di Catello, 1902.

Matthew Paris. *Chronica majora.* Ed. H. R. Luard. 7 vols. Rolls Series, vol. 57. London, 1857.

McLaughlin, Terence, ed. *The Summa Parisiensis on the Decretum Gratiani.* Toronto, 1952.

McNeill, John T., and Gamer, Helena M., eds. *Medieval Handbooks of Penance.* New York, 1965.

Meyer, Paul, ed. *Histoire de Guillaume le Maréchal.* 3 vols. Paris, 1891–1901.

Migne, J. P., ed. *Patrologiae cursus completus. Series latina.* 221 vols. Paris, 1841–1864.

de Montaiglon, A., and Raynaud, G., eds. *Recueil général et complet des fabliaux des xiii*[e] *et xiv*[e] *siècles.* 6 vols. Paris, 1872–1890.

*Monumenta germaniae historica. Leges.* 5 vols. Hanover, 1835–1889.

*Monumenta germaniae historica. Scriptores.* 32 vols. Hanover, 1826–1913.

Müllenhoff, Karl, and Scherer, Wilhelm, eds. *Denkmäler deutschen Poesie und Prosa aus dem viii-xii Jahrhundert.* 2 vols. Berlin, 1892.

Muratori, Ludovico, ed. *Rerum italicarum scriptores.* 34 vols. Città di Castello, 1900 ff.

Nicolaus de Ausmo. *Supplementum Summae Pisanellae.* Nuremberg, 1478.

Nicholas of Lyre. *Postilla super totam Bibliam.* 4 vols. Strassbourg, 1492.

Orderic Vitalis. *Historia ecclesiastica.* Ed. August Le Prevost. 5 vols. Paris, 1838–1855.

Othloh of St. Emmeram. *Liber de cursu spirituali.* In *PL* 146:139–242.

———. *Liber de suis tentationibus.* In *PL* 146:23–58.

Paul of Hungary. *Liber de poenitentia.* In *Bibliotheca casiniensis,* vol. 4, pp. 191–215. Monte Cassino, 1880.

Peckham, John. *Divinarum sententiarum.* Paris, 1513.

*Pentateuch with Targum Onkeles, Hapthorath, and Rashi's Commentary.* Ed. and trans. M. Rosenbaum and M. Silberman. 5 vols. New York, 1929–1934.

Peraldus, W. *Summa de virtutibus et vitiis.* 2 vols. Lyons, 1668.

Peter Cantor. *Summa de sacramentis et animae consiliis.* Ed. J. A. Dugauquier. 5 vols. Louvain, 1954–1967.

———. *Verbum abbreviatum.* In *PL* 205:22–554.

Peter Celestine. "L'Autobiografia di Pietro Celestino." In *Celestiniana,* Frugoni, Arsenio, ed., pp. 56–57. Rome, 1954.

Peter of Chartres. *Manuale.* In V. L. Kennedy, ed., "The Handbook of Master Peter, Chancellor of Chartres," *Medieval Studies* 5 (1943):1–38.

Peter Damian. *Liber Gomorrhianus.* In *PL* 145:159–90.

Peter Lombard. *Libri IV Sententiarum.* In *PL* 192:522–962.

———. *Sententiarum libri quattuor.* Ed. PP. Collegii S. Bonaventurae. 2 vols. Quaracchi, 1916.

Peter of Vaux-de-Cernay. *Hystoria albigensis.* Ed. P. Guébin and E. Lyon, 3 vols. Paris, 1926–1939.

Peter the Venerable. *De miraculis.* In *PL* 189:851–954.

Philippe de Beaumanoir. *Les Coutumes de Beauvaisis.* Ed. A. Salmon. 2 vols. Paris, 1970.

Pierre de Langtoft. *Chronicle.* Ed. Thomas Wright. 2 vols. Rolls Series, vol. 47. London, 1866–1868.

Pontal, Odette, ed. *Les Statuts synodaux francçais du XII e siècle. I. Les Statuts de Paris et l'Ouest (XII e siècle).* Paris, 1971.

Powicke, F. M., and Cheney, C. R., eds. *Councils and Synods.* 2 vols. Oxford, 1964.

Rabanus Maurus. *Commentarium in Ecclesiasticum.* In *PL* 109:673–1126.

Rabanus Maurus. *Commentarium in Ezechiel.* In *PL* 110:493–1086.

Ranulf de Glanvill. *Tractatus de legibus consuetudinibus regni Angliae.* Ed. G. D. Hall. London, 1965.

Ranulf Higden. *Polychronicon.* Ed. T. R. Lumby. 9 vols. Rolls Series, vol. 41. London, 1869.

Rapetti, P.N. *Li Livres de jostice et de plet.* Paris, 1850.

Raymund of Penyaforte. *Summa de poenitentia.* Verona, 1744.

*Recueil des historiens des Croisades.* 16 vols. Paris, 1846–1906.

Regino of Prüm. *De Ecclesiastica desciplina libri duo.* In *PL* 132:175–400.

Rinaldi, E., ed. *Statuti di Forlï dell' anno MCCCLIX con le modificazioni del MCCCLXXIII.* In *Corpus statutorum italicorum,* vol. 5. Rome, 1913.

Robert of Courson. *Summa.* In V. L. Kennedy, ed., "The Contents of Robert of Courson's *Summa,*" *Medieval Studies* 9 (1947):81–107.

———. *Summa.* Part 1. In V. L. Kennedy, ed., "Robert Courson on Penance," *Medieval Studies* 7 (1945):291–336.

Robert of Flamborough. *Liber poenitentialis.* Ed. J. J. Francis Firth. Toronto, 1971.

Robert Manning of Brunne. *The Story of England.* Ed. F. J. Furnivall. 2 vols. Rolls Series, vol. 87. London, 1887.

Röhricht, R., ed. *Regesta regni Hierosylmita MXCVII–MCCXCI.* Innsbruck, 1893–1904.

Roswitha of Gandersheim. *Passio metrici S. Pelagii.* In *PL* 137:1093–1102.

———. *The Sufferings of Pelagius.* In *The Non-Dramatic Works of Hrosvitha,* ed. and trans. M. Gonsalva Wiegand, pp. 128–157. St. Louis, 1936.

Rothwell, Harry, ed. *Historical Documents, 1189–1327.* London, 1975.

de Saint Martin, Léandre, ed. *Biblia sacra cum glossis ordinaria.* 6 vols. Anvers, 1634.

Salimbene de Adam. *Cronica.* Ed. O. Holder-Egger. In *Monumenta germaniae historica. Scriptores,* vol. 32. Hanover, 1913.

Schannat, J. F., and Hartzheim, J., eds. *Concilia germaniae.* 3 vols. Cologne, 1760.



Segarizzi, A., ed. *Historia fratris Dulcini heresiarche.* In *RIS,* vol. 9, pt. 5. Città di Castello, 1907.

Socii Bollandiani. *Acta sanctorum quotquot toto orbe coluntur . . .* New ed. 66 vols. to date. Paris, 1863–1940.

Sperling, H., and Simon, M., trans. and ed. *The Zohar.* 5 vols. London, 1931.

*Statuta civitatis Cremonae.* Cremona, 1578.

*Statuta urbis Ferrarae.* Ferrara, 1567.

*Statuto del commune di Lucca dell' anno MCCCVIII.* Lucca, 1867.

*Statutorum magnificae civitatis Paduae libri sex.* 2 vols. Venice, 1767.

*The Theodosian Code.* Ed. and trans. C. Pharr. Princeton, 1952.

Thomas of Chobham. *Summa confessorum.* Ed. F. Broomfield. Louvain, 1968.

Turner, C. H., ed. *Ecclesiae occidentalis monumenta juris antiquissima.* 2 vols. Oxford, 1899–1939.

J.-M. Vidal, ed. *Bullaire de l'Inquisition française au XIV*[e] *siècle et jusqu'à la fin du Grand Schisme.* Paris, 1913.

Vincent of Beauvais. *Speculum maius.* 4 vols. Douai, 1624.

Viollet, P., ed. *Les Établissements de Saint Louis.* 4 vols. Paris, 1881–1886.

Warnkönig, Leopold August. *Flandrische Staats- und Rechtsgeschichte bis zum Jahr 1305.* 3 vols. Tübingen, 1839.

Wasserschleben, W. H. *Die Bussordnungen der abendländischen Kirche.* Halle, 1851.

William of Auvergne. *Opera omnia.* 2 vols. Paris, 1674.

William of Malmesbury. *Gesta pontificum anglorum.* Ed. N.E.S.A. Hamilton. Rolls Series, vol. 52. London, 1857.

Yves of Chartres. *Correspondance.* Vol. 1. Ed. J. Leclercq. Paris, 1949.

———. *Decretum.* In *PL* 161:47–1022.

Zdekauer, L., ed. *Il Constituto del Commune di Siena dell' anno 1262.* Milan, 1897.

———. "Il Frammento degli ultimi due libri del più antico constituto senese (1262–1270)." *Bulletino senese di storia patria* 3 (1896):79–92.

———, and Sella, P., eds. *Statuti di Ascoli Piceno dell' anno MCCCLXXVII.* Rome, 1910.

## Secondary Sources (Books)

Amann, Emile, and Dumas, Auguste. *L'Église au pouvoir des laïques (888–1057).* Paris, 1948.

Anciaux, P. *La Théologie du sacrément de penitence aux laïques.* Louvain, 1949.

Bailey, Derrick S. *Homosexuality and the Western Christian Tradition.* London, 1955.

Baldwin, J. W. *Masters, Princes, and Merchants: The Social Views of Peter the Chanter and His Circle.* 2 vols. Princeton, 1970.

Baudrillart, Alfred, et al. *Dictionnaire d'histoire et de géographie écclésiastiques.* 17 vols. to date. Paris, 1912–1969.

Bloch, Iwan. *Die Prostitution.* 2 vols. Berlin, 1912.

Borst, Arno. *Les Cathares.* Trans. Ch. Roy. Paris, 1974.

Boutruche, Robert. *Seigneurie et féodalité.* 2 vols. Paris, 1970.

Briffault, Robert S. *The Troubadours.* Trans. Laurence F. Koons. Bloomington, Ind., 1965.

Buchberger, Michael, et al. *Lexikon für Theologie und Kirche.* 14 vols. Freiburg-im-Breisgau, 1957–1967.

Bullough, Vern L. *Sexual Variance in Society and History.* New York, 1976.

Bultot, Robert. *La Doctrine du mépris du monde.* 6 vols. Louvain, 1963.

Cheyette, Frederic L., ed. *Lordship and Community in Medieval Europe.* New York, 1968.

Cleugh, James. *Love Locked Out: A Survey of Love, License, and Restriction in the Middle Ages.* London, 1963.

Curtius, E. R. *European Literature and the Latin Middle Ages.* Trans. W. Trask. New York, 1963.

Dahm, G. *Das Strafrecht Italiens im ausgehenden Mittelalter.* Berlin, 1931.

Davidsohn, Robert. *Geschichte von Florenz.* 4 vols. Berlin, 1896–1927.

Denifle, Heinrich. *Die Entstehung der Universitäten des Mittelalters bis 1400.* Berlin, 1885.

Douais, Célestin. *L'Inquisition, ses origines—sa procedure.* Paris, 1906.

Duboys, A. *Du Droit criminel de l'Espagne.* Paris, 1870.

Duby, Georges. *The Early Growth of the European Economy.* Trans. Howard B. Clarke. London, 1973.

———. *Rural Economy and Country Life in the Medieval West.* Trans. C. Postan. London, 1968.

Duvernoy, Jean. *Inquisition à Pamiers.* Toulouse, 1966.

Eck, Marcel. *Sodome: Essai sur l'homosexualité.* Paris, 1966.

*Encyclopedia judaica.* 16 vols. New York, 1971–1972.

Epstein, L. M. *Sex Laws and Customs in Judaism.* New York, 1967.

Flandrin, J.-D. *L'Église et le contrôle des naissances.* Paris, 1970.

Fliche, Augustin, et al. *La Chrétienté romaine (1198–1274).* Paris, 1950.

———. *Du Premier concile du Latran à l'avènement d'Innocent III.* 2 pts. Paris, 1948–1953.

———. *La Réforme grégorienne et la réconquête chrétienne (1057–1123).* Paris, 1950.

Fournier, Paul, and Le Bras, Gabriel. *Histoire des collections canoniques en occident depuis les Fausses Décrétales jusqu'au Décret de Gratien.* 2 vols. Paris, 1931–1932.

Frati, L. *La Vita privata di Bologna dal secolo XIII al XVII*. Bologna, 1900.

Garde, Noel I. *Jonathan to Gide: The Homosexual in History*. New York, 1964.

de Ghellinck, J. *L'Essor de la littérature latine au XII^e siècle*. 2 vols. Paris, 1946.

Ghisalberti, A. M., ed. *Dizionario biografico degli italiani*. 17 vols. to date. Rome, 1960–1974.

Gibbs, M., and Lang, J. *Bishops and Reform, 1215–1272*. Oxford, 1934.

Ginzberg, Louis. *Legends of the Jews*. 7 vols. Philadelphia, 1910.

Glorieux, P. *Répertoire des maîtres en théologie de Paris au XIII^e siècle*. 2 vols. Paris, 1933.

Godefroy, Fréderic. *Dictionnaire de l'ancienne langue française*. 10 vols. Paris, 1880–1902.

Graham, J. *The Homosexual Kings of England*. London, 1968.

Green, V. H. H. *Medieval Civilization in Western Europe*. London, 1971.

Grinell-Milne, Duncan. *The Killing of William Rufus*. Newton Abbot, 1968.

Guilhermoz, P. *Essai sur l'origine de la noblesse en France au moyen âge*. Paris, 1902.

Helfer, Ray E., and Kempe, C. Henry, eds. *The Battered Child*. Chicago, 1968.

*A Homosexual Miscellany*. New York, 1975.

Hyde, H. M. *The Love That Dared Not Speak Its Name*. Boston, 1970.

Hyde, J. K. *Society and Politics in Medieval Italy*. London, 1973.

Karlen, Arno. *Sexuality and Homosexuality*. New York, 1971.

Katz, Jonathan, ed. *Documents of the Homosexual Rights Movement in Germany, 1836–1927*. New York, 1975.

King, P. D. *Law and Society in the Visigothic Kingdom*. Cambridge, 1972.

Lacroix, Paul. *Histoire de la prostitution*. 6 vols. Brussels, 1851–1853.

de Lagarde, Georges. *La Naissance de l'esprit laïque*. 3d ed. 5 vols. Louvain, 1956.

Lampe, G. W. H., ed. *The Cambridge History of the Bible*. 3 vols. Cambridge, 1969.

Landau, Peter. *Die Entstehung des kanonischen Infamiebegriffs von Gratian bis zur Glossa ordinaria*. Cologne, 1966.

Langlois, Ch. V. *La Vie en France au moyen âge de la fin du XII^e au milieu du XIV^e siècle*. 4 vols. Paris, 1924.

Lauritsen, John. *Religious Roots of the Taboo on Homosexuality*. New York, 1974.

———, and Thorstad, David. *The Early Homosexual Rights Movement (1864–1935)*. New York, 1974.

Lea, Henry Charles. *A History of the Inquisition of the Middle Ages*. 3 vols. London, 1963.

———. *A History of Sacerdotal Celibacy in the Christian Church*. 3d rev. ed. 2 vols. New York, 1907.

Le Bras, Gabriel. *Institutions ecclésiastiques de la Chrétienté médiévale.* 2 pts. Paris, 1959–1964.

Leff, Gordon. *Heresy in the Later Middle Ages, c. 1250–c. 1450.* 2 vols. Manchester, 1967.

Lerner, Robert. E. *The Heresy of the Free Spirit in the Later Middle Ages.* Berkeley, 1972.

Le Roy Ladurie, Emmanuel. *Montaillou, village occitan de 1294 à 1324.* Paris, 1975.

Lindsay, Jack. *The Normans and Their World.* New York, 1974.

Livingood, John M., ed. *National Institute of Mental Health Task Force on Homosexuality: Final Report and Background Papers.* New York, 1976.

Luchaire, Achille. *Innocent III.* 6 vols. Paris, 1905–1908.

Maddicott, J. R. *Thomas of Lancaster, 1307–1322.* Oxford, 1970.

Maisonneuve, Henri. *Études sur les origines de l'Inquisition.* 2d rev. ed. Paris, 1960.

Martines, Lauro, ed. *Violence and Civil Disorder in Italian Cities.* Berkeley, 1972.

de Mause, Lloyd, ed. *The History of Childhood.* New York, 1974.

May, Geoffrey. *Social Control of Sexual Expression.* London, 1930.

Mollat, M., and Wolff, P. *The Popular Revolutions of the Late Middle Ages.* Trans. A. L. Lytton-Sells. London, 1973.

Moorman, John R. H. *A History of the Franciscan Order.* Oxford, 1968.

Mundy, John Hineln. *Europe in the High Middle Ages, 1150–1309.* London, 1973.

Naz, Raoul, et al. *Dictionnaire de droit canonique.* 7 vols. Paris, 1924–1965.

Nelli, René. *L'Érotique des troubadours.* Toulouse, 1963.

———. *La Vie quotidienne des Cathares du Languedoc au XIII$^{e}$ siècle.* Paris, 1969.

Noonan, John T. *Contraception.* Cambridge, 1966.

*Oxford English Dictionary.* 13 vols. Oxford, 1933–1970.

Pollock, F., and Maitland, F. W. *The History of English Law before the Time of Edward I.* 2d ed. 2 vols. Cambridge, 1968.

Poole, Austin L. *From Domesday Book to Magna Carta.* Oxford, 1958.

Postan, M. M., ed. *Cambridge Economic History of Europe.* 3 vols. Cambridge, 1952–1966.

Pugh, Ralph B. *Imprisonment in Medieval England.* Cambridge, 1968.

Rosner, Fred. *Sex Ethics in the Writings of Moses Maimonides.* New York, 1974.

de Rougement, Denis. *Love in the Western World.* Trans. M. Montgomery Belgion. New York, 1974.

Russell, Josiah C. *Late Ancient and Medieval Population.* Philadelphia, 1958.

Ryan, J. J. *Saint Peter Damiani and His Canonical Sources.* Toronto, 1956.

Slater, Philip E. *Microcosm.* New York, 1966.

Slicher van Bath, B. H. *The Agrarian History of Western Europe.* Trans. O. Ordish. London, 1963.

Smalley, Beryl. *The Study of the Bible in the Middle Ages.* Oxford, 1952.

Steakley, James D. *The Homosexual Emancipation Movement in Germany.* New York, 1975.

Stone, Lawrence. *The Crisis of the Aristocracy.* Oxford, 1965.

Teetaert, A. *La Confession aux laïques dans l'Église latine depuis le VII*[e] *siècle jusqu'au XIV*[e] *siècle* Paris, 1926.

Thouzellier, Christine. *Catharisme et Valdéisme en Languedoc à la fin du XII*[e] *et au début du XIII*[e] *siècle.* 2d rev. ed. Louvain, 1969.

A. Vacant et al. *Dictionnaire de théologie catholique.* 15 vols. Paris, 1908–1950.

Vanggaard, Thorkil. *Phallòs.* New York, 1972.

Vidal, J.-M. *La Poursuite des lépreux en 1321.* 2 vols. Toulouse, 1899–1900.

———. *Le Tribunal d'Inquisition de Pamiers.* Toulouse, 1906.

von Schulte, J.-Fr. *Die Geschichte der Quellen und der Literatur des kanonischen Rechts von Gratian auf die Gegenwart.* 3 vols. Stuttgart, 1875–1880.

Waddell, Helen. *The Wandering Scholars.* London, 1927.

Westwood, Gordon. *Society and the Homosexual.* London, 1952.

## Secondary Sources (Articles)

Anciaux, P. "La Sacrement de pénitence chez Guillaume d'Auvergne." *Ephemerides theologicae lovaniensis* 24 (1948):98–118.

Anonymous Norwegian scholar. "Spuren von Konträrsexualität bei den alten Skandinaviern." *Jahrbuch für sexuelle Zwischenstufen* 4 (1902):244–63.

Baroja, Julio Caro. "Honour and the Devil." In *Honour and Shame: The Values of Mediterranean Society,* ed. J. G. Peristany, pp. 79–137. Chicago, 1970.

Bowsky, William. "The Medieval Commune and Internal Violence: Police Power and Public Safety in Siena, 1287–1355." *American Historical Review* 73 (1967):1–17.

Breitscher, Jane K. "'As a Twig Is Bent . . .': Children and Their Parents in an Aristocratic Society." *Journal of Medieval History* 2 (1976):181–91.

Brundage, James A. "Concubinage and Marriage in Medieval Canon Law." *Journal of Medieval History* 1 (1975):1–17.

———. "Prostitution in the Medieval Canon Law." *Signs* 1 (1976): 825—45.

Bullough, Vern L. "Heresy, Witchcraft, and Sexuality." *Journal of Homosexuality* 1 (2):183–201.

Crompton, Louis. "Gay Genocide from Leviticus to Hitler." Forthcoming (in *The Gay Academic*).

Delehaye, Hippolyte. "Les Lettres d'indulgence collectives." *Analecta Bollandiana* 44 (1926):342–79; 45 (1927):97–123, 323–44; 46 (1928):149–57, 287–343.

Delhaye, P. "Deux adaptations du 'De amicitia' de Cicéron du XIIe siècle." *Recherches de théologie ancienne et médiévale* 15 (1948):304–31.

Delisle, Leopold. "Notes sur les poésies de Baudri, Abbé de Bourgeuil." *Romania* 1 (1872):23–50.

Dietterle, J. "Die Summa confessorum . . ." *Zeitschrift für Kirchengeschichte* 24 (1903):353–74, 520–46; 25 (1904):248–72; 26 (1905): 59–81, 349–62; 27 (1906):70–79, 166–68, 269–310, 431–42; 28 (1907):401–31.

Duby, Georges. "In Northwestern France: The Youth in Twelfth-Century Aristocratic Society." In *Lordship and Community in Medieval Europe,* ed F. L. Cheyette, pp. 198–209. New York, 1968.

———. "Structures de parenté et noblesse dans la France du Nord aux XIe et XIIe siècles." In G. Duby, *Hommes et structures du moyen âge,* pp. 267–85. Paris, 1973.

Duemmler, D. "Zur Sittengeschichte des Mittelalters." *Zeitschrift für deutsches Altertum* 22 (1878):256–58.

Erikson, Eric. "Ego Development and Historical Change." *Psychoanalytic Development of the Child* 9 (1946):359–96.

Flandrin, J. L. "Contraception, mariage et relations amoureuses dans l'Occident chrétien." *Annales. Sociétés, économies, civilisations* 24 (1969):1370–90.

———. "Mariage tardif et vie sexuelle: Discussions et hypothèses de recherche." *Annales. Sociétés, économies, civilisations* 27 (1972):1351–78.

Forsyth, Ilene. "Children in Early Medieval Art: Ninth through Twelfth Century." *The Journal of Psychohistory* 4 (1976):31–70.

Goodich, Michael. "A Profile of Thirteenth-Century Sainthood." *Comparative Studies in Society and History* 18 (1976):429–37.

Haskins, G. L. "A Chronicle of the Civil War of Edward II." *Speculum* 14 (1939):39–81.

Kay, Richard. "The Sin of Brunetto Latini." *Medieval Studies* 31 (1969):262–86.

Kellum, Barbara. "Infanticide in England in the Later Middle Ages." *History of Childhood Quarterly* 1 (1973):367–88.

Lancaster, L. "Kinship in Anglo-Saxon England." *British Journal of Sociology* 8 (1958):230–50, 359–77.

Lavaud, R. "Éclaircissements sur la vie et l'oeuvre d'Arnaut Daniel." *Annales du midi* 23 (1911):5–31.

Leclercq, Jean. "Modern Psychology and the Interpretation of Medieval Texts." *Speculum* 48 (1973):476–90.

Leonhardt, W. "Die Homosexualität in der altesten deutschen Dichtkunst." *Jahrbuch für sexuelle Zwischenstufen* 12 (1912):153–65.

Meersseman, G. G. "Études sur les anciennes confréries dominicaines." *Archivum fratrum praedicatorum* 20 (1950):5–115; 21 (1951):51–196; 22 (1952):5–176.

Michaud-Quantin, P. "À Propos des premières summae confessorum." *Recherches de théologie ancienne et médiéval* 26 (1959):264–306.

Monter, E. William. "La Sodomie à l'époque moderne en Suisse romande." *Annales. Sociétés, économies, civilisations* 29 (1974):1023–33.

Oakley, Thomas P. "Alleviations of Penance in the Continental Penitentials." *Speculum* 12 (1937):488–502.

Palandri, E. "Andrea de' Mozzi nella storia e nella leggenda." *Giornale dantesco* 32 (1929):93–118.

Robertson, D.W. "Frequency of Preaching in Thirteenth-Century England." *Speculum* 24 (1949):376–88.

Robinson, C. "Was Edward II a Degenerate?" *American Journal of Insanity* 66 (1910):445–65.

Ruggiero, G. "Sexual criminality in the Early Renaissance: Venice 1338–1358." *Journal of Social History* 8 (1975):18–37.

Saffady, William. "Fears of Sexual Licence during the English Reformation." *History of Childhood Quarterly* 1 (1973):89–97.

Schmid, K. "Zur Problematik von Familie Sippe und Geschlecht: Haus and Dynastie beim mittelalterlichen Adel." *Zeitschrift für die Geschichte des Oberrheins* 107 (1957):1–62.

Stanley-Jones, D. "Sexual Perversion and the English law." *Medical Press and Circular* 215 (1946):391–98.

Ulrichs, Karl H. [Numa Praetorius]. "Ein homosexueller Ritter des 15. Jahrhunderts." *Jahrbuch für sexuelle Zwischenstufen* 12 (1912):207–30.

———. "Die straflichen Bestimmung gegen dem gleichgeschlechtlichen Verkehr." *Jahrbuch für sexuelle Zwischenstufen* 1 (1899):97–158.

Vauchez, A. "Une Campagne de pacification en Lombardie autour de 1233." *Mélanges d'archéologie et d'histoire* 78 (1966):503–49.

von Vershuer, Undine Freiin. "Die Homosexuellen in Dantes 'Göttlicher Komödie.'" *Jahrbuch für sexuelle Zwischenstufen* 8 (1906):353–63.

Vicaire, M.-H. "Les Cathares albigeois vus par les polemistes." In *Cathares en Languedoc: Cahiers de Fanjeaux,* vol. 3. Paris, 1968.

# Index